Do
Share
Inspire

Also by Kylie Dunn

Living With Intent: The 10 Steps to Defining Your Why from My Year of TED

Write to Launch: A Step-by-Step Guide to Self-Publishing

Praise from TED Speakers

Having given several TED talks, I can speak from experience that very few speakers expect that anyone will take what they say seriously enough to act on it. Kylie Dunn did, launching a courageous year of taking TED talks to heart and translating them into action. This book is an inspiring account of Kylie's "Year of TED." I hope that people will read the book and learn from it that life change is possible. And I hope that future TED speakers will read it and learn that they really need to mean what they say, as lives may hang in the balance.

> **Barry Schwartz is professor of psychology at Swarthmore College. He has given three TED talks, watched by more than 10 million people. His most recent book, based on a TED talk, is "Why We Work."**

What I really appreciated about Kylie's project, was that she opened up a broader discussion with these TED Talks. As a speaker, I enjoyed the connection to Kylie during her activity on leadership, and seeing what she's done overall. It's the sort of thing I wish happened more often.

> **Dave Logan is the President of CultureSync, and teaches at the USC Marshall School of Business. His TED Talk on tribal leadership shares the ideas from his bestselling books on the topic.**

Love the idea of going beyond the quick hit of a TED talk to test the ideas in real life. A brave, smart and fascinating experiment.

> **Carl Honoré is an award-winning writer and TED speaker. He has written a number of bestselling books on slowing down in all aspects of life.**

Even the lucky few who attend the expensive TED conference tend to head home without making any change in their life. I so admire what Kylie has done here, and so glad she's shared her story, in this charming, captivating, and inspiring book.

> **Derek Sivers is a creator, writer, speaker and entrepreneur who has delivered a number of popular TED Talks.**

KYLIE DUNN

DO
SHARE
INSPIRE

The Year I Changed My Life Through **TED** Talks

dinkylune

First Published in Australia in 2015 by dinkylune

Copyright © 2015 by Kylie Dunn

Activity artwork created by Matthew Dunn (www.matthewdunnart.com) – copyright Kylie Dunn

The moral right of the author has been asserted.

All rights reserved.

No part of this publication may be reproduced, stored in a retrieval system, or transmitted in any form or by any means, without the prior permission in writing of the publisher, nor be otherwise circulated in any form of binding or cover other than that in which it is published and without a similar condition including this condition being imposed on the subsequent purchaser.

National Library of Australia Catalogue entry:
Dunn, Kylie Louise, 1972- author.
Do, share, inspire : the year I changed my life through TED talks / Kylie Dunn.
ISBN: 9780992358334 (paperback)
Self-actualization (Psychology) -- Anecdotes.
Self-actualization (Psychology) in women.
920.72

Printed and bound in Australia by
IngramSpark, Lightning Source Inc.

CONTENTS

INTRODUCTION 1
OCTOBER 2011 – SETTING UP THE PROJECT 4
   Activity 1 • 30 days of fashion 11
NOVEMBER 2011 – LET'S GET THIS STARTED! 14
   Activity 2 • 30 days of Thanks, Praise and Mindfulness 19
   Activity 3 • 30 days of Better Listening 28
DECEMBER 2011 – ONE DOWN 31
   Activity 4 • 30 days living the 3 A's 38
   Activity 5 • 30 days of an Asian Diet 46
JANUARY 2012 – NOT A GREAT START 54
   Activity 6 • 30 days of Drive 59
   Activity 7 • 30 days of Slowing Down 71
FEBRUARY 2012 – HUGE LEAPS AHEAD 78
   Activity 8 • 30 days of Simplicity 87
   Activity 9 • 30 days with Less Meat 96
MARCH 2012 – GRATEFUL FOR THE RECHARGE 100
   Activity 10 • 30 days of More Happiness 106
   Activity 11 • 30 days of Preconceptions 120
APRIL 2012 – HARD TO BE HAPPY 126
   Activity 12 • 30 days of Letters 138
MAY 2012 – A LITTLE OFF TRACK 155
   Activity 13 • 30 days of Starting a Movement 163
   Activity 14 • 30 days of Leadership 171
JUNE 2012 – DIFFICULTY LEVEL RISING 174
   Activity 15 • 30 days of Remembering 176
   Activity 16 • 30 days of Choice 183
JULY 2012 – THE MONTH I TURNED 40 187

Activity 17 • 30 days of Being Wrong 193
AUGUST 2012 – WHY AM I DOING THIS? 206
Activity 18 • 30 days of Vulnerability 212
Activity 19 • 30 days of Time 221
SEPTEMBER 2012 – TURNING A CORNER 225
Activity 20 • 30 days of Compassion 233
Activity 21 • 30 days of Balance 243
OCTOBER 2012 – THE FINAL PUSH 245
END OF 2012 – STARTING TO SUM IT UP 254
THE EXTRAS 266
THE FINAL CHAPTER – FOR NOW 289
ACKNOWLEDGEMENTS 292
ABOUT THE AUTHOR 296

This book is dedicated to Derek, without whom I would never have thought this journey possible.

Introduction

I never intended collecting the blog posts from My Year of TED into a book. I'm not entirely sure why I made the decision not to. I'm not even sure I made that decision at all – you'll see that's a bit of a theme for me, one I thought I'd addressed. Thinking about it now, as I finalise this book, I think there were three sub-conscious reasons I didn't pursue this option.

The first is pretty simple. I wasn't sure people would be interested in reading through this journey as an 'after the fact' collection of experiences. So much of the blog was focused on the 'in the moment' responses to what I was doing; taking that out of the moment felt a little weird and disconnected for me. Of course, that makes sense **for me**. You aren't me though, so there's no disconnect for you.

Secondly, I forgot how extraordinary this entire project was. You see, I lived it, so it's quite ordinary in my world. We all have experiences, knowledge or skills that fall into this category. Once they become part of our story, we forget that not everyone shares the things we know how to do; concepts or knowledge we have acquired for ourselves; or the unique experiences we've had. My Year of TED, and what I learned from that experience, has become such a large part of who I am; I forgot that it's not known or understood by everyone else.

Lastly, there is the fear of collecting this together and publishing it into the world. As a blog, I didn't promote it, and I can make it disappear if I choose. Putting it into the printed word is something altogether different. It makes all of these admissions about my faults and failings permanent, which is an incredibly scary reality. There is another fear, well two more fears I guess: the fear that no one will want it, that I've put this together and no one will want to read it; or the scarier option that lots of people will want it, and the success will expose me even further.

The other book

There was, of course, a much more obvious and conscious reason for not spending time on this blog book; I've been writing another book about the experience. This other book takes the deeper approach to everything I learned and discovered. It's a consolidated collection of the ideas that had the biggest impact, and provides advice on how you can make some simple changes to your own life. It also contains more details about my life, details I didn't want to share on the blog, and what comes after experimenting with your life for a year.

That book is a work in progress, but is getting close to finished now. It needed me to take the time for all of these experiences and knowledge to settle into my life; so I could see the long term impact they had in my world. My plan was for that book to not be 'self-published'; I think the experience of this book will dictate how I feel about that moving forward.

What is TED?

I should start by explaining TED, for any of you who might be unfamiliar with it. TED stands for Technology, Entertainment and Design; and is a wonderful 'nonprofit devoted to Ideas Worth Spreading'. A couple of TED conferences run annually, and franchised TEDx events occur throughout the world. It pulls together groups of fascinating speakers on a wide range of topics. The format is that the idea must be shared in under 20 minutes – many talks are under 10 minutes. Many conference talks are available for free on the TED website ted.com; TEDx Talks are available on YouTube.

There are a number of other activities and projects in the TED business, like the TED Prize, TED Books and TED Ed. Visit the website to find out more about the organisation and everything they offer.

The Wizard of Oz analogy

About halfway through My Year of TED I realised the project was my own little Wonderful Wizard of Oz. This classic children's story seemed to have all of the elements of the project. I've included the blog post from January 2013 where I finally explained this to the readers. But I held onto the idea for much longer than that.

Basically, I wanted the same things as Dorothy and her companions:
- A Brain – wisdom to understand myself and what I want from my life.
- A Heart – the ability to connect with people through compassion and self-compassion.
- Courage – the strength to action the changes I needed to make in my life, and be braver.

- A Way Home – to return to my authentic self; to rediscover the true Kylie and how I want to contribute to the world.

The journey was full of witches: wicked ones that represented my own limiting thoughts and my internal critic; and good ones that were mainly friends, family and TED speakers who encouraged and supported me.

I love this analogy. It has given me an even deeper understanding of some of the lessons from My Year of TED. It might be interesting for you to keep it in mind as you follow the journey. Remembering that I wasn't aware of it for much of the project itself.

For now...

Regardless of the reasons why I didn't do this earlier, which are many and varied; it is done now, and I've released it into the world. Be kind with it. The woman who started this journey all those years ago was more broken than she realised. But she took on this amazing adventure, having no real idea where it might lead her – I'm forever grateful it led her to me.

So this is the story of My Year of TED. It started in July 2011, when I decided I wanted to do something different for my 40th year on the planet; when I decided it would be good to sort out my life. What you are holding is a collection of most of the posts from the year, and a few additional ones that close out the story.

The blog is ongoing, as the lessons continue to seep into my life. I share ongoing discoveries from that incredible year, along with additional lessons from new TED Talks, and from the new life I've created. Come and join me at kyliedunn.com to learn more about it, after you finish the book that is.

For now, sit back and enjoy the insanity that comes from trying to change your life; discover your Why; and generally become a better person through TED Talks.

October 2011 – Setting up the project

Day –20: My TED Project

The concept

To dedicate myself to applying some of the inspirational and insightful TED Talks I have been watching for the last five years. Or to use two of the talks: to try something new for 30 days [Matt Cutts] and immerse myself in a topic, because changing your behaviour can change your mind [AJ Jacobs].

Implementation

Over the course of a year I will apply the advice, insights and concepts of a number of TED Talks into my life – undertaking each for 30 days. I'm currently trying to refine the list as there are still about 60 talks I would like to include, but I can't do them justice by starting one every week so…

- There are a small number of 'concept talks' that will inform the entire project – I'll outline these throughout the project.
- I will start applying a new talk every two weeks, continuing them for 30 days. So at any given time I'll be doing two different concepts, which I feel is manageable and will allow me to dedicate enough time to each.
- In some instances, the activity will use a couple of TED Talks on a similar topic.
- There are also 'opportunity talks', where I'm not guaranteed the right circumstances will arise to allow me to use the lessons in the talk, for example, *Aimee Mullins: The opportunity of adversity*.

How I see this working

I mentioned this project to my boss recently and she thought it was amusing how prepared and controlled I was being with it all. She also made me realise during our conversation that starting one each week would not allow me to give some of the activities the time they deserved. I don't see the control aspect of this as a major flaw; it is, after all, how my brain is wired to work.

The idea is that I will take the parts of the talks that a) I feel have the most resonance for me and my life, and b) are able to be applied within a relatively short timeframe. I will write a further post about the subjectivity aspect of this. Particularly how I am not saying this is the speaker's 'message' but what I have taken from their talk – as misinformed and misguided as it might be.

I will start a new activity on the first of each month, writing a blog entry the Sunday prior to introduce the new concepts and how I plan on integrating them into my life (or allowing them to take it over – one or the other). I will post other entries during the 30 days about how it's going, and then at the end of the 30 days a reflective post about whether I felt it was something I benefited from; what I learned; whether I will be keeping it; and other points of interest. I realise for some activities the actual impact and lessons may take longer to hit me, so of course there may be epiphany posts that come later.

I won't have the entire year scheduled when I start – partially because that's too anal, even for me. But mainly because I want to leave slots open for any new, inspiring talks that might come along during the year.

The blog

I have decided to blog about this for a number of reasons, but the most important ones are to allow me a method of reflecting on what is going on, and because TED's motto is *Ideas worth spreading*. This blog is my way of spreading the wisdom and brilliance of these speakers beyond my immediate circle of influence.

There is another underlying reason, I have always wanted to write and this is the perfect project to use as a vehicle for that. Depending on the success of the project, how I feel about the blog, and what I have learned from the entire experience, there may very well be the opportunity to turn it into a book.

This is where you come in

For anyone who decides to follow this potentially ill-conceived experiment with my sanity, I would appreciate honest feedback on the blog posts. I plan on making all comments visible, without editing, unless you ask me not to – or I think that they are too offensive to include (that is not a challenge!).

So that is the outline of My TED Project or A Year of TED; I'm open to suggestions on what I will call this. I expect it will be a complete mixture of emotions throughout the year, and I will try to be as honest as I can on what I learn about myself throughout this process. I'm incredibly excited about the whole thing, and quite scared at the same time.

Day -16: How to choose a presentation

For the last eight weeks I have been watching and re-watching TED Talks, to decide which ones I want to use in this project. I subscribed to TED through iTunes a number of years ago, so I watched a lot while commuting in Sydney. But not all talks have appeared on iTunes. So I copied the All Talks list from the website as a starting point to work out what I might want to include.

At the time that I did this there were 994 TED Talks on the list. This does not include all of the curated talks that appear on the website, like *Randy Pausch: Really achieving your childhood dreams* talk from Carnegie Mellon; a must watch in my opinion. This led to my first decision on the project – I would try to only include TED Talks, not other talks that might appear on the website (excluding AJ Jacobs' concept talk). Excellent, one decision about talk selection down, only 300 more to go!

I then went through the list of 994 talks and marked whether I thought I might be able to apply it; based on whether I had watched the talk or by title alone. If I thought I could use it, then I would watch it during this evaluation period. I had already begun re-watching my favourite talks, so there were a few I had already decided I would include. But there were just over 220 talks I thought I should watch, or re-watch.

As of today, I have watched 231 TED Talks in the last eight weeks to prepare for this project. Now, I will admit there are a few of these I haven't watched all the way through. Over the last two weeks I've been quite ruthless with them. But the partially watched ones are generally talks I had watched years ago and when I got a few minutes in I worked out they weren't right for this. There have been a few where I just couldn't get past the first three minutes. They were too dense in content for me or the presenter didn't inspire me to keep listening. But all of the talks did get a three minute minimum listen, which I think is fair.

How I made the decisions

So how did I decide who made the cut? As I mentioned in the first post, there were different categories of talks, but they all had to meet a set criteria:
1. They had to be something that piqued my interest and I could see might enhance my life – that sort of goes without saying.
2. They had to have something for me to take away and apply to my life – even if it wasn't a direct action that was mentioned. Something

in the talk had to inspire me to think 'oh, that's sort of like this thing in my life, maybe I can make a change by doing X'.
3. That something had to be actionable within 30 days – this one wasn't hard and fast, but I had to be able to evaluate its impact on me in 30 days.
4. The last consideration was that it had to be something that challenged me – challenged my current behaviours or actions with the aim of calling me on my crap and/or making me a better person.

There are currently 71 talks in the list, as mentioned I will start a new activity every fortnight and do them for 30 days. So that only leaves room for 23 activities; if I want to finish the last 30 day period as close to the end of 12 months as I can.

Some of the talks are concept talks that inform the whole process, some are opportunity talks, and some talks can be combined, since the concepts are similar. I do still have some culling to do, especially since I want to leave room for new, inspiring talks that might come up during the year.

That cull is well underway, as I have decided the project will commence on 1 November. I contemplated starting on Halloween but starting with the beginning of a calendar month works with my structured brain.

From the 71 talks I have listed at the moment I created the following Wordle today. It only includes the words that appear more than once, but I think it's a fair summation of where this is heading.

Day -12: More on concept talks

I've spent most of today going through a process of sorting and choosing talks for the project. In my usual 'structured' manner I have grouped talks into categories, and today I have gone through another grouping exercise.

What I've realised is there are more talks I wanted to include that won't work as 30 day activities – instead they underpin the whole concept, like Matt Cutts' and AJ Jacobs' talks. They apply to the whole project, or they are the reason some of the other talks are being included in the project.

So I have selected 11 talks that are part of the underlying concept of this project. Their learnings apply to the whole process, the changes I'm making, or help define the project parameters.

The concept talks

These are, in alphabetical order, because that's just as good as anything else:

- *AJ Jacobs: My year of living biblically* – the whole concept of experimenting with my life, and the idea that changing my behaviour can change my mind.
- *Adam Savage: My obsession with objects and the stories they tell* – eye opening realisation there are many people in the world with random collections of ideas they would like to create/develop. This also led me to place more structure in the collection of project material (if that's possible).
- *Caroline Casey: Looking past limits* – everyone needs to watch this talk, but the concept she gave me is: when I believe in myself and everything about me, then extraordinary things can happen. If Caroline can achieve all of that, then I can achieve this project. This is only one of the many things I got from this talk, but maybe I will talk about the others later.
- *Dan Dennett: Dangerous memes* – this is a great talk explaining memes, and how they can infect the world. I've included this because it is basically what I am doing: taking the ideas of others, outlined in their TED Talks; using them; and passing them on again. Hopefully none of the speakers are too concerned with how I use their ideas, or how I interpret them.
- *Derek Sivers: Keep your goals to yourself* – this made me think about how and when I should share the project. It was interesting to understand that my mind can play tricks on itself, something to be aware of.
- *Elizabeth Gilbert: Your elusive creative genius* – I love this talk and it is one I need to apply to the project, especially in the writing, so I can protect myself. I like the concept that it isn't all down to me and my abilities; the failure and success of creative endeavours isn't all about the individual.
- *Matt Cutts: Try something new for 30 days* – the idea that this is a good way to create or remove habits from your life. Long enough to try it on, not so long that you can't stick at it.
- *Matthew Childs: 9 life lessons from rock climbing* – there are some great points in this that struck a chord with me, particularly Fear sucks and

Know when to let go. So I will be using these lessons as a tool to structure the project and how I work within it.
- *Nic Marks: The Happy Planet Index* – the particular aspect I'm using is the Five Ways to Wellbeing. I listened to this for the first time almost a year ago and have been thinking I need to work harder at these things. A lot of the activities I have planned cover these topics, so rather than including this talk in every third activity, I thought I would have it as an overarching concept.
- *Richard St John: 8 secrets of success* – these will also underpin how I approach the project and in particular the latter part of the writing around it. I am particularly fond of the last one 'Persist', especially the CRAP acronym (Criticism, Rejection, Assholes and Pressure).
- *Ze Frank: My web playroom* – last, but by no means least, is a Ze talk. It could be dangerous to put this one out there, as people may know what I'm humming in the office now, but this is what the project is all about – Connecting and Sharing. I could have done this project within the confines of my own world, not telling anyone what was going on. Sharing the experiences, learnings and the wisdom of TED with others; possibly connecting to other people who have been inspired by these speakers; these are some of the reasons for this blog.

I know this may seem like a lot, but I wanted to make sure I didn't leave any of them out. Remember this has been brewing for a number of years, so it shouldn't be surprising that there are a lot of influential talks.

Day −9: The subjectivity clause

There's probably no need for me to write this post, since it should be quite clear that this is a subjective project. However, I thought I should take the opportunity, up front, to acknowledge the extent of that.

As I've mentioned, what I am taking from these talks and how I am applying them to my life may not be the main topic or message the speaker was putting out there. I know I am applying a subjectivity filter around them, I have taken what I want; in most cases what I need. Some people may even feel what I've taken from the talks wasn't there in the first place, that I've missed the point. For them that might be true but, as many of the speakers note, we have our own mental models and bring our own interpretation into all interactions.

I'm more than happy for a speaker to tell me if I have entirely missed the point of their talk, but for everyone else – how can you be sure your interpretation is more or less valid than mine? A truly inspirational speaker will resonate with an audience on many different levels and in many different ways. Since I have chosen inspirational talks to include in my project I expect my takeaways will be different from other people's; given my focus and experience.

In short, I am happy to engage in a discussion about why I have taken one aspect over another, or how I came to a particular learning from a talk – but you can't say I am wrong to include it for a particular reason, just like I can't say you are wrong for thinking that I might be wrong.

So, circular discussion over with, remember this is a practical exercise. This means what I have taken from the talks also has to be easily applicable to my life, within a 30 day period. So while there were some incredibly inspiring and thought provoking talks I would have loved to include, there weren't any practical or tangible takeaways for me. That is why there are so many concept talks and why I have a category for opportunity talks.

Day –7: One week to go

The countdown is on now, with the first 30 day activity starting next week. This one required me to do a little preparation, which I'm enjoying. I will do a post about the chosen topic on Sunday, outlining the concept from the talk that I am applying and what I hope to get from the 30 days.

I have also just contacted the speaker of the talk, which is something I've chosen to do for all of the activities – so yes, I did have a busy day last week emailing all of the concept talk speakers.

Update on the schedule

I had decided to start a new talk every second Monday, but I will go back to dates instead. The schedule will now be starting an activity on the 1st and 15th of each month. I felt this would be a little tidier, since I am doing 30 days, not 28. The 'launch' post will go up the Sunday before an activity starts, unless it starts on a Sunday – in that situation I'll do it a few days earlier.

Day –4: Subconscious plans are sometimes the best kind

When I first read the title of *Derek Sivers: Keep your goals to yourself* talk I wondered what the hell it would be about. Most modern wisdom is about sharing what you want to achieve so other people help keep you motivated. The crux of the talk is that sharing can convince your brain you have already started achieving (or even achieved), lessening your drive and enthusiasm.

So why am I talking about this now?

Well, I've made a lifelong habit of not sharing my goals with others, and the way I feel at the moment is the reason why. There are many things in my life I have started thinking 'Yeah I could do this, it will be great', and then my confidence wavers and I stop. That is why I don't share, because once it's out there I have to keep going, or own up to the failure – and those who know me, know I don't fail gracefully.

I understand Derek's wisdom, and have used it in small ways – I'm not sharing all of my goals and activities up front, I'm keeping some things to myself. But I also need to apply the lessons I got from Caroline Casey, and have enough confidence in myself; believe I can do this project.

Quite frankly, if I had been my normal 'me', I would not be starting next week. I'd feel it was a great idea and would be a lot of fun but… well I've just read a post by Tommy Walker on Chris Brogan's blog '106 Excuses that prevent you from ever becoming great', and I'm sure I'd have gone through about 60 of these to convince myself this is a bad idea by now.

This is a major reason for the blog, and setting the whole project up this way – which I'm only now consciously understanding. I set myself up to succeed, because I knew if I'd kept it quiet it would never have happened.

I'm not sure whether I want to hug my subconscious now and thank it – or take it outside and smack it around a little bit. I hope that when this current rush of fear and self-doubt passes I'll be happy with it.

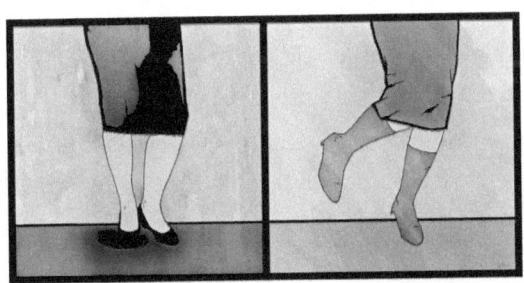

ACTIVITY 1 • 30 DAYS OF FASHION

The first 30 day activity is based on *Jessi Arrington: Wearing nothing new*, which may seem like a very simple concept but will challenge me in many ways.

The talk

I will admit that I skipped over the talk a number of times before I started planning the project, because I don't have a huge interest in fashion. I am extremely glad I did watch this talk, just for the energy and enthusiasm of the speaker alone. It is very worthwhile to visit Jessi's website and see some of her other 'finds' as well.

The basic concept from the talk is conscious consumption, so second hand clothes shopping. For me the deeper concept is that I should have more fun with my clothes and be more confident with my appearance; the section on fitting in being overrated strongly resonated with me.

Jessi's explanation that 'surrounding yourself with the right people' gives you the freedom to be yourself, and they may even appreciate the quirkiness, definitely hit home. After all why should I care what everyone thinks of me, it's the people I choose to include in my life whose opinion I value – and given some of you are *very* quirky; why shouldn't I feel free to be?

The challenge

This one struck a chord with me because I'm not overly confident with my clothes/appearance – my subconscious mantra seems to be 'just don't stand out', and not only with my clothing. Clothes are a way of fitting in and effectively hiding myself – which is a broader issue around confidence, taking risks and putting myself out there. Since this is a major component of the things I want to change about myself; how I look might be a good start, and it's also a simple first concept. To ease me into the project if you like.

This talk is also about sustainability and conscious consumption, which is why I'm only adding to my wardrobe through op shopping. The main thing for me is about not hiding myself through my clothes, not caring whether people think I'm a little odd for dressing a certain way – and adding some more colour and fun to my life.

This may not sound like a big deal to all of you extroverts out there, but for a little introvert like me this will be confronting. After all, the majority of my wardrobe is actually black, white and shades of grey, with only small bits of colour and not a lot of very 'feminine' pieces.

I think it will be a fantastic way to start the project, because I will hopefully learn to be more comfortable with standing out and stepping outside my comfort zone. This is important since I'm putting all of this out there for anyone to consume, and I do have to find a way to be comfortable with that concept.

The activity

I've decided that for the 30 days of this activity I will have four completely new outfits either through items bought second hand or things I already own that people have seldom, if ever, seen me wear (underwear is excluded from this). This will give me a new outfit for each week.

As well as the complete outfits I will also wear something more colourful or out of the ordinary for me, each day. This might be a more colourful article of clothing or accessories/jewellery (which I also seldom wear).

This may get quite interesting given some of the more fashion conscious people I work with, but that will make it all that more amusing; if I keep the right attitude. Importantly, I have decided not to tell everyone what I am doing, not only with this activity but with the project as a whole. If they find out on their own that's fine, but I think it is a cop out for me to give everyone an 'excuse' for my weird behaviour and/or changes in the next year.

The only part I can't take on from Jessi's talk is her universal truth – I can't see that 'Gold sequins go with everything', well not for me anyway. And yes I did try something sequined on, I just cannot do it.

The blog will include a number of photos about some of the gems I added to my wardrobe, like funky purple boots from the Salvos – Derek is already sick of me talking about the boots. And while we're on the topic of my lovely, supportive partner please spare a thought for him throughout this project. He is very tolerant but I think this will stretch even his patience at times.

> A note before we start, since this is a black and white printed book there are a number of photos and other images I have not included. Visit www.kyliedunn.com/dsipics if you want to see some of the fashion photos, and colour versions of the other images from the book.

November 2011 – Let's get this started!

Day 1: It begins, the first full outfit

So it is finally Day 1 of My Year of TED – but I think that I should say Day 1 of 30 Days of Fashion, because otherwise it's a little bit daunting.

For everyone who won't see me today I thought I would share the first outfit. Well you didn't expect bright pink and yellow did you?

The dress ($7.99), cardigan ($5.99) and funky purple boots ($9.99) are all from the Salvo's store in Hobart. The linen jacket was an afterthought I bought on Saturday from Vinnie's ($8.99) since the first week of November in Hobart will not be exceptionally spring-like weather – I know that must come as a shock to most of you.

The necklace was $3.99 from Salvo's in Bellerive and brooch was $8 from the Hobart Resource Collectables. Just under $45 for the whole thing, and I think it's come out pretty well.

And don't worry, you won't have to see a photo of me every day of this activity, since I hate having my photo taken (that should be obvious). Maybe the full outfits, and if I think anything is particularly noteworthy – but not every outfit, not every day.

Day 2: $5 earrings are a hit

Today's outfit was mainly things I already owned, but don't usually wear together. I did pair it with a little bit of a gold sparkly cardigan and the new for me earrings.

I received about half a dozen compliments on the earrings, which is particularly noteworthy for me since I always wear the same earrings on a daily basis. They are a very lovely pair of ruby earrings Derek bought me about six years ago; I've worn them nearly every day since.

It's not that I don't own other earrings, I guess it's just indicative of how little I bother accessorising my outfits. It's one of the areas I will be focusing on this month, adding a bit of colour and movement through the use of accessories.

And how do I feel after Day 2? Well I must admit it has been quite nice being a bit more dressed up and colourful for work, but there is certainly an underlying level of stress around it. It's not natural for me to be receiving compliments on my appearance – as sad as that looks in type.

> What I didn't share at the time was the complete meltdown I experienced that afternoon heading back to my car – and I mean tear-filled meltdown!

Day 4: Settling in, no really

Day 3 wasn't overly eventful, partly because I did have a black and white day and partly due to a shocking headache for most of it. Now before you think 'it's only Day 3 and she's already back in black and white', it was still quite different to what I usually wear and did include different earrings and a colourful necklace. But when I woke up this morning, a little chirpier than yesterday, I got to thinking about the colourful clothes and whether forcing myself to wear more colour yesterday would have affected my mood at all?

Having said that, quite a few headache pills didn't improve it, so I think it's unlikely a brighter top would have improved the day – but I don't know that for sure. So the little sub-challenge in the next 26 days is when I don't feel colourful, I need to force myself into it to see if it lifts my mood.

A bit of sparkle for Day 4

For Day 4, I'm not bright, but I am a little sparkly. I found a cute silvery-type top at Vinnies for $5.99, and I'm wearing a fairly colourful necklace.

I'm going to do some more op shopping at lunch today, I need to find more shoes to do this activity. I've definitely worked out the shopping part is the bit I love – actually wearing the outfits for others to see and judge… not so much.

In many ways I find it odd that it's been so stressful, and I don't think it is all down to the activity alone. I think some of the stress comes from blogging about it and making my thoughts/feelings open to others. And my osteopath is not going to be happy with me on Monday. My shoulder and neck are killing me (this is where I store my stress), and I've probably gone backwards in treatment about eight weeks in the last four days!

It is getting a little easier each day, partly because people seem to be getting used to seeing me in different things, so there are less comments. I think it may take a little longer to get used to blogging about it, and I have come to realise I need to add another concept talk – but that's a post for the weekend when I have more time to think about it and try to explain it.

Vulnerable (adj) capable of being physically or emotionally wounded

You know how sometimes you think you've planned something quite well, but then once you start the actions you realise there was this incredibly obvious thing you missed – well I've hit that point in this activity (realisation hit at Day 2, that is how obvious it was).

Actually there have been two realisations. First, I probably should have started with Activity 2 – and why is that? Well Activity 2 is about asking for praise/thanks (which I have already had to do with Derek for Activity 1); and the importance of thanking and praising others, which is something I've felt a need to do more often as people comment on my outfits.

I don't want to pre-empt the launch of Activity 2 too much here, but in hindsight that might have been a better starting point.

How did I miss this?

The second thing, I have to add *Brené Brown: The power of vulnerability* into my concept talks. I had overlooked including it in the concepts because I want to use it as an activity. But thinking through why Activity 1 is freaking me out so much I realised this whole project is an exercise in embracing vulnerability in my life.

I am a control freak, no surprise to people who know me and should be no surprise to anyone reading the blog. This includes, where possible, controlling how much people know me and the ability they might have to impact my life.

I make no bones about this, I'm pretty broken – and I'm not unique in this, you are all broken in your own special ways. Go on, admit it, I won't tell anyone. I won't get into the background of this too much but, like many people (well pretty much everyone I would suspect), I have spent my life developing mechanisms to keep me safe from being hurt by other people.

As a result of these feelings I hate being vulnerable. I hate exposing myself in any way where I could be open to ridicule or give people power (even perceived power) over me.

That is why I hide myself in my clothes, why I don't take risks with my outfits, just in case I get it wrong. I know I shouldn't care, I should just be able to laugh things off but it doesn't work that way. This also explains a lot of other behaviours I have, but that's for another time.

Brené's talk has always resonated deeply with me, especially defining it as 'excruciating vulnerability'. I'm not going to get into the rest of it, as it comes down to me not feeling worthy of love and belonging, and like I said, that is for a later activity. BUT given everything I'm doing from Activity 1 onwards, I need to practice Brené's talk – I need to have the courage to be imperfect; have compassion for myself; become authentic to who I am; and above all else to embrace the vulnerable position that all of this puts me in.

Remind me again why I am doing this project? It feels a little crazier every time I think about what's happening and what's to come. Seriously, why on earth am I doing this myself? All I can say is that it had better be worth it.

Day 7: A swishy sort of day

The end of week one, and I'm feeling a little better about how it went, well as I write this post anyway.

Today's outfit is brought to you by Vinnie's North Hobart, and my wardrobe. The dress is new, and the most expensive single item to date at a whopping $12.50. You can't tell very well in the photo but there is another swishy layer under the last cream one, which makes it very frilly and feminine – not my usual fare, but I love it.

I know it's still quite black and white, but remember I am sourcing clothing from quite a small population base here, so there are limits. Added to this, the challenge is about stepping outside my comfort zone, but that doesn't mean I have to be dressed atrociously. I think it is a requirement that I also like the clothes, otherwise I will never feel comfortable and confident in them, and that is supposedly key to this whole thing. Trust me, tomorrow's complete outfit will be a lot lighter and brighter – well the one I have planned at the moment.

Day 8: Second complete outfit

Today is the unveiling of the second complete outfit. This is not what I intended to wear today. The one I had chosen was summery and the weather here today just didn't match (it's raining). So here is the alternate outfit.

The shoes are the funky purple boots from last week. The skirt is a cool layered design, you can't tell in the picture, which cost $6.99. The top was $5.99 and the camisole I found on Saturday for $2.50. The jewellery is stuff I already had, because I haven't found a lot of nice second hand jewellery.

This is a limitation of op shopping: if you're looking for something very specific, it is a lottery. But that also makes it very relaxing in a way, because I don't have an expectation I will find what I want. Jessi talks about it being her own 'personal treasure hunt'; if she finds something that meets all of her criteria then she feels like she's won. I completely get this feeling, and it is probably why I enjoy op shopping so much.

I'll talk about the stress of choice in another activity, for now I'm getting into the joy of the treasure hunt. Now all I have to do is get to a slightly bigger population centre to increase the chances of finding treasure.

Day 10: Preparing for the next Activity

I've started preparing for Activity 2, trying to work out how that will look and feel for me, since it is not as practical as 30 days of Fashion. This next activity incorporates three talks. I've contacted two of the speakers but am struggling to find appropriate contact details for the third. I have committed to contacting each of the speakers prior to using their talks, but I think this might have to be 'where possible', because some people are not easy to find.

The post for Activity 2 will be up on Sunday, and this one will certainly be more challenging than the current one – oh yeah!!! I am looking forward to seeing how I cope with it though, since it's something I want to improve.

Activity 1 is still going well. Yesterday I wore my Day 1 outfit again, but without the boots as it was a lovely, warm day here in Hobart. Today is another low ebb day, maybe I just have an issue with Thursdays. Or more likely I know I won't get home until about 9.30 tonight; I'm currently doing a Letterpress course on Thursday nights. Maybe I feel drained in anticipation.

Whatever it is, I decided that I would still be a little more colourful even though I don't feel it. So today I am in a red top with the cool earrings from last week. It hasn't picked up my mood at the moment, we'll see.

Day 12: Letting go of objects

One of the other things Jessi spoke about was letting go and not developing emotional attachments to things. Today I decided I should practice this and did a pretty major cull of my wardrobe. You know all of those things that you keep 'just in case' – in case I manage to lose that extra five kilos, in case I need a black top to go under a jacket, in case I suddenly forget how uncomfortable it is and decide that I have to wear it again – that sort of thing.

I now have a garbage bag full of clothes to donate, which hopefully means someone else gets to enjoy them rather than having them live under my bed in a storage bag. This took a little time since the majority of these items came with us last year when we moved to Tassie, so I obviously had a strong enough attachment to cart them to another State.

But I do feel surprisingly cleansed by the whole experience. I guess Jessi's other point has also rung true for me – I have found some amazing outfits and articles of clothing just in the last few weeks. This has left me feeling quite confident that I don't need to hold onto these things any more 'just in case', because I will always be able to find something else if I need it.

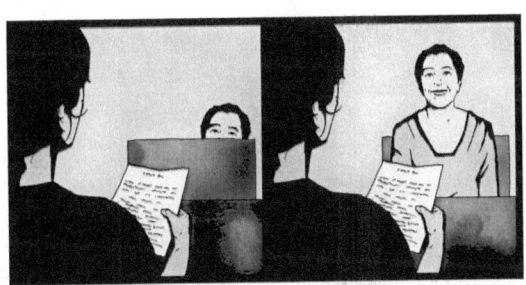

ACTIVITY 2 • 30 DAYS OF THANKS, PRAISE AND MINDFULNESS

When I heard Laura Trice explain how she was bad at giving praise, that she really wanted to do it but found it hard; I knew this was a talk for me. I am shockingly bad at praising and thanking people. I feel very uncomfortable and self-conscious doing it, and I always feel it sounds stilted and forced. But rest assured, if I have ever actually thanked you, it is always genuine – it is so uncomfortable for me that I wouldn't even attempt to fake it!

This is one thing about myself I've never understood because I am a people pleaser, and it's not like thanking or praising someone makes me vulnerable – but I'm still crap at it.

Maybe it isn't strange that I'm bad at receiving thanks and praise. I never know quite how to respond to it – the standard response is to dismiss my achievement as nothing much, even if I worked my fingers to the bone for it. If it's a compliment; well I think I've been pretty clear about those feelings.

The talks

Activity 2 addresses some of these issues as it is 30 days of Thanks, Praise and Mindfulness. That means applying three talks into my day-to-day life.

- *Mark Bezos: A life lesson from a volunteer firefighter* – I am taking the lesson that every day offers us the opportunity to affect someone's life. So this will be a mindfulness thing where each day I have to think about something simple that might positively affect someone around me.
- *Karen Armstrong: Let's revive the Golden Rule* – ignoring some of the more in depth 'compassion' elements of the talk for the moment, and totally ignoring the religious aspect of it (I'll talk about that later), I will try to apply the 'do unto others…' rule in my everyday life. Again this is a mindfulness thing, but as Karen explains the other way of expressing the Golden Rule is in the positive 'Always treat all others as you'd like to be treated yourself', which I am taking to be more proactive – involving praise, thanks and possibly doing positive things for people.
- *Laura Trice: Remember to say thank you* – this is about asking for the praise you want to receive as well as praising others. As I've already mentioned this will involve breaking two traits I am not good at; giving praise and thanks to others, and asking people to praise me.

The challenge

Giving, receiving and asking for praise is not something I do well, which was why I realised at Day 2 of Activity 1 I probably should have done this activity first. I have received quite a few compliments in the last two weeks and, while I'm getting better at acknowledging them, my usual internal response is 'aarrrggghhhh!' – and these are just compliments not real praise!

More importantly, I had a minor (yes Derek it was minor!) meltdown last week about the blog and my writing with Derek. It was at that point I realised I hadn't given Derek any idea on the praise I might or might not require. I had mentioned to him that I needed him to comment on the clothes I was wearing a little more than he usually does (so more than never). What I had failed to mention was anything about the blog and my writing, which is considerably more important to me and my feeling of self-worth than my physical appearance – I know that must shock you all!

What I want from this challenge is to be one of those people who can spontaneously and comfortably thank and praise others, without feeling self-conscious. More importantly, doing this without thinking about myself, just focusing on them and having a positive impact on their day.

The activity

For the next 30 days I will focus on praising and thanking others, and finding other ways I might positively affect them. I will also try, notice the use of the word try, to open up with people and let them know how and when I need to be praised. Since I don't receive praise all that well, I subsequently don't require a lot of praise in my life. I think what I need to work out is how I want to be praised/thanked, and how am I comfortable receiving that.

This will require a great deal of mindfulness about the people around me, but that will be good because over the last two weeks I have felt that I am focusing way too much on me. This activity gives me an external focus again.

I also want to try to apply the Golden Rule for the 30 days, to see if I can keep it in mind, particularly around some of the people in my workplace.

Multi-tasking and Day 14

Tomorrow I start Activity 2, and with it I start the process of focusing on two activities at one time. I don't think this will become too difficult for me, I like to believe I'm at least capable of multi-tasking[1] two things at once, but it means I do have to try to schedule things appropriately moving forward.

For instance, it may be difficult to do a very internal focused activity with a very external focused one – it might become a little schizophrenic.

I'm comfortable that I've settled into the 30 days of Fashion, so adding a focus on praising, thanking and having a positive impact on others shouldn't be too difficult. And by this I mean it shouldn't be difficult to focus on it. Actually doing it... well the launch post covered my hesitation with that.

Fashion

As I mentioned, I'm feeling pretty settled into this. I'm feeling more confident with my outfit choices, although my complete outfit this week will be interesting.

Day 14 is the purple boots and black skirt from last week with a creamy floral top and cute purple tights. Feeling very feminine today, but wasn't alert enough for a photo this morning (maybe when I get home, maybe not).

---

[1] Yes, I know that no one can actually multi-task; but you understand what I mean.

Derek has found the positive aspect of this activity. When we went shopping for him, and a birthday present for our nephew on the weekend, he didn't have to put up with me stopping and looking at clothes. He thought it was a lot more enjoyable than the usual shopping expeditions with me, which still usually result in me not buying anything, but require lots of browsing and trying on.

Day 15: Halfway a little brighter

Well today is officially halfway in 30 days of Fashion. The weather is much nicer in Hobart today so I am wearing the outfit I planned last week.

The top was $5 from Lifeline, the singlet is one of mine (since finding a nice one in a light colour was impossible), the pants were $4.99 from the Salvos, and the shoes were a massive $2 from the Salvos (half price).

You can't tell in the photo but the top has a sequin pattern on it, so I'm sparkly today. I am also feeling quite self-conscious in white pants (which I can't remember ever owning before buying these ones). But they are very comfortable, so I'm hoping that means I just stop thinking about them.

Praise, thanks and mindfulness

That also means it's day one of Activity 2, which is not off to an auspicious start; there is a motorbike that keeps parking in my paid space. Today I wrote him a nice note asking him not to do it anymore, since he doesn't seem to be taking the hint, so we'll see if explaining the situation to him calmly helps.

Day 16: Feeling pretty good

Activity 1 is going pretty well. Today I wore the swishy outfit from Day 7 again, except had a different necklace on. I've actually broken Jessi's rules a little with that outfit, because I am developing an emotional attachment to it. It's just so 'pretty', and I own very few pretty things – especially for work.

I felt very confident in it today though, which was great; getting my hair cut might have influenced that too. I could have lived with less wind when walking to and from work though; a short, flouncy 'dress' is not the sort of outfit you can easily hold down in strong winds.

Activity 2

And how is Activity 2 going? Well I'm glad you asked. I'm not being over the top with it since I think that would be disingenuous, and the aim is to become comfortable in giving the praise I want to give. So at the moment by focus has been more around the Golden Rule, because apart from Derek I haven't felt anyone else has warranted my praise – jokes!

Seriously though, I'm trying to be more mindful when I am interacting with other people, and I feel it has made an immediate difference. Do I feel like I am doing this all of the time? Not at all, but I'm trying to be more thoughtful about my interactions with others, and focus more on how I might be able to positively impact the person.

Like the car parking incident I mentioned yesterday – which I should mention resolved the problem. By dealing with it from an assumption that the person who owned the motorbike didn't realise the spot was a paid car park (my parking spot is a little random, so I can fully understand the potential for confusion), I got the outcome I wanted and hopefully the person didn't feel too confronted by the incident – my car is still intact so that's a good start.

I'm also trying to be more attentive with people, because if I'm talking to someone I would hope they were giving me their full attention, so I should do the same. This may sound obvious, but a lot of people come to talk to me at my desk, and switching off from the emails coming in, or the work I have to do can be quite difficult at times.

It's just the beginning of what is likely to be a long 30 day activity, but I'm feeling quite confident about the start of the process. Having said that, I haven't addressed asking for praise and thanks yet, so I know it will become a lot more challenging. Added to that I'm in a pretty good mood at the moment, so it's easier to be attentive and mindful of others; wait until I have a bad day and we'll see how well it works.

An example to follow
As a side note, I was in a meeting today with a team of managers – they invited me to discuss our records project (don't ask!). Anyway, one of the team started with the statement, 'I just want you to acknowledge up front the great job I did getting the Minutes of the Statewide meeting done'. This was met with a few chuckles but also with 'great job', 'thanks for that' and a few other comments. Now that's how you ask for praise and thanks!

Day 18: Pink flowers and praise

Thought I should do a status update today. Things were a little too hectic yesterday, and with Letterpress course going to 9pm; you know how it goes.

Activity 1

Yesterday was quite plain, mainly black but with a very bright magenta top, so didn't completely break the rules. Today I went a bit more bright and sunny, since the weather people promised us 27 degrees today – right now I am looking at a rainy, windy 17 degree Hobart day; we won't dwell on that. Today I'm in a pink and white floral skirt and white top, so feeling quite girly. The skirt is another op shop find, off the top of my head I think it was $4. The people at work are quite amazed at some of the things I have found.

I also went shopping at lunch and for the whopping price of $29 I managed to get six more articles of clothing. There are a couple of very special items in there, as well as some basics. Undoubtedly I'll have a few on next week, and there are a couple that will warrant photos.

I still haven't decided on the complete outfit for next week yet, but I probably have enough items to put one together without more shopping (don't try hold me to that Derek).

Activity 2

This is going better than I thought it would. Not going into too much detail, for the other person's sake not mine, I was presented with an opportunity to offer someone praise yesterday. The world had sort of shifted on its axis overnight, and they weren't feeling very sure about where they stood. Rather than thinking too hard about it I thought to myself, 'If that were me what would I need to hear?' I just wrote down a couple of quick points about how talented and well respected this person is.

I felt quite good about it, but then I remembered the not-being-present aspect has always made praise easier for me, so I took myself off to see the person and give them the praise verbally. I didn't feel self-conscious about it; I was truly focused on supporting a friend rather than on my own feelings – which I think might be the trick.

On the negative side, I have been far too involved in... well I guess it is fair to say gossip, with some of the people around me. At the moment though it is a coping mechanism to some of the changes occurring in our environment, and it isn't malicious gossip – *more factual with judgemental overtones* (I need a sarcasm font!).

Seriously though, that is something I am going to have to curb if I'm trying to apply the Golden Rule, as I would not like to be gossiped about. That might be the focus for next week – reduce the involvement in idle gossip. Looks like I'm in for a quiet week then.

Day 19: A little clarity

So, after adding Brené Brown's presentation into my concept talks I decided I should probably buy her book and get into this a little more, in preparation for the later activity I plan to do.

The Gifts of Imperfection: Let Go of Who You Think You're Supposed to Be and Embrace Who You Are arrived yesterday, and since I am at home alone today I thought I would take the opportunity to start reading.

This is going to be a bumpy ride, since I completely fall into the 'Don't' action category. But I take heart in knowing this is where she was when she started the Wholeheartedness work.

I made it all the way to page 15 before have a mini-breakdown, just a few tears nothing major. It's because I realised I have spent the majority of my life not feeling connected to people and that is because of who I am (which is something I have always suspected, but not in the way outlined in the book). What does that mean? It means I've always felt it was because I wasn't enough – interesting enough, pretty enough, funny enough, smart enough, nice enough, kind enough, and the list goes on.

What I have failed to realise is feeling this way about myself, I've effectively been creating barriers that have stopped the connections. I am a judgemental perfectionist – I am also a lot of wonderful nice things, but that's not relevant. This is gaining the realisation so I can resolve these traits.

This resonates strongly with the current activity – the Golden Rule is about compassion, and while I haven't made this an activity explicitly about compassion, this is largely what it is all about. Being compassionate to others and being self-compassionate as well. Maybe not surprisingly, I am usually less harsh on other people than I am on myself. I don't allow myself any leeway to fail or be less than perfect – but trust me I am far less than perfect. This results in very negative self-talk. My internal dialogue is nicer to my ex-husbands than me – now there's something I really need to work on. And yes I did mean ex-husbands (plural), but that is a whole other blog!

I should go back to page 15 and keep going. I think I will learn a lot from this book, it might just take a while to get through it.

There is a line in the preface of the book which resonates with this growing feeling I have had in since starting this project:

> It's an unraveling – a time when you feel a desperate pull to live the life you want to live, not the one you're 'supposed' to live.

This might seem obvious to people outside my mind, but I don't think I had realised until I read this line that this is exactly what My Year of TED is all about. I'm trying to work out who I am, what gives me meaning and trying to define the life I want to live. Not a bad epiphany for Day 19, but makes this whole thing a little scarier at the same time.

Day 22: Something very different

This is the last complete outfit for the 30 days of Fashion activity. It's VERY different to my normal style of dress, but I sort of like that it's out of the ordinary – can you tell by the photo I'm not all that comfortable?

The black top/coat is the first thing I bought, yes something black and white was my first purchase; it was $7.99 from the Salvos. The maroon camisole was $4.99, grey skirt $5 and of course the purple boots. The tights are new, they count as underwear. The earrings you've seen before.

Shoes have been the biggest challenge, hence the purple boots have been part of three full outfits. I have bought other shoes, but they haven't matched outfits. I am going to try to wear them before the 30 days are up though.

A special thank you goes to my patient photographer this morning. Taking this was a bit of a challenge, mainly because Lily was attention seeking. In hindsight we should have just put her outside for two minutes and got it done, but between feet licking (one of her less acceptable behaviours), sitting in front of the flash and rolling around in the middle of the floor with her stuffed toys (cracking me up) it was a bit of a challenge. You can see a little bit of her at my feet in the photo. So thank you Derek.[2]

Activity 2 is going well, but I still catch myself reflecting on times I should have said or done something different. They aren't big things, but that is the point of the whole activity. I need to be doing this for the small things as well, so I can get better/natural at the big things.

I have given praise a couple of times, and haven't felt self-conscious about it. I haven't had conversations with people about how I want/need to be praised and thanked. Okay, Derek and I have had a conversation about this, yes 'conversation', but I haven't done this with anyone else yet. This is partly because I don't know what I want, and partly because I'm probably avoiding that aspect of the activity. I plan to spend time thinking about it this week though, to see if I can come up with at least one conversation to have.

---

[2] I failed to mention Lily is our gorgeous fur child – it reads a little strange if you don't know that.

Day 23: More colour and doubt

I must say that I ended up feeling quite comfortable in yesterday's outfit. Initially I felt a little exposed, but I think that was mainly the shorter skirt than usual and the stockings. By about the middle of the day I was loving the coat/top (whatever you call it).

Today is a dramatic change in look, still not my usual fare but in the opposite direction. Today I feel very pretty, soft and flowy in a way.

The top was one of those 'treasures' that I've spoken of before. I almost didn't look at the back rack, since I was looking for more summery clothes, and when I saw the material I thought there would be no way that was my size. Happily it was, and at $6.99 how can you go wrong.

As for Activity 2, I continue to feel I'm not doing enough, which probably means I'm not. I think the main problem is the Fashion activity is very tangible, either I am wearing brighter/colourful clothes or I'm not. Whereas Activity 2 requires me to focus on it during the day, not just set and forget.

This is important because the majority of activities I have planned are more like Activity 2, so I have to find some way of focusing and capturing things as I go along. I need to think some more about it; suggestions would be greatly appreciated.

Day 26: Activity 1 almost complete

I'm coming to the end of 30 days of Fashion, only three more working days left. I say working days because I haven't changed my weekend wardrobe much. Partly because we've been quite domestic the last few weekends. So while I have incorporated more colour I've also been in jeans a fair bit.

We did do one last shopping trip today, well last for a little while. I've kept track of all purchases over the last six weeks, so in the reflection post I'll include details of what I've spent, and what I've acquired in total.

I'm feeling a sense of satisfaction in the first activity, but I will be glad when it is finished. Not so that I can go back to black, white and grey; that isn't going to happen. More because I feel I haven't spent a lot of time on Activity 2, and this will let me shift focus.

I've picked Activity 3 to complement Activity 2, so there will be more of an inward/self-awareness thing happening (I hope).

I think the problem I am having is Activity 2 is quite difficult to write about. I feel if I write about having praised or thanked someone that it means the compliment wasn't real; it was just something I did for the sake of the activity. I know that is not the case, but it makes it seem disingenuous.

For instance, there was a woman at work the other day who had taken a little more trouble with her appearance than usual and was in a new dress that was very flattering. Knowing that she struggles with her weight I did the mindfulness thing and thought 'I know that she likes compliments about her appearance, and she looks really nice today, so I'm going to say something'. Where usually I'd just think 'she looks nice today'. When I told her, her face lit up with the compliment.

So, I am doing more around Activity 2 than I'm documenting here. The other issue is a few people I work with are reading the blog, so I don't want to go into too much detail about incidents. I will try harder to document them though, or else the next couple of weeks as I wrap up Activity 2 and start Activity 3 could get quite dull in the blog post department.

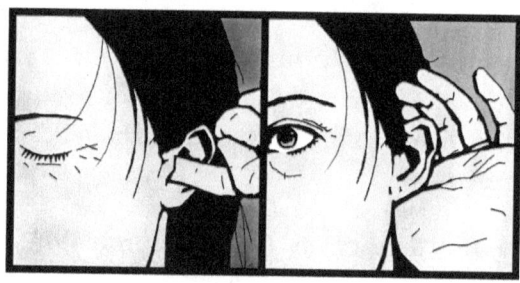

ACTIVITY 3 • 30 DAYS OF BETTER LISTENING

The talks

Julian Treasure has two TED Talks about sound that have informed this activity – *Julian Treasure: 5 ways to listen better* and *Julian Treasure: Shh! Sound health in 8 steps*. The talks complement each other, and they both contain practical exercises to improve listening. However, the bulk of the activity is based around the first talk, the five ways to listen better.

The concept of improving my quality of hearing intrigues me since hearing is not something I had thought all that much about. Yes, I have learned active listening techniques, and I do sometimes apply them. But I think, like most people, I am an 'unconscious listener' for the most part. I also think that the five practical exercises he outlines to improve conscious listening are a little more practical than the eight steps in the other talk.

Some of the actions do align, and I may try to undertake the eight steps at some point in the 30 days. But they are not the focus of the activity.

The challenge

I know I don't listen to others as well as I could – Derek has stated that he is looking forward to this activity. I have already said I will try to be more attentive for the mindfulness aspect of Activity 2, which is one of the reasons I scheduled this activity alongside it.

This is much more than 'active listening', it's about improving your quality of hearing and ability to channel and enjoy sound. Even more than that it's about connecting to and understanding your environment and the other people in it.

The challenge for me is to become a conscious listener – to become better connected with my environment and also find appropriate ways to control my soundscape when I need to.

The activity

For this activity I will ensure I mindfully practice the five exercises:

1. Silence – for three minutes a day I will seek silence to reset my listening.
2. The Mixer – at least once a day, when I am in a noisy place, I will listen to how many channels of sound I can hear and identify them.
3. Savouring – once a day I'll try to enjoy a mundane sound, like the dryer.
4. Listening positions – I will play around with listening positions, trying to use the most suitable one to each situation. I need to learn more about this.
5. RASA (Receive, Appreciate, Summarise and Ask) – much like standard active listening, I will apply this to important conversations, particularly where things are being asked of me.

Day 29: Mindfulness vs Ignorance

Activity 2 has raised a quandary for me around mindfulness, and in particular the application of the Golden Rule. At what point is someone being so ignorant/rude/frustrating that you are allowed to just give up on treating them well? I think this is an important thing to be clear on within yourself.

So, if the concept is to treat others as you would like to be treated, well I would expect to be treated poorly if I was acting like an ignorant moron. And if I were being so self-absorbed that I was having a serious negative impact on those people around me, I would want someone to tell me (that is not an open invitation to all of the 'comedians' I know, thank you).

A lesson from Buddhism

This reminds me of a sign at the Buddhist temple in Wollongong when I did a weekend retreat eight years ago. So many people talk about the pacifism of Buddhism, there is this general feeling they aren't supposed to be annoyed at others or fight back.

The sign on the bathroom door taught me this was not always the case. The fire alarm in the room was triggered by steam from the shower. The sign explained this and politely requested guests close the bathroom door to avoid a fire department call out. The last part explained that if you decided to be ignorant of this request and the fire fighters came, you would pay their fee.

When the Golden Rule does not apply

I like this concept and it's how I've been applying the Golden Rule. Basically I give people the benefit of the doubt, assume they might not know the steam sets off the alarm. But if I explain the situation to them, or if I know they are already aware of the situation, well they're choosing to act in an ignorant manner that is negatively impacting me so I don't have to be nice to them.

This has been working for me so far with the few frustrating situations that have occurred since starting this Activity. It is a definition in progress, but I think that it has a pretty solid grounding.

It means I am less judgemental of others, more willing to take a breath and explain the real situation to them. Unfortunately it doesn't mean that I haven't had ignorant morons in my life, but there seem to be fewer.

> I was taken to task for this in the blog comments – that I couldn't pick and choose, I always had to apply the Golden Rule.
>
> While that is the goal, I respectfully disagree that it holds in every case. Bullies are bullies, and sometimes you need to protect yourself from damaging individuals.

Day 30: The end of Activity 1

It's the final day of Activity 1. I'll be writing a more complete reflection post in the next few days, but a couple of things I will mention up front:

- Op shopping and having more fun with my clothes will stay in my life
- While this was extremely challenging at times, overall I enjoyed it.

Since I am a complete information geek I'm including an infographic in the reflection post about all of the clothes I purchased, and other details.

December 2011 – One down

Day 31: More on the Golden Rule

I should probably explain the Mindfulness vs Ignorance post from the other day, and maybe work a little more on the definition in progress.

This was always going to be a challenge when I got to a day like Tuesday, where there were just too many people in too short a timeframe pushing my buttons. And I do agree with the premise of the commenter on that post, that the Golden Rule should always apply, and I have fallen a little short of the activity with the post.

So, here is a question to all of you readers out there, how do you deal with the people who are being extremely ignorant and selfish? I had three incidents on that day of people I internally wanted to slap. Of course I did nothing of the sort, and instead chose to ignore them, which is fairly standard operating procedure since I am non-confrontational by nature.

Is that enough though? Is it appropriate for me to just ignore them and not go out of my way to assist them, or are these the people I should be striving to be mindful of?

I felt I was going okay with this part of the activity, as I've tried to be more mindful in doing nice things for others, focusing on their needs and being more considerate of my impact on them – but is that enough for me to say I am practicing the Golden Rule?

It is far easier to be my natural people pleasing self without analysing any of this, but that part of my personality is not conducive to personal growth. So we come back to the conundrum…

I think more thought is required; any advice would be gratefully accepted.

Day 32: Start of Activity 3

30 days of Better Listening began yesterday, I failed to mention anything about it in the Golden Rule post.

It got off to quite a good start, although the dogs over the road seem to know when I'm trying to have three minutes of silence. I figure that since it isn't possible for me to have complete silence in the house/car/work, then it is enough for me to remove all the sound I can.

I was focusing on active listening components, although I didn't fully practice RASA as I didn't feel it was appropriate to any of the conversations I was having. However, when Derek needed to talk to me last night I made sure I removed all distractions and focused on him and the conversation we were having. That might sound completely normal to all of you, but there is often a distraction of TV or the iPad or something going on that means all of my attention isn't on the conversation; this is why I need to change.

This morning I spent a few minutes 'enjoying' the mundane sound of the bathroom fan. This is quite difficult for me, because that sort of white noise usually irritates me a great deal. But instead of thinking of it as an annoying background noise I have to try to tune out I spent a few minutes listening to it, and it does have its own melodic – quality in a way.

Update on Activity 2

We're now onto day 18 of Activity 2 and I think that overall it is going quite well. I'm not about to change this all in 30 days, but making it a focal point has made me think; obviously, given the recent posts about the Golden Rule.

I have actively tried to do/say at least one thing a day to positively impact someone's life, and I think I've been achieving that. Most of them have been little things, but that is the point of Mark Bezos' talk, the little things that you may think are inconsequential might have a big impact on a person.

I'm yet to have a conversation asking for praise/thanks, but I'm getting a good idea in my head of how I might want that to happen. Hopefully I will be ready to have one of those by the end of the activity.

REFLECTION – 30 DAYS OF FASHION

As mentioned in the End of Activity 1 post I've enjoyed this activity; the changes in my appearance and consumption will stay in my life now that it's finished. Actually I more than enjoyed this activity, I found it to be a very freeing experience. I feel like I've rediscovered a more playful part of myself that's been lost for a while now.

I think I knew this, but just hadn't acknowledged. It's not like I've always been this boring with my clothes, I actually culled a fair amount of colour out of my wardrobe when we packed up to move down here. But the move interstate, to a whole new life and new job, rattled my self-confidence more than I had realised, and it had already taken a hit from my last job as well.

So right now, I feel more like myself than I have for a couple of years, but I can't attribute that to this one activity. The fact I'm actually doing this project is having a huge impact. There have been so many things in my life I've thought about doing, even planned out but didn't take the leap. Not only have I started My Year of TED project, but I've completed Activity 1.

In hindsight, 30 days of Fashion was a wise choice for the first activity. It helped move me into a different mindset, with a daily external awareness that I was making changes in my life. I think it has also helped me feel a bit more connected to some of the people at work. Yes that has meant more conversations about clothes than I have ever had, but it is a connection I haven't felt since making the move to Tasmania almost 18 months ago.

For the few friends I had made, it feels like those connections have strengthened as well. I feel more comfortable with them, even though they know some of my flaws and failings a little better now.

Overall I feel a lot more relaxed, much less like I need to be perfect and more accepted for the crazy/odd person I am. I've even stopped some of my internal beatings for getting simple things wrong, something I know do far too much.

I realise I'm unlikely to have this level of growth with every activity, especially since it is only partially due to Activity 1. But the positive feelings that have surrounded this first activity will help me move onto the more challenging activities to come.

A note on op shopping

It's funny how we forget things about ourselves. Doing this activity reminded me how I used to op shop at university, and how much I enjoyed it then. I'm not entirely sure why I ever stopped doing it, but I'm so grateful to Jessi for inspiring me to take it up again. It was the price aspect of buying the clothes that let me take some

Do Share Inspire 33

'risks', because if I felt uncomfortable in something and wouldn't wear it again, well it was generally around $5 so who cares – I'll just donate it back.

Surprisingly, I had a tiny percentage of misses, and they cost me far less than some full price fashion disasters I've left of stores with, in the past.

Belief systems and definitions

I've been reading Brené Brown's book *The Gifts of Imperfection: Let Go of Who You Think You're Supposed to Be and Embrace Who You Are*. I'm loving it; there are a lot of 'it's not just me' moments in it, which I always find reassuring.

It was a little challenging for me because there is a lot about reliance on God, prayer and the like. It doesn't concern me that other people are religious and this is a way they seek comfort and support, but it gets challenging separating some of the messages from the religion.

Overall Brené is inclusive in her definitions, and there is no requirement to follow any particular dogma or belief to benefit from her book. But there are two problematic sections, Spirituality and Faith.

- The definition of spirituality on page 64 of the book says 'we are all inextricably connected to each other by a power greater than all of us and that our connection to that power and to one another is grounded in love and compassion'. While this does not clearly state the 'power greater than all of us' is a higher being, it's a little too implied for me.
- The definition of faith on page 90 says 'Faith is a place of mystery, where we find the courage to believe in what we cannot see and the strength to let go of our fear of uncertainty'. Brené includes a quote from Richard Rohr that scientific hypothesis is more attuned to faith than the certainty of some religious people, which I quite like.

Atheism, spirituality and faith

I've spent the last couple of days mulling this over in my head, how these definitions do/don't work for me, and why I find them problematic. As an atheist I don't like the words spirituality and faith, as there are religious connotations about higher beings and afterlife. It's the use of the phrase 'power greater than all of us' that gives me the most trouble.

Note: What follows is a brief view into my atheism, and not what all atheists believe.

I believe all living things are 'inextricably connected' to each other, as we are part of an amazing web of life, evolved over millions of years to bring us to today. That connection is not only with the people around me, but with every living thing on this planet, from all times of this planet's life.

I am but one tiny, and somewhat insignificant, part of an amazing history of life and of an incredible species that has the capacity to contemplate these issues; adapt and adjust the world around it; create beauty (and unfortunately horror); and form these sort of connections. For me there is a 'power greater than all of us' that is grounded in scientific laws, and in our genes.

We are wired to want to connect with each other, to share and learn from each other, and to generally be compassionate to each other. As an atheist I don't believe in 'God' which means I don't believe in the 'Devil'. I believe we are all capable of doing good things for each other and bad things to each other. It is part of the competing priorities we have in our heads to function as part of a society but to also survive well. So I do agree the connection is 'grounded in love and compassion', but also in survival.

It is only through connection to each other and working together that human beings have been able to survive and evolve to the level we have: by developing societies with people who support and assist each other; by sharing thoughts and ideas that germinate and grow into something larger than any one person could come up with themselves.

This is where things like TED come into the process; they contribute to the collective consciousness in a way unprecedented at any time before the digital age. The fact that I am doing this project, applying knowledge and wisdom from people I would never have had a chance to meet in my life. That I'm potentially communicating my thoughts and feelings about it to people all over the world – it is connection on a gigantic scale.

As for faith, I do have faith in other people and our society as a whole. I continue to believe, even with a mountain of evidence to the contrary, that we are capable of finding a way to join together and dig ourselves out of the mess that we have placed the world in.

So while I have struggled for a few days with the religious content in Brené's book, I think her definitions can fit into my non-theistic worldview.

I will leave it for about a month to germinate and then read it again, so I can turn the messages into something tangible. But from the first go round, I think there is a lot of validity in the book and I highly recommend it.

Day 35: Changing mindset and silence

The human brain is an interesting thing. This morning I was picking what I would wear to work and settled on the outfit I wore on Day 23. As I was getting the top out of the wardrobe my 'old' brain kicked in and started telling me not to be ridiculous! I couldn't wear that because it was way too dressy for work etc.

I'd had a discussion with my previous boss about this last week, how she bought this beautiful top but feels it would be too dressy for work, and as a result hasn't worn in yet. It is a very interesting mindset. We buy these pretty articles of clothing but then feel we can't wear them. We keep them for 'good', but I know my life has few occasions that would fit that category. So the most beautiful things I own seldom get worn, which seems a real waste.

You should be happy to know I pushed through that negative internal voice and I am wearing the outfit.

Driving differently

I had also forgotten to recharge the iPod over the weekend, and actually left it inside the house this morning. As I left for my half hour commute, Triple J was playing a song that annoyed me. So thinking about my Better Listening I decided I would turn the radio off entirely for the drive in this morning.

That allowed me to get some morning silence, since I hadn't focused on that earlier, but it also allowed me to do a focus exercise on a mundane sound. I spent about 10 minutes just listening to the sound of the tyres on the road, and how it changed depending on the road surface.

It made for a very different driving experience this morning, I felt much more focused than usual. I couldn't do it all the time though, the commute is a little too boring to not have some sort of diversion.

Day 37: Better listening at work

I'm sure the universe is conspiring against me on this activity; I've had far too many meetings since I started this one. And while meetings can be good, since I can focus on listening positions and focus on listening to the person talking, they are not the best environments for maintaining focus.

I long ago realised I have some kinaesthetic learning traits, which for me means I need to be doing things with my hands to absorb and engage the ideas people are presenting to me. I'm also visual, so if the visual presentation is fascinating enough the tactile need diminishes.

This means I'm a rabid doodler, my diaries and notebooks are full of little pictures and patterns. While many people think this is rude, or a reaction to being bored that is not even close to being true.

A few months ago TED posted up *Sunni Brown: Doodlers, unite!*, which is a fantastic talk for me, since it validated my need to incessantly doodle during meetings and other forums. It also validated my feeling that I absorb the content far better when I indulge myself in this activity.

But, this is a problem with the Better Listening activity, since there isn't a listening position of 'doodling while listening attentively'. It means I've been fidgeting a lot more in the meetings, and as a result I don't think that I have gotten as much out of them as I might have otherwise.

There has to be a happy medium, I'm just yet to discover it.

Day 39: Really practising the Mixer

Today I had an end of year lunch with one part of our organisation. This was held in a nice restaurant in Hobart, which is also a very noisy restaurant. Why restaurants have no soft furnishings *at all* I will never know! It did allow me to practice the Mixer more than any day so far.

I should have prefaced this whole activity by mentioning I have problems with my right ear, since having transphenoidal surgery over eight years ago. This presents in a few ways, but one of them is I find it hard to separate just one sound in very noisy places, part of the reason for the activity.

Today I felt I did well with this. By identifying all of the various channels I felt it was easier to remove them as distractions, and there were a LOT of channels going on today. So I was pretty happy with how this went.

I'm also doing well with the silence and savouring activities, I'm enjoying my few minutes of silence in the morning before the day starts, and I've been using the sound of the engine/tyres/wind while commuting for savouring.

Activity 2 update

I can't believe I'm only a few days off finishing Activity 2, which means I'm only a few days off starting Activity 4 (wow!). I'm trying not to think about that at the moment, and I'm feeling quite good with how Activity 2 is going.

I'm still yet to have a conversation requesting praise, and I'm unlikely to do that before the end of the activity. But I have been thinking very hard about who and how.

What I'm very happy about is how well I have transitioned into giving others thanks and praise. I can comfortably say I've done something nice for someone every day. Some of them have been significant nice things, but on the whole it is about being a little more attentive to others needs. I guess what I need to do is ask the people who are around me all the time whether they've noticed a difference. So for those of you who read the blog feel free to add a comment and rate my performance with this one – hey, does that count as asking for praise?

ACTIVITY 4 • 30 DAYS LIVING THE 3 A'S

The talk

This activity is based on *Neil Pasricha: The 3 A's of Awesome*. I enjoyed this talk for two reasons; on a very basic level it allowed me to discover Neil's blog, *1000 Awesome Things*, which is very cool. More importantly though it presented a set of very inspiring but seemingly simple ways to try to achieve greater joy in your life.

The 3 A's of Awesome are Attitude, Awareness and Authenticity:

- Attitude – life doesn't go according to plan but you always have two choices: sink or swim. You can choose to have a good attitude and try to rise above.
- Awareness – small children are completely aware of the world since they are experiencing it for the first time. Remember that sensation and try to re-embrace that enthusiasm.
- Authenticity – be you and be cool with that. Follow your heart and get more joy out of life, leading to fulfilment.

The challenge

This challenge is about trying to rediscover the simple beauty and joy in the world and bring more happiness into my life.

This is another challenging activity that will focus on the basic way I deal with the world and the people in it. I don't think Awareness will be overly difficult, especially on the back of mindfulness and the listening exercises.

Attitude will be interesting, particularly around Christmas since I am going 'home' for five days. Like most people, my family has a complicated history which makes for some intriguing relationships. For the majority of the time it will just be a case of keeping my cynicism in check, but over that five days it will be more of a struggle.

The aspect that will be more complex is Authenticity. Since I've come to realise that being more authentic is one of the underlying themes for this entire project; I don't expect I will come to peace with it in this activity. I figure if I focus on it in a number of different activities, from different aspects, then I might be able to find a way to reach my peace with being me and being happy with that.

The Authenticity part will also be particularly challenging when I go home. I don't think it will do much for my relationship with my parents if I am truly authentic during that period of time – that never works. But that's only five days out of the entire 30, and if I can identify when and why I am not being authentic during that time I'll still be happy with my progress.

The activity

So what does this all mean? It means practising the following:

- Attitude – I will try to maintain a positive attitude during this activity, and choose language and actions to express that.
- Awareness – maintaining more wonder about the world around me and seeing the beauty in things I now take for granted, which will hopefully be fun.
- Authenticity – I'm not going to go all out on authenticity for this one, since it's an underlying theme of the entire project. I will focus on being more aware of when I stop myself being myself, and if I am stopping myself then why. I think it is quite a slow process to truly discover the authentic me, especially after hiding her for so long.

Day 43: Activity 2 almost finished

Tomorrow is the last day of 30 days of Thanks, Praise and Mindfulness and at this point in time I'm not sure how I feel about that. I will do a reflection post later in week, after I've had a little time to think about it all and consider what this activity has or has not given me.

What I do know is that today is day five of a bad mood that won't go away, no matter how hard I try. I've kept up the colourful exterior, in the hope that would lift my spirits, but that hasn't worked. It's not like I'm thoroughly miserable or anything, I'm just in a bad mood. Since I start the 3 A's on Thursday, one of which is a positive attitude, I have to find a way out of this mood.

My hope, it's just a reaction to being up North doing information sessions, which I don't feel like doing at the moment. But then again they are conversations about introducing a new system into the areas, so I'd never feel like these conversations. Also, the morons on the road yesterday didn't help at all – what sort of illness is it when you drive 20kms under the speed limit on the single lane section of road but then speed up to be just on or over the speed limit when I have an overtaking lane and can safely pass you!

As you can see some of the mindfulness has fallen by the wayside on the drive up, and the drive back today is a longer stretch. I should be in fine form by the time I get home tonight (I can hear Derek cheering from here).

This wasn't so much a post as a bleat, but to be entirely honest through this project I think I need to capture these episodes as well – there will be more of them, I can guarantee that. We'll see if sharing the bad mood helps bring me out of it at all, because nothing else is working at the moment.

Day 44: A brief reflection on Activity 2

Fortunately my mood has picked up; considering the 3 A's start tomorrow and I have to try maintain a positive attitude, this is a good thing. I think it might have had a lot to do with being back home from my trip up North, but also I feel like I achieved a fair bit at work today, which always makes me feel good.

Today is the last day of Activity 2, and I'm a little relieved this one is over. Don't get me wrong, I've found it very inspiring and freeing in some ways, and I will be carrying the principles and skills forward. But the problem with focusing on these things for such an intense period is I feel a lot of pressure to make sure I am doing the activity – which was taxing for this topic.

Initial reflection

So my initial thoughts about this are:
- I feel quite happy with how comfortable I've become praising and thanking others. I find I'm not second guessing myself as much, and I don't feel as self-conscious about it, which is great.
- I still feel uncomfortable receiving thanks and praise in most instances, but it has become a little easier over this period.
- I did not manage to have a conversation to ask someone for praise and thanks, or explain how I would like to receive it.
- I do feel like I was more mindful of others and did try my best to have a positive impact on at least one person each day.

- I haven't yet resolved how I feel about the compassion aspect of this, and it's something I will continue to work on.

Day 46: Update on Activities 3 and 4

Activity 3

I commuted to work on public transport today, which is not a regular occurrence for me since moving to Tasmania. When I lived in Sydney I always commuted on the train, and the noises (and smells) were just a common part of my day. But it's been quite a few months since my last bus trip into town, and it was a great opportunity to practice 'the Mixer'.

After about 10 minutes identifying all the different bus sounds, conversations, songs on the radio I found it was all getting a bit too much though. So the iPod went on and I tried to block out the other noise.

We also had another Christmas lunch today, benefits of working with two operational units. This one was noisier than last week's, and it was a real struggle to hear people on the other side of the table talking, something a lot of people mentioned. I don't know who's designing restaurants these days, all hard surfaces with no soft furnishings to absorb anything. At least today was a little more understandable, being a pub – and the food was good.

Activity 4

Positive attitude has been going well, but it is only Day 2. With the Awe part of this I've been focusing on nature as a starter. Derek and I moved to Tasmania in July last year, and we're yet to grow tired of the natural beauty in the area. I often find myself caught up in the beauty of the valley, the clouds over the mountains and the expanse of stars at night.

I do intend on making awe more about finding the childlike joy in things as well, but more than anything this project has taught me to start out slow with these activities – ease into them if you will.

I haven't caught myself being inauthentic in this short time frame. Someone mentioned today that I was extremely tactful, we were talking about some of the other people we work with. I thought about this afterwards and whether in those comments I was being inauthentic about how I felt; I don't believe I was. I might not have mentioned all of the negative thoughts I had, but then again I don't think venting in that way would have added to the conversation – and not who/how I want to be. I still think it was very clear how I felt about the people we were discussing, which wasn't entirely negative I should add.

REFLECTION – 30 DAYS OF THANKS, PRAISE AND MINDFULNESS

Giving and receiving thanks and praise

Overall, I'm happy with how this activity went and how I feel about myself as a result of it. I don't understand why I'm so uncomfortable with this, because it wasn't as hard as I thought it would be. I think it's a confidence thing, in particular having the confidence that I won't say the wrong thing and screw it up. It might also have to do with the fact that, as mentioned a few times, I am shocking at receiving praise and thanks. As a result I think I project this onto others, hesitating because I would feel uncomfortable if someone made a fuss.

It wasn't that hard though; instead of projecting the feelings of embarrassment I feel I projected the other feelings, when I know someone genuinely appreciates or sees value in what I do. The compliments I had been receiving as 30 days of Fashion helped this process, so I think I was primed to do this activity.

So for this aspect of the activity I achieved what I wanted – I am more comfortable giving praise/thanks and am also more comfortable receiving it, to the point that there were even times I sought it out a little.

Asking for thanks and praise

I had a discussion with people in my work unit (all two of them) the other day about the end of this activity. I mentioned I hadn't asked for thanks or praise, and we talked a little about why. I think the main reason was that nothing came up where I felt I had to ask. The people I work with, and particularly my boss, are quite complimentary anyway, so I didn't feel I needed to discuss being thanked or praised.

I'll keep this in mind moving forward, as I'm sure something is bound to come up, and I would like to see how this works for me. Very early in the project, I did have two conversations with Derek asking for praise. I asked him to pay a little more attention to what I was wearing during 30 days of Fashion, and be a little more complimentary if he did like the outfit.

Then there was the discussion about providing positive feedback about the writing for the blog, since this is a very important element of the project for me. So I have asked for praise, but these discussions were with Derek. And while they were still challenging and vulnerable discussions, I think that doing this with someone who is not my partner would be different.

Mindfulness and the Golden Rule

There are two parts to this, the mindfulness part where I was trying to have a positive impact on others and applying the Golden Rule. We'll start with the mindfulness part first, since this is easy to reflect on.

I loved focusing on others and trying to have a positive impact on their lives. These were mainly small things, but there were a few days where I feel like I did something that influenced a person's day (and maybe even more).

The Golden Rule continues to challenge me in some respects. Using it as a means of achieving the mindfulness activity above, yep no problems there. The issue is about continuing to apply the Golden Rule, or continuing to be compassionate when people are being less than considerate of others. But I've come to a level of peace about this because I had always considered doing a 30 days of Compassion activity.

So I've purchased Karen Armstrong's *Twelve Steps to a Compassionate Life* in the hopes that I have a better working knowledge when I get to that activity. It sounds odd to me, reading that back, since I think I am a genuinely compassionate person, but I'm hoping that Karen's book covers off the issues I've been having.

In summation, I will continue to try to do Thanks, Praise and Mindfulness but without the singular focus. I like having a positive impact on other people's lives and think the world would be a better place if we were all a little more focused on being nice to others.

Day 49: Listening exercise progress

I'm almost two thirds of the way through Activity 3 at the moment and I'm feeling a little lost. On one hand, I do feel that I am more consciously listening, but on the other hand I don't know what I am achieving.

- The few minutes of conscious silence a day does make me feel calmer, but it feels more like a meditation than a listening exercise.
- I've found the Mixer to be probably the most worthwhile part of this activity. I'm finding it easier to dismiss extraneous sounds in a noisy environment after I have identified all of them. Not sure whether this is the point of the exercise really, but it has been helpful.
- Listening to mundane sounds does help me appreciate, and as a consequence be less annoyed by, pesky noises that drone away.
- The listening positions is probably the one I haven't been conscious of enough. For the last third of the exercise this will be a focus area

for me. I think there are times I am too expansive and empathetic in the work place. This results in difficulty disengaging from some conversations I need to learn how to shut down more effectively.

- I have tried RASA in the few important conversations I've had so far. But I think I need to practice it more before the exercise ends. So I'll start doing this for less important conversations – I apologise in advance to the people around me that might start to find the 'summarise' tedious.

I think this is one of those activities I won't truly appreciate until I've finished it and have a good chance to reflect on what I have learned.

As a side note, focusing on the music and the breathing of the beautician while having my eyebrows waxed did make the whole process a little less painful. I don't think I've ever been more aware of someone else's breathing, except when I've been trying to sleep and someone is snoring nearby.

Day 51: The 3 A's vs my parents

I've been doing pretty well achieving a positive attitude. I even managed it yesterday when I was going to have a pretty full on day, and not in a fun way.

However, any semblance of positivity was sucked out of me after something my Mum said yesterday. I don't know how I will manage to keep a positive attitude over Christmas when my Mum has decided to be a little bit needy and selfish at the moment – remember compassion Kylie.

I've thought a lot about how much I should talk about my past and my family in this blog. My brother and sister both read the blog but my parents don't have internet access – so there is a sense of freedom in some respects.[3] I can't honestly go through a process around authenticity or discuss topics like vulnerability, courage, confidence without at least providing some context around upbringing and family. So as much as possible I will make this about me, and not necessarily about others, but sometimes they'll come in – like this post for instance.

I always knew that doing the 3 A's with my parents, in my childhood home, would be a challenge, but it's starting a little earlier than expected. It's good in a way because I know I'm going to have to dig deep to get through it, and it is likely to bring up things I probably need to deal with.

---

[3] Yes, they will get a copy of the book though – which wasn't planned at the time I wrote this.

By that I mean internal things. I've long since learned that it is not worthwhile to challenge my parents too much, the cocoon of denial they've built around themselves is impermeable.

At this point, I should mention my parents are not awful people, or bad parents – they are a product of their upbringing, and had us very young. I love my parents, and generally enjoy spending time with them. Like many people though, that relationship can be challenging at times.

So we fly to Wollongong on Friday and come back on Tuesday. This will be the longest period of time I've spent in their house for over a decade. The challenge is to find a way to make peace with it and go with the flow. I won't be writing on the blog during that time (the Activity 5 launch is scheduled to publish Sunday) but I will make notes and do a big post when I get back.

If anyone has any parental coping mechanisms, besides alcohol and violence, please feel free to chuck them in the comments – I may need help.

Day 52: Childlike wonder

About a month ago Derek Sivers put up a post called '32 sand dollars'. I knew when I read this that I would be doing the 3 A's of Awesome, and this struck me as the type of experience I should remain open to for this activity. You know those things you did as a kid that were so awesome but you lose the wonder of them as you grow up and get more cynical.

I haven't entirely lost that in my life and I think there are three things that help me keep an element of wonder and joy. I wasn't really thinking of them in that way, but doing this activity I'm thinking differently.

The creative/crafty things I do

There is a little buzz I get when I create something. It's a childlike sense of pride in the things I create combined with a sense of wonder that I was able to make it. I think it's one of the reasons I have so many crafty hobbies, to keep that sense of pride. There are a bunch of other reasons as well, but being able to experience the 'I made that' moment is a big thing.

Having a pet

There is something about having a pet that is fun and full of wonder. I had sort of forgotten that, since I didn't have one for over a decade. But Lily has reminded me how awesome a pet can be. Watching her discover things for the first time, watching her go into her insane playful moments and even training her to do something are all activities that help me retain childlike wonder of the world.

Building our dream house

Okay, there are times this is incredibly stressful, but it's usually a very positive and awesome experience for us. This is partly related to the first point on creativity, but it's a whole other level of that, as Derek is building us a home. I'll feel more re-engaged with it when I get more hands-on involvement in the build, but to see the photos and go out to see the progress as our house grows out of the ground certainly allows me to practice awareness.

I am still looking for more daily activities where I can engage my awareness for the 3 A's. Maybe I should keep Louis CK's comments on Conan about *Everything's Amazing and Nobody's Happy* in mind when we fly to Wollongong tomorrow – would make for a very interesting trip.

ACTIVITY 5 • 30 DAYS OF AN ASIAN DIET

The talk

This activity is based on a talk by *Dean Ornish: The killer American diet that's sweeping the planet.* The talk presented a very simple premise that an Asian diet is healthier than a Western diet. Looking at Dr Ornish's website – this should include a significant reduction in red meat, sugar and white flour, coupled with an increase in Omega 3 oils, fruits and vegetables.

On the website, Dr Ornish also talks about the benefits of meditation, exercise and connection.

The challenge

This challenge is about seeing if I can improve my health and well-being through a rather radical change in diet, increased exercise and introducing meditation into my daily routine.

The success of this activity will be measured by two things, my weight/fitness and how I feel about my levels of stress.

The activity

So what does this all mean in relation to actions? Well there are four areas:

- Diet – for 30 days we will be completely changing our diet into an Asian diet. We have been collecting recipes over the last month or so, but if you have any suggestions please let me know.
- Supplements – I will go back to taking fish oil tablets on a daily basis to increase my Omega 3 intake.
- Exercise – ensuring that I get about 20 minutes a day of exercise, and longer sustained exercise at least 2 days a week.
- Meditation – incorporate five minutes of meditation into my daily routine.

I'm looking forward to seeing how I feel on a fully Asian diet, noting that the definition of Asian for this exercise includes South-East Asian and mainland Asia. So we will be including Indian and Nepalese food with the Thai, Malaysian, Chinese and Japanese food.

Day 57: Activity updates from festive season

I did get to tweet a little while we were in Wollongong, but I've missed writing anything substantial about the project while I was away. I hope that everyone had a lovely festive period, we had a nice time but we're very glad to be home. Onto the activity updates.

Activity 3

Practising silence everyday was almost impossible while I was away, even while I was lying in bed in the morning – but listening to mundane sounds was something I got to practice, a lot. I rapidly lost the ability to enjoy these sounds, particularly the constant sound of the fan and cooler in the house. They were required though, it was very muggy up there and we are definitely not used to that weather system since living in Tasmania.

I did get to practice the Mixer, a lot! Particularly around my gorgeous but very hyper nephews and niece. It was great to catch up with them all, they are growing so quickly and I miss seeing them more often.

We went to visit the Nan Tien Buddhist temple for a couple of hours yesterday morning, which gave me a chance to get a few minutes of peace and silence practice. Sitting around the lotus filled lake was particularly serene, and a great recharge to take on the rest of the day.

Activity 4

I was happy with how positive I was able to be during the trip. I should mention it wasn't as bad as I had thought it might be, and I think a large part of that was due to the way I thought about it. I had decided to dismiss the little things about my parents and their house that drive me completely nuts – dripping taps, the fact that the kitchen renovation is not finished (after two years) and so on. Instead I focused on simply being with them, and my sister and her family, trying to remain positive in all interactions.

The Awareness part of the activity was quite easy, being around the kids helps you see things with renewed enthusiasm. Also, being at the Nan Tien temple and trying to appreciate the beauty of it all fitted in with this activity.

The biggest part of the challenge was always going to be authenticity. There were a few times I had to bite my tongue, particularly when Mum was talking about her relationship with her own mother. I was reminded a couple of times of the Julie Metz quote *Hypocrisy has its own elegant symmetry* while I listened, but felt it wouldn't achieve much by pointing out similarities of some of her own behaviours. I did make a few comments to both Mum and Dad I wouldn't have made previously, so a little more authenticity.

There was one incident when we were playing cards that reminded me that being with my parents can bring out the worst in me – which hopefully is not my authentic self. Derek pulled me up on one comment, and I realised that hyper-competitive part of me had come out without me even noticing. I don't like that particular 'Kylie' but it is such a deeply ingrained behaviour from my childhood it's hard to be aware of and stop. I did remain more vigilant about it for the rest of the time we were there, but I think that I fell a bit short of being my authentic self.

Activity 5

I have posted the launch of Activity 5 and can't wait to start this on 1 January. We'll be getting a lot of recipes together and doing some shopping over the next few days in preparation. It will be nice to do a practical activity again, take a bit of a break from analysing my thoughts and actions so much.

Day 59: Julian's other listening exercises

As mentioned in the Activity 3 launch, there was another TED Talk from Julian that also informed this activity, *Julian Treasure: Shh! Sound health in 8 steps*. Since this is the second last day of 30 days of Better Listening I thought I would reflect on the steps I have been incorporating into the activity.

Julian lists seven things we can do right now to help ourselves are:
1. Listen consciously – this has been a big part of the Activity, so I don't think that I need to expand on this one.

2. Protect your ears – I long ago replaced my iPod earphones with a decent pair of noise reducing buds. I realised the first time I used them how much better they were. Not only the sound produced, but also because their design meant I could turn the volume down.
3. Befriend silence – this is part of the Activity from the other talk.
4. Train your voice – when I was in primary school I was in the choir, and we did receive basic training and instruction. I'm not the best singer, but I can carry a tune and there is an absolute freedom in singing that I used to enjoy by being part of a choir. We didn't have a choir in our high school, and I have never really sung publicly since that time. I do sing in private though, it is one of the joys of commuting in the privacy of my car rather than public transport. During this Activity I have been more aware of the technique of singing during my commute.
5. Make music – this is explained above for me.
6. Design soundscapes – I work in an open plan area which is very noisy and disruptive. I don't know why this continues to be an office design, as it definitely has a negative impact on productivity. My iPod is a part of my work soundscape, particularly required when I'm trying to write more detailed documents. But sometimes even music is too disruptive, so I have a couple of websites that I now use as well. One of them I found just before starting this activity, Rainymood which is a fantastic site since I love the sound of a rain storm. The other I found after Julian's recommendation from this talk to listen to more bird song, Bird Song Radio.
7. Speak up! – a few times during this activity there's been a disturbing noise I've been able to ask someone to minimise or stop. I've been more aware of doing this, and taking positive control of the sounds in my environment. This has been where possible of course, the incessantly barking dogs on Xmas day, crying kids on the flight home and other such things just have to be endured sometimes.

I'm feeling pretty happy that I've been more conscious of listening so far in the activity. There will of course be a full reflection on the activity a few days after I finish, and there is a part of me that will be glad it's over. It's tiring spending so much time focused on the sounds/noises which constantly assail us. So while I feel I've learned a lot from this activity and I will keep some ideas/actions with me, I am looking forward to having a break from the Mixer and mundane sound exercises.

Concept talks – Richard St John's 8 to be Great

One my concept talk is *Richard St John: 8 secrets of success*. The reason I included this talk was that it's such a simple yet obvious set of characteristics he came up with after interviewing hundreds of successful people. So I felt it would be a good idea to use these as a guide for undertaking the project.

The *8 to be Great* are Passion, Work, Focus, Push, Ideas, Improve, Serve and Persist, and Richard outlines these quite basically in his short talk. When I was including the talk I did a little more research into this, to see if there was more to it. I went to Richard's website and ended up buying a copy of his book, *The 8 Traits Successful People Have in Common: 8 To Be Great*. I've put a basic review on the Other Material page of my blog, but I wanted to comment on a couple of points in more detail, with a focus on how they relate to this project for me:

- Passion – many TED speakers talk about following your passion and how that is the way to really enjoy what you do and feel like you are contributing. I like Richard's 'following many paths' to find your passion since it can be difficult to discover. I think I've been doing this for a long time, but this project is the first thing I've felt truly passionate about for a number of years.
- Work – you need to work really hard to be successful, which is not a shock but I think many people forget this fact. I'm doing this project alongside my full-time job and while we are building our dream house. So I always knew its success would rely on a lot of hard work, and that's just the time consideration. Let's not start on the introspective nature of most of the activities and the challenges they will bring me.
- Focus – this was an important chapter for me to read, because I can get distracted by bright, shiny things. Although I was relieved that Richard talked about going wide and then focusing, so ensuring you raise your head for a broad view but then focus back on one thing. I know I have to work more on this, particularly eliminating distractions, to keep this up for another 10 months.
- Push – this is something I have been doing for quite a while in my life, but it was great to read about how so many successful people need to push themselves beyond their shyness, self-doubt and other limitations. Again I think at a basic level we all know other people have the same sort of struggles as we do, but it's so nice to read it. The whole project is very much pushing me outside my comfort zone, so I hope that I'm on the right track with this part.

- Ideas – have a lot, have them often and maybe one of them will be good, is the basic lesson from this chapter; well that and methods for stimulating ideas. Getting ideas while doing this project is not the hard part, getting good ideas and having time to do something about them may be a little more difficult, we'll see how I go.
- Improve – practice makes perfect, but there's always room for improvement. This is something I have not excelled at in the past, however reading the focus chapter allowed me to understand that a lack of interest in what I was pursuing might have been a factor. Doing the project, and particularly writing this blog, is all about improving myself and my writing skills – so I guess that's a bit of a tick.
- Serve – the project is a personal development activity, but it does also have a large aspect of serving others. Writing this blog is about sharing the things I learn, and sharing TED Talks with others. This involves being open and honest (and therefore vulnerable) which scares hell out of me, but I can't do it any other way. I have already had a few people tell me they've been inspired by the project. The aim is to keep the project and blog interesting enough to inspire others, that's how I'm hoping to serve.
- Persist – the ability to push through time, failures, mistakes, criticism and rejection are the main points Richard discusses. Undertaking a very public, personal development program of 23 activities in one year, well I'm bound to come across a lot of these issues. But Richard has some great strategies to help with this, and I will undoubtedly use them during the year.

I would recommend Richard's book. You might already 'know' some of the content, but it helps to read about it and have it explained through the wisdom of successful people. It validates that knowledge and for me, the approach I'm taking to this project. There are also a couple of important points I had never considered, and all packaged in a nice easy read.

REFLECTION – 30 DAYS OF BETTER LISTENING

I'm glad that this activity finished when it did, only because I have a bad head cold that's blocked my ears and I'm not listening very well at the moment.

This was an interesting activity to do. Maintaining a heightened awareness of listening and my soundscapes did provide me with some insight into things I do well and not so well in listening. What do I mean by that? Take the mundane sounds exercise, I realised there are sounds in my environment

I find very distracting and annoying. I am not a white noise person, I much prefer complete silence. But since I started focusing on them and finding their melody I've become better at tuning them out. Don't get me wrong, I still hate white noise, but by learning to appreciate it I'm finding it less irritating. There is still a way to go on this, of course, but the fan in the bathroom no longer irritates me of a morning and I don't find road noise in the car as distracting – which is a good start after only 30 days.

Another thing has been a better ability to focus on conversations in a very noisy environment, which is always something of a struggle. We had a few loud work gatherings in the weeks leading up to Xmas, and I was marginally better at hearing the conversations I was involved in over all of the other noise. I know I'm not alone with this one, I'm sure that everyone at some point has nodded a response to something that they were just unable to hear at the time. But since one of the bigger 'learning experiences' in my life started because I couldn't hear what someone said to me in a bar, this is something I would like to do better (long story).

Overall I think this has made me more aware of the existence of a soundscape, and my ability to control it. That revelation in itself has made this a worthwhile activity. I will keep some of the exercises in my life, and will try to continue to be a conscious listener. I'm sure the people in my life would appreciate me continuing to be more attentive when they talk.

Day 62: Activity 5 begins YUM!

I can confidently say that this is the first activity Derek has been looking forward to. We eat a lot of Asian food anyway, but given the carb reduction diet I've been on for a while now I think he's looking forward to getting back into more rice.

We've been preparing for this one for the last week, looking through cookbooks and shopping at the local Asian grocers. There are some limitations, I'm not a mushroom person and there's a lot of seafood I won't eat. But we'll still have a lot of options, especially since I'm willing to give tofu another try (never been a big fan).

The biggest issue is likely to be breakfast, since toast and cereal are out of the picture. But we've been doing poached eggs and dhal of a weekday for a number of months now, so I don't think we have to change weekdays. The change will definitely be around weekends, since that usually includes toast.

The one thing I will need to manage is biscuits, cakes and sweets in general. I'm prepared though, I have found some substitutes from the Asian grocery stores that will fill that gap. After all, it is unrealistic to assume I can do 30 days without sugar along with the other changes. I don't think Derek would be nearly as keen for the activity if that was part of it.

Tomorrow I'll be making rice paper rolls for the first time, which is likely to become a lunch standard for the activity. I'm also going to try making roti for the first time, which is something I've always wanted to be able to do. I have four different recipes so I'm hoping one of them will work for us.

Mostly, I'm looking forward to doing a very practical, external activity. Maybe it's just the head cold but I'm feeling a little weary at the moment, and since I know what Activity 6 is, I know a recharge will be needed.

January 2012 – Not a great start

My wholehearted Letterpress piece

I mentioned I was doing a Letterpress short course through the Polytechnic for the last couple of months, which was fantastic by the way. I managed to get a lot of things done during the 10 weeks including little notebook covers, bookmarks, bookplates and, my favourite item, a piece based on Brené Brown's *The Gifts of Imperfection*. The piece used some of the important words from Brené's book.

I'm very happy with how this came out and framed it as a Christmas present for a few people. It was great to combine something from TED with one of my creative outlets. I might even try to do a little more of this sort of thing as I continue through the project.

Day 63: My 3 words for 2012

This is inspired by Chris Brogan:

> I've been challenging people to forego the idea of a resolution, and instead, to come up with 3 words that will help you define your goals and experiences for the coming year.

This year I thought that I should give it a try, well I'm trying everything else why not this wisdom as well.

So my 3 words are Do. Share. Inspire. – shouldn't be that surprising.

- **Do.** This could have been action or a number of other words but I like the simplicity of 'do'. This of course applies to the project, but also life in general. I feel I overthink and end up procrastinating on things too much. The project has been a huge step in the right direction – taking action on all of these inspirational talks – but it should apply to all aspects of my life.
- **Share.** This is not only around sharing my experiences from the project but also sharing in other ways like contributing to online forums (personal and professional interests), finding ways to share more in my workplace and community (time and knowledge), and

generally being more open to sharing things about myself I usually keep hidden (that whole vulnerability thing).
- **Inspire.** There are a lot of things I would like to achieve from this project, and this year. I had chosen quite a few words here around growing and learning, but I settled on inspire as an extension of this. In order for me to inspire it means there has been growth and learning that I've shared with others, so it ties in nicely. I've realised how important it is for me to inspire others, which is more than I had thought. I'll just leave it at that for now, but I will expand on this later.

So, instead of just reading Chris' words for the third year in a row I've decided to do it myself this year. I'm sharing my words with you, but also the concept and, for some of you, possibly the existence of Chris Brogan. And maybe this will inspire some of you to think about your own three words for 2012, or to visit Chris' site and learn more from him.

Happy 2012!

Day 64: Activity Updates

Activity 4

It was my first day back at work from leave, so maybe awesome wasn't on my mind so much today (jokes people). It hasn't been hard to keep a positive attitude of late, you know apart from the self-pity around feeling sick and all. And today I'm feeling a lot better, so positivity was right up there.

There have been so many little awesome things over the last 20 days that I've taken delight in. Simple things like watching Lily swim for the first time; the pleasure of finding some great new flavours already with Activity 5; fresh sheets; clean towels; not having to iron most of my clothes off the line; Doctor Who coming on five nights a week; a close encounter with a wedge-tailed eagle; getting more Twitter followers; trains running on time in Sydney; little things that the kids did at Xmas (you know the things kids say and do that crack you up) and many, many more.

As for authenticity, I have been aware of a few times when I haven't been my authentic self. Most of these are where I have bitten my tongue and avoided saying things simply because I didn't want to engage with the person, but I don't feel bad about any of them. On reflection the only time I have felt bad about not being the authentic me was when the nasty, competitive nature came out playing cards. Let's see how the remaining 10 days go.

Activity 5

It's only Day 3 of this activity but I can tell it's going to be a fun one. So far we've have Prawn and Mango Salad, Crispy Tofu, Chicken and Cashew, Rice Paper Rolls, Chicken and Basil and Brown Rice with Lemongrass to name a few dishes. We have many more yummy meals planned for the next 27 days.

I started my meditation a day late, a very runny nose doesn't assist focus. It's going to take me a while to get back into a meditation mindset. I might use the guided meditation podcasts I've downloaded to assist me. It was peaceful just trying to meditate though. I've forgotten how good that feeling of quiet is – it will be even better when I feel like I'm doing it properly.

All in all I'm feeling pretty good at the moment about the project as a whole – what I've done, what I'm doing and the challenges yet to come.

I am not alone

I have another group of talks that I had called my advocacy talks, they are like opportunity talks but they require me to speak out about certain things. One of these talks is *JD Schramm: Break the silence for suicide attempt survivors*, which is a very personal account of surviving a suicide attempt and how the silence that we put around these sort of events just makes it even harder for people to rebuild their lives.

This came to mind earlier this week in a tweet 'The hardest post I ever had to write', which took me to the *Bloggess* blog. That post is one of the most honest and courageous things I've read in a long time. When I got to the site I wrote comment 288, as I write this there are 2174 comments on the post, and thousands of tweets (see #silverribbons). It is a very courageous commentary on her depression and the other actions associated with it. Yesterday there was another tweet with the follow up post, just titled 'Wow'.

My personal struggles

When I put JD Schramm on my list of potential talks I knew it meant talking about my depression, which on one hand isn't scary since I've open about the fact I get depressed. But talking about it so publicly is daunting.

I suffer from what I lovingly refer to as depression-lite. I call it this because after my neurosurgery a number of years ago I suffered clinical depression, and everything after that time doesn't compare to the darkness of those few months. For that period of time every day was a struggle not to end my life, and I think it's really important that people who don't suffer from these sort of issues understand how that works. It's not that I hated life, it's not that I didn't value the people in it, it's not that I wanted to lash out and hurt anyone – it's simply that being alive was so painful and I couldn't see how that pain would ever go away. I didn't want to die, I just didn't know if I was strong enough to keep living. Fortunately I was.

My depression-lite is far less all-encompassing, it's an emptiness (like the lack of fulfilment that started all of this) that I sometimes refer to as my soul is crying. It doesn't stop me from being able to function – if my clinical depression didn't stop me from functioning then this is unlikely to impact. More importantly though it isn't so all encompassing that I ever consider ending my life. But it does impact my ability to feel joy, to really engage with things and people in my life and basically to feel connected.

What helps me get through all of this is my understanding and supportive partner, and the fact that I have a lot of people in my life who have suffered from depression, anxiety etc. and we talk about things. So while I don't open up when I am depressed I know that I am not alone, even though that is one of the strongest feelings when I am depressed.

We are not alone
The power of knowing you are not alone is amazingly strong, which is why we need to talk about it. I think it's also important to talk about it so the 'normal' people who are fortunate enough to not experience this don't judge us for it. As I said, I have a lot of people in my life who also suffer from depression, anxiety and a number of associated mental health issues. Maybe I attract people like this into my life because of how I am, but I don't think that is the case. I think there a lot more people suffering from these issues than society likes to acknowledge. And these are strong, capable, professional, loving, funny, wonderful people who generally struggle with their demons in silence; occasionally popping their heads up and letting those of us who understand their problems know they're doing okay.

The point of this post is to add to a conversation that for me was started by JD Schramm and this week was added to in a huge way by Jenny Lawson (The Bloggess). That conversation saved at least one person from taking their life this week, imagine how many more we could save if we removed the power of silence from mental illness. If we made it okay for all of the strong, capable, amazing people in the world who suffer from these issues to say 'Hey, me too. You aren't alone.'

Thank you JD, thank you Jenny and thank you to all of the wonderful people in my life who survive.

Day 69: Catching up

Just a quick catch up post on the status of the current activities. I just realised I should be launching Activity 6 today, but I had thought I'd be launching next Sunday so I am not prepared for it. As a result I will launch it mid-week, gives me a chance to do all of the things I do before writing the launch post – a final think through of the activity, getting in touch with the speakers and getting the artwork done.

This means it's only five days until the 3 A's activity is complete. I don't feel I have written very much about this activity as I've been doing it, but I guess there is a bit about Xmas and Wollongong I've included. I'm looking forward to writing the reflection post; I've realised some things about myself with this one which may seem at odds with some of the other posts of late.

Activity 5 is continuing along nicely, in parts. The food has been great, I've been sticking closely to the Asian diet. We had a dumpling feast last night and Chinese Scallion Pancakes for breakfast this morning, which were pretty nice (though fiddly). But I haven't meditated for two days, simply because I forgot. It's not a habit yet, so it's easily forgotten when I'm absorbed in something (it was watching *Cowboys and Aliens* last night). Simple remedy though, today I'm sticking a big note up 'Have you meditated today?' to remind me, until it becomes more of a habit. To make up for the last two days, today I'm doing a 15 minute podcast meditation.

I think being unwell for the last week has really worn me out, but I need to find some energy for the next activity, it has the potential to be draining.

The power of a personal mantra

Many years ago, at a particularly pretty crappy time in my life, I came up with a mantra for myself – *forza e corraggio* – quite simply 'strength and courage' in Italian. I use it whenever things get particularly difficult, I take a deep breath and either say it out loud or in my head (depending on the situation).

This has been very powerful for me, but I don't think I've thought much about the word choice. They were just the qualities I felt I needed to have to get through the bad things that were happening.

Recently, as part of this project and the wisdom I am absorbing, I've started thinking about these little words in more detail. Why did I choose them and why do they give me so much comfort? After all *forza* is not the best word for personal strength in Italian; I like that it also means force.

I'm strong but do I have strength?

I know I have a great capacity to endure and come out the other side of adversity a stronger person. If the saying 'what doesn't kill you makes you stronger' is even partially true, well I must be pretty damn strong. But a lot of my strength comes from an overwhelming need to not be vulnerable, to not fail or falter, to be perceived as strong, to being unable to ask for help. It also tends to come from the need to prove myself, and to not let anyone get the better of me – not a very positive place at all. So while I may be strong and resilient, in many ways I do not feel like I have positive strength.

I also don't feel that I'm courageous, being that I'm extremely non-confrontational (and I mean extremely). I have the strength to endure but I don't often have the courage to remove myself from situations where I am forced to endure. I don't stand up for myself, and others, as much as I should and I do not have the courage to be my authentic self a lot of the time.

That is why I still chant the mantra, and until the day I feel I have the courage to do and say the things I believe in without being so diplomatic and scared, I will continue to say the mantra. So I think it's with me forever, although hopefully, through this project and all of the activities involved, I can become more authentic and I won't feel like I need it as much.

Your personal mantra

I encourage everyone to come up with their own little mantra, if you don't already have one. I translated mine into Italian because it was a language I knew, and I feel there is added strength to everyone not understanding what I am saying; it makes it feel more special. And if you don't have your own feel free to borrow *forza e corraggio*, it's been doing a great job for me.

ACTIVITY 6 • 30 DAYS OF DRIVE

The talks

Activity 6 is based upon two talks, *Simon Sinek: How great leaders inspire action* and *Tony Robbins: Why we do what we do*. Simon's talk presents the concepts that great leaders and inspired organisations start from a point of WHY and then move out to the How and What, which applies to individuals as well. Tony's presentation is about individual focus, target, belief system and fuel, and how these things define a person's drive.

The challenge

This challenge is about understanding my drive and defining my Why. There are many TED Talks that discuss the concepts that doing what you are meant to do is when you're truly happy. My issue is that I have no clear concept in my mind of what I am meant to be doing.

Little things reveal themselves to me at different times, and I have certainly had enough experiences to know things I shouldn't be doing, but my purpose has yet to reveal itself. By purpose I mean the direction I would take that will help me to feel fulfilled.

The activity

This is a shift back to an internal focus, for the most part. There are many tools available on the web, I have already done the assessment on Tony's website, and many books to read on the topic. It's not the first time I've tried to work this out for myself, so I guess I have a bit of a head start on it.

For the 30 days I intend to ponder this further, maybe publicly pondering some of these issues will help bring me some insight. I have Simon's book, *Start With Why: How Great Leaders Inspire Everyone to Take Action*, to read as well as a lot of resources from his website. And hopefully I will find my Why, along with some of the things that drive and inspire me to action.

I have already started to work this out a little. By undertaking this project I have already discovered things about myself that I hadn't consciously realised before.

The other part of the activity is about seeing if I can apply this to work, and at least defining some of the Why in my work environment. It would be timely to be able to articulate this as we'll start business planning in the next few months.

Day 74: Last day of Awesome isn't

I've been a bit introspective in the last few months, which isn't surprising. Something I was looking at the other day must have stuck in the back of my mind and it caused a random thought to pop into my head overnight: that my ex-husband, Craig, had passed away. A Google search this morning confirmed that he had passed away in August 2010.

I don't know how he passed away, I've contacted a few people who might be able to shed some light on that for me. Ours was not an amicable separation, which was a real pity, and that means he hasn't been in my life for over seven years now. But I did love him and he was of course a big part of my life for four years, and I wanted him to be happy. He left behind a wife and child, so he must have found something of what he wanted in life.

Anyway, all of this is to say two things:
- My last day of the 3 A's is probably not going to be all that awesome, there are a few too many tears for that.
- More importantly though, life is short and we never know when or how it might end.

I need this to sink in a little more before I truly understand what it means for me, and I need to know what happened to make sense of it. I think I just needed to write this in case I do go off the reservation for a few days, and to make it real for me (it's very surreal at the moment).

I doubt that anyone from this period in my life is reading this, but if you are and know what happened please leave a comment – I won't publish it.

Not mourning, just sad

I had a whole fun awareness activity planned for my final day of Living the 3 A's. I planned to find 10 awesome things for the day; little things. Instead it was mostly very teary after finding out about my ex-husband. So I focused on the other two A's for the day – attitude and authenticity.

A quiet reflection on yesterday

It saddened me that I couldn't think of an obvious person to contact to find out what happened to Craig. It's not that I didn't think of people, but they have been out of my life for so long there was no way to easily contact them. And a lot of the people I thought of had been my friends too, completely independent of Craig, but he was staying so I let them all go.

I eventually thought of Leigh and Dawn, surely they would still live in the same place, they would know how Craig had died and they are the sort of people who can be out of your life for years but be just the same. I broke down in tears when I asked Leigh what had happened, he took the time to explain what he knew (Craig had died of cancer, at only 36 years old), then talked with me a little about Craig.

I stayed at work, not incredibly productive but managed to get a few things done, and it was better than being home alone. This was where the positive attitude had to come in. I kept thinking about how happy Craig must have been in his last few years with his wife and child; he had always wanted to be a dad and he had that. It wasn't for long enough, but from the outside he had the life he always wanted.

Then there was authenticity – I've thought a lot about how to articulate this so I wouldn't sound like a complete bitch, but I'm hoping you will all understand. You see, the fact that Craig is dead has no impact on my life. He was no longer a part of my life and would not be a part of my life ever again. So it isn't that I am mourning his loss, because there is no loss for me. I am extremely sad for him, his wife, his child, his family and friends, who were once a big part of my life too. I just feel that, if I am being authentic, it would be hypocritical of me to say that the loss was anything more than that – how can it be when he is nothing more than a memory.

Full reflection on the 3 A's

I had planned on doing the full reflection today, but I want to distance it from this one event – I don't want the whole activity and the things I have learned about myself to be caught up in this one day. So I will post up a full reflection in a couple of days, when I can focus a little more clearly.

REFLECTION – 30 DAYS OF LIVING THE 3 A'S

This activity was awesome; seriously though, it was a great 30 days. I didn't find it exceptionally difficult to incorporate into my day-to-day life, mainly because I think on the whole this is my general nature. But let's look at it in more detail.

It's all in the Attitude

On the whole I would say I'm a positive person. Neil talks a lot about attitude: when life doesn't go according to plan, at those times we can make a choice about the attitude we adopt. And in those situation I'm generally a pretty positive survivor.

Having said this, internally I know I spend far too much time considering the worst case scenario, how things could go wrong and how I might deal with those outcomes. I also spend far too much of my life thinking about things that have gone wrong in the past, and how I might have stopped/changed that outcome. This will be a whole other activity later, so I won't dwell on it here.

So how did I go with this part of the activity? I think it worked well for me focusing on being more positive for the 30 days. It certainly made

Christmas easier, and I think, it made a difference to how I generally approached things in my life. I wouldn't pretend that I kept it up for the full 30 days, there were times I caught myself talking in less than positive ways about things, but when I did catch myself I would correct my language to be more positive.

Awareness enhances appreciation

I didn't struggle with this part of the activity, enjoying the small pleasures in life is something that I do try to do on a regular basis. This might have a little bit to do with suffering from depression, where it helps to find those little bits of joy in a day, because finding joy in the bigger things is more difficult (for me anyway). I was more aware of doing this though, and that helped with the positive attitude at times as well.

I think this is something that everyone should do more of. There are a lot of first world problems we gripe about in our lives, and the vast majority of people able to read this blog should do more to remember this simple fact: we live in an amazing world that makes our lives simple and comfortable. Doing this awareness activity is a fantastic way to become more appreciative of how great our lives are.

I'm not saying that I didn't make any first world problem statements during this time, but if I caught myself saying something like 'my phone is taking forever to connect to the internet' I would smile to myself and think 'my phone connects to the internet, how cool is that!'

Being my Authentic self

I predicted this would be the hardest part and I was right. There are a lot of activities I've done and will doing that are about discovering my authentic self and being authentic to that self. Being so early in the project I knew that this would be a struggle, since I've spent so much of my life as a non-confrontational people pleaser – and not surprisingly that requires me to suppress my authentic self.

I have spent a lot of the last decade trying to change this, since these are things about myself I don't like. I have allowed myself to go through awful situations, or miss out on wonderful opportunities, because of these characteristics; that is something I need to change.

There were a number of times I did say something I normally wouldn't; spoke up in an environment I would usually stay quiet in; and identify times I wasn't being authentic. Simon Sinek says that being authentic is 'saying and doing the things that you actually believe'. I think that this is a very simple and clear definition of the word, and it is how I think of authenticity.

I require a lot more practice with this, and I need a lot more self-confidence before I can consistently do it well; I am proud of the small steps I made during this activity.

Overall analysis

So will I keep this in my life? I will keep focusing on trying to be authentic. Activity 6 that started today requires me to work harder on discovering more about my authentic self, so this part of it is definitely in.

With attitude and awareness I want to maintain more focus on these, but probably not as much as the last 30 days. I think this one will require a second reflection in a month or so, to see if I am able to retain these characteristics without having them as a focus activity.

I would recommend this activity to everyone, just to reset yourself and regain awareness of all of the positive things that are part of your life – especially if things don't appear to be going to plan.

Day 77: Where is the time going

January just seems to be disappearing at a rapid pace at the moment and I must admit to feeling slightly overwhelmed by it all. I thought I should try to slow it down a little with a status update on Activities 5 and 6.

Activity 5 – The food has been great

I've been sticking to the diet very well, although we did have morning tea with our neighbours yesterday so there was a little bit of cake and a biscuit that aren't part of the deal. I'm halfway through the activity though, and that was the first thing that wasn't Asian; so I think I'm doing okay.

I finally made roti for the first time on Saturday, to have with our first curry of the activity. We've been trying hard not to go for the coconut milk based curries, as much as we love them I don't think they're in the spirit of this diet. Anyway, the rotis turned out quite well. The first two were a bit of a flop but I worked out that resting them a third time before the last roll out worked well, so the rest were great.

Retreating into my brain too much

The exercise and meditation haven't been going as well. It wouldn't be surprising to anyone who knows me, or has seen the photos from Activity 1, that I live much more in my head than in my physical body. I take a lot more time to cultivate my thoughts and my knowledge than I do making sure that I am fit; I like to say that I am built for comfort not speed. So it isn't surprising for me that the exercise component would be lagging.

I have pushed myself to be more physical than usual, just not as physical as I could be. I need to focus more on that in the last half of the activity.

After the last post I did quite well at meditation practice for a couple of days, but with everything that happened on Friday my brain was too addled to focus on meditation. I know this is the time I should put extra effort into it, and on Friday night I did try, but on the weekend I lapsed again. So more needs to go into this as well, looks like I'll be doing a few more guided meditations to see if that helps.

Activity 6 – Starting on my Why

I've started planning the best approach to this. I've been consuming more from Simon and Tony's websites in the last few days and I think I have an initial plan of attack. This one is likely to involve a lot of mind mapping and drawings, so there will be some more graphics to include.

There are some simple things I already know about myself; things I know are triggers for me; things that inspire me, motivate me, and make me feel good about myself. A lot of these are around learning new things; sharing those learnings with others; being able to explain complex concepts in simple ways; and feeling like I have influenced someone else's understanding on how something is. I know these are all a big part of me, and I think this area is probably the best place to start.

I've got a few things to listen to from Tony, and I can't wait for Simon's book to arrive to help with this – but in many ways I want to discover a process for this in my own way. I figure I will have about a third of the activity done before Simon's book arrives, and depending how I feel about it then I can get a free coaching strategy session from Tony's website. For now I'm trying to absorb their online wisdom and nut out some of what makes me tick.

This is going to be a fun ride, hopefully I end up at a nice destination.

Day 80: I want a brioche!

For some reason this morning I woke up craving bread. As I got closer to town, this became an obsession for a brioche from the bakery near work. I started the whole rationalisation about the French in South East Asia and how that would surely allow me to have a brioche. But you'll be happy to know I resisted temptation, well for now anyway.

Activity 6

I've been spending a lot of time in the last few days reading and listening, I'm feeling a little tapped out actually. Tony Robbins is a very energetic person and I find it draining when I spend too long listening to him. Don't get me wrong, he is very inspiring to listen to as well, but after about 30 minutes my brain shuts down a little bit – it retreats from actively listening.

A couple of months ago my boss introduced me to enneagram personality types. Taking an online test I found out I am a big ol' 5 in the enneagram world. Reading through the enneagram descriptions, I could have guessed that without the test. She recently loaned me a book with more information about the personality types and it's quite spooky how well this describes me.

The other thing I did just prior to starting this activity was the 'Personality Strengths Profile' from Tony Robbins' site. Again, nothing in this that surprised me, but it's interesting seeing your personality in black and white.

I've been trying to absorb these results to see how they might help me identify my purpose, cause and belief – which are the three things Simon Sinek says we need to understand our Why. I envy people who seem to know this from a young age, the people who at five years old declare they want to be an X and that is what drives them throughout their life.

Fortunately I have come to understand they are the vast minority in this world, and while I spent the majority of my 20s wondering why everyone seemed to have this all worked out and I didn't, I've come to realise in my 30s that virtually no one has this worked out.

So I guess the update for this is I haven't had any epiphanies about what drives me – apart from the need for a sweet, buttery brioche!

Day 82: Starting to outline my Why

Doing this project has allowed me to understand far more about some of my inner workings. This has been partly to do with the amazing content I've consumed to date, and partly the process of blogging.

Activities and the skills to do them

One of the first areas I've been focusing on with drive is 'what are the things that I get a buzz from?' or what makes me feel fulfilled. This list is not all that surprising. But writing it down like this in one place makes it a little surreal, don't ask me why. So here are the things I know fulfill, drive and inspire me:

- **Learning/Understanding** – I love learning new things, which is probably why I love TED so much. I've always craved new information and knowledge in my life. Now, learning from experts is great but I think I probably enjoy learning through discovery a little more. When I'm able to work something out for myself; reaching my own conclusions provides fulfilment. But this sort of thing doesn't happen in a vacuum, and involves reading and being exposed to a lot of intelligent people's ideas.
- **Teaching/Explaining** – when I understand something I get a certain amount of joy from it, but when I can explain it to someone else and teach them about it – that's a whole other level of fulfilment. For me there is no point learning if I'm just going to keep it all for myself, and as frustrating as explaining things to others can be, there is a distinct joy in the moment they understand it as well. This is also something I think I do quite well, the explaining part of things.

  There is a little part of this that is inspiring/mentoring others. I get great enjoyment from being able to help people in my life when they are trying to sort problems out and deal with issues in their lives. This surprises me to some degree, knowing some of my internal workings.
- **Discovering/Sharing** – this is a little like the two points above, but also different. I love discovering new things. I particularly love it when I am the first in my social group to do so. This is why I enjoy StumbleUpon so much. I have discovered so many sites I would never have known about without that wonderful community. And when I discover particularly fantastic things (mind blowing ideas, cool music or art) I enjoy sharing it with people who I think would also love it.

  Maybe this explains that librarian-side of me, but I get a real buzz from being the person who has introduced someone to something new. A little like teaching/explaining I guess. This also applies to discovering things about myself/human nature and sharing it with others. I have learned so much from people who are brave enough to share things about themselves, like Brené Brown, and I'd like to think by sharing things I learn about myself I might be helping someone else come to a realisation. Even if that realisation is simply that they are not alone.
- **Designing/Simplifying** – from a young age I've always enjoyed being creative; drawing, painting and generally making things. In high

school I did graphic design for work experience. If I ever had something I felt I should be doing it was graphic design. Sadly, I listened to the careers adviser and decided against it; it was the career *du jour* and I was convinced there would be a glut of graphic designers by the time I graduated. Added to this nobody else in my year wanted to do art for their HSC, so I would have had to do it by correspondence – and so in Randy Pausch's discussion of brick walls, obviously I didn't want it enough to push through the barriers.

All of that aside, I have always enjoyed the parts of my jobs where I get to create – designing and creating conference brochures, forms, documents, visualising concepts, training documents, websites and the like. I think this is what led me into information management. I find it to be a very design-related job, where the design is supposed to simplify the process of storing and locating information within an organisation. This also leads me to have a lot of creative hobbies like jewellery making, card making and bookbinding. In some ways I wish the hobbies were able to be my full time job. But I think I would miss the other things too much. I don't think I have the right balance around this though.

Things I need from my environment

To set things straight, this blog contains information I haven't previously acknowledged to myself, let alone shared with close friends and family. It scares the hell out of me to be so open about the broken parts of me, but at the same time, as I do this it becomes a little less scary. And after reading the above I think you might all realise this feeds into the sharing/teaching. This section might explain it a little more.

We all have triggers, things that we need from the environment around us to make us happy. This section is a brief outline of some of the things I need from my environment to feel fulfilled. I'm hoping by writing these out, like the points above, I will get some more clarity about my drive.

- **Feeling appreciated** – this is based around receiving acknowledgement and thanks for the things that I do. These are fundamental for pretty much everyone, I'm sure there are some people who can function without it, but I'm yet to meet them. In particular I need people to acknowledge things that have taken me a great deal of effort to do or are uniquely mine – yeah I know that's not an incredibly clear definition, but I never claimed this would make sense.

- **Belonging** – I didn't realise how much I crave this. I've always spent so much time in my own head, that I didn't understand how much I need that sense of belonging. I don't need to be with people a lot, but I need to know I belong somewhere. Realising this, I think I might finally understand my career in the air force. I'm not a very military-oriented person so that career choice was always a little odd for me; maybe it is better explained by the next need.
- **Contributing/making a difference** – I need to feel like I am making a difference in the world, that I'm contributing to something larger. Again, this is not something unique to me, I think that the majority of us need to feel like we are making a difference in some way.
- **Time alone** – I am an introvert, I can't wait to read Susan Cain's book *Quiet* and to see her talk at TED2012. This means I need time alone to recharge; to give my brain a chance to absorb and process the events and learnings of the day. This also translates into needing time alone during my work day to process and get my work done.
- **Ownership** – I need to own the activities I am responsible for and have a level of control over what I do and do not achieve.

So what does all this mean in relation to my drive and my Why? I'm not entirely sure yet, like I said this is the beginning of the process. If you have any insight into what you think this might mean, feel free to let me know.

Day 85: Left out respect

respect: To feel or show deferential regard for; esteem

I've been thinking about the list I wrote the other day and realised that in the 'Things I need' list I neglected one of the most important elements – respect. I am a little surprised I failed to include it, but it's so fundamental I don't think of it as an option. So maybe not surprising at all.

I think everyone likes to believe they have the respect of the people around them. I always try to earn the respect of people in my life, and I think I've been pretty successful; you may have a different opinion.

It's also important for me to have respect *for* people in my life; I know I work harder for a boss I respect than one I don't. Maybe the importance of this is more of a commentary on my judgemental nature, but the loss of respect for my husbands definitely led to the end of both of my marriages.

It's great that my brain is coming up with these things; waking me at 4am to tell me about it isn't very conducive to a restful night though.

Day 87: So how are we doing?

Activity 5 – food glorious food

I am glad I love Asian food, because it's starting to get a little tiring. What do I mean? I want some vegemite toast and potato chips! I don't know why but these are the things I'm craving at the moment, hmmm salt. I've realised 30 days is a long time to go without vegemite, another fact I just learned about myself.

I am still enjoying it though, and on Tuesday morning I fully expect I will assuage the craving for vegemite. Some of the meals we've enjoyed of late are: Asian crepes; a crispy tofu noodle thing with homemade satay sauce (drooling just writing it); our favourite pad thai; more rice paper rolls (great with new wrappers); and a marinated Tasmanian salmon with noodles.

I admit to breaking the diet yesterday, we had a work function to celebrate Australia Day – sausages, chico rolls, sausage rolls, pavlova and Anzac biscuits were the standard fare. I didn't eat very much but enough to say that I definitely broke the diet. Twice in 26 days is not a bad effort though.

I continue to fail in the meditation stakes, and I don't completely understand why. I'd say it was mainly due to the fact that in my failed attempts to date I haven't been able to calm my brain down at all. This is making me feel like it's a waste of time, so I think this is driving behaviour. I do need to resolve this, as meditation will be part of Activity 7 as well.

Activity 6 – are we there yet?

I'm a few chapters into Simon's book at the moment, finding it interesting but will write more when I finish. A lot of this activity is very internal and mulling things over, so I don't feel like there is much to write at the moment.

I am doing one of my project talks at the moment as well, I will post up more about that soon. This project is the sort of thing I love doing, I think that it's all included in the previous post starting to outline my Why, but I'm trying to be aware of things about it that might not have been captured.

It's tiring being this hyper aware of everything, maybe that is contributing to my failure to meditate.

Quarterly reflection

I will be doing my first quarterly reflection at the end of the month – so exciting just saying I'll be a quarter of the way there. Knowing all of the activities I have yet to do, I'm nowhere near a quarter of the way through the effort required, but I'll take any milestone I can get at the moment.

ACTIVITY 7 • 30 DAYS OF SLOWING DOWN

The talk

This activity is based around the talk *Carl Honoré: In praise of slowness*. In his talk Carl explains some of the various slow movements around the world, and about how he engaged in a raft of slow activities to write his book *In Praise of Slowness: Challenging the Cult of Speed*. Things like the Slow Food movement, the Slow Cities movement, and a number of other ideas based around the general concept of savouring time instead of counting it.

The challenge

I'm really looking forward to this activity, given that I've been feeling a bit stressed and weary of late. It will still be happening in parallel with 30 days of Drive, but being forced to slow down will be a great focus for me. I'm hoping it will help me recharge my batteries a little.

The main challenge for this will be, well the whole concept; I don't do slow well. I have a nasty habit of doing too many things at once and not giving things my whole attention.

The activity

This is going to sound so simple, and yet I know it will be difficult for me to apply. For this activity I will being doing the following things:

- Meditating – because this worked so well for me in the current activity! I'm hoping the overall focus of slowing down helps me do this better.
- Stop multi-tasking – this will include a whole heap of things like not watching TV while eating dinner, not playing with the iPad while I watch TV, and only checking email at work when it is convenient (so closing Outlook until I'm ready).
- Stop eating lunch at my desk at work – taking an actual lunch break and leaving my desk; when possible, leaving the building.
- Enjoying slow food – the slow food movement is about cultivating, cooking, and consuming food in slow ways. That means using the local farmers' markets to get fresh, organic produce; finding recipes

about enjoying the preparation and cooking of the food; and then consuming food in a slow, purposeful manner. We won't eat like this for every meal, but we'll at least do this on the weekends.
- Relaxation – I will make time to relax in my day. Hopefully taking a proper lunch break, not multi-tasking, and meditating will address this. If not, I'll need to make more time to relax (walk Lily, read etc).
- Give up StumbleUpon – this will be one of the more difficult things, since I am slightly addicted to it, like many other Stumblers.

There will undoubtedly be other things I will change in this month. I feel the main idea of this activity is to be more meaningful with how I spend my time and to savour the activities I'm doing. I know there is a high likelihood of doing a lot of little things wrong with this activity, but I also feel this is an incredibly important lesson for me to be able to learn.

Day 91: Last day of Asian diet

A quick post to acknowledge the last day of an Asian Diet. As usual, there will be a reflection post in a couple of days with my initial reactions to the activity and how I think it went. For now, I know I didn't do as well with some areas of this as I would have liked, but that's what this is all about. If I was successful with every activity, where would the challenge be?

Tomorrow morning I will be having vegemite toast for breakfast, I can't explain how much I'm looking forward to that. I also intend on having chocolate tomorrow; this is the other thing I've missed in the last 10 days.

Activity 7 will start tomorrow, it has to start a day early so it will still finish at the end of February. Slowing down will be a big challenge for me, but one I am looking forward to.

QUARTERLY REFLECTION – THE PROJECT SO FAR

I've completed five activities so far in the project. It seems like I've done so much but there is still such a long way to go. I thought that it might be timely to re-reflect on some of these, and whether they have had any longer lasting impacts so far. This reflection won't include Activity 5, since it has only just finished and will have its own initial reflection post.

30 days of Fashion

I learned to have more fun and take more risks with my appearance. It's not that scary – neither is being more visible to the world.

I still think this was the best activity to start the project. It was extremely confrontational to make such a big change to my wardrobe overnight, but I'm extremely glad I did.

I had such a great time op shopping, found some amazing bargains, and continue to do so. Just the other week I bought two dresses, two tops, and a skirt for $27 – post-Xmas shopping spree. One of the dresses is particularly pretty, although it is black and cream so it's not that out there; the lime green dress on the other hand…

I haven't reverted back to my standard black/white/grey wardrobe, although some more of those pieces have come back into use since the activity. I have caught myself a couple of times thinking in my old mode, but I continue to push myself through the doubt.

This activity brought me out of myself and gave me a lot of confidence to launch into some of the more personal and revealing activities I have undertaken – and continue to undertake.

Thank you again Jessi for such an inspiring talk, I continue to keep the principles in my life and I can't see that changing back.

30 days of Thanks, Praise and Mindfulness

I learned to be more comfortable praising and thanking others; but I need to learn more about compassion because I wasn't doing enough.

This was more of an internal struggle for me, but I'm happy with the outcome. I managed to overcome a little of whatever it was that stopped me from being able to compliment and praise others, but I still don't feel I've gotten the hang of compassion.

I still try to do at least one thing a day to have a positive impact on someone, but I am not as mindful of others as I was during the activity.

I am reading Karen Armstrong's *Twelve Steps to a Compassionate Life*, but I've struggled to get through the First Step – Learn about compassion. This is mainly due to the fact that it is a lengthy theological discussion about the presence and importance of compassion within each major religion. I'm through this chapter now so hopefully the rest picks up a bit.

This activity did teach me a few things about myself and I feel I grew a little in the 30 days. It didn't happen in isolation though, doing the 30 days of Fashion at the same time made this a bit easier.

Thank you to all of the speakers, I am trying to remain mindful of keeping this focus in my life; I feel much more connected to people when I do.

30 days of Better Listening

> The big idea from this activity was the theory of soundscapes and the concept I can create and control mine – so simple, but so powerful.

This had a lot more of an impact on my life than I thought it was going to. To be honest, I thought this activity would give me a bit of a break from being so focused – nothing could be further from the truth.

I do still find myself trying to appreciate mundane sounds when they're annoying me, the bathroom exhaust fan is a classic example. I think I'm much more conscious about the sounds in my environment and try to be a more active listener.

Thank you for all of the talks Julian. They've made me think about listening in a very different way. I still have a long way to go to be a good conscious listener, but I continue to try, and that's the point at the moment.

30 days of Living the 3 A's

> I learned I'm generally positive but I need to do more, because my life is great, and it's only going to get better.

As I mentioned in my reflection post on this activity, I think I was already a pretty positive person going into this, but I just hadn't realised it. That would probably be due to my cynicism and sarcasm, which I had felt meant I was negative in the way I viewed the world. I no longer think that is the case.

Focusing on finding the joy in the little things in life is also something I generally do already, but focusing on it for 30 days was a very positive activity I think everyone would benefit from. It's far too easy for us all to get caught up in our own lives and be annoyed or upset by things that are not important, or catastrophic. The majority of my day-to-day problems are first world problems; I need to take a step back and remember how good my life is.

Finding out my ex-husband had passed away from melanoma at the end of this activity made that hit home for me. I have a great life, with an amazing partner, loving family, and wonderful friends. It may not always go to plan, there are times things aren't as bright as they could be, but on the whole it's great, and I need to appreciate it more.

I still need to work on authenticity, but I had no preconceptions that I'd feel like I had this sorted by the end of the 30 days. After all, I don't know who my authentic self is; I have spent most of my life as a people pleasing, non-confrontationalist, so she's pretty lost. I've spent the last five or six years trying to turn that around, and feel I understand myself a lot more than I ever have, but finding my authentic self, and learning how to be authentic, were always going to be challenges for the project as a whole.

Thank you for this talk and your website Neil. I honestly believe everyone would benefit from doing 30 days of Living the 3 A's. It makes you look at things a little differently – and even as I write this I realise I had all too quickly forgotten the lessons. I need to make sure that I continue to focus on this in my life, because my life is pretty damn awesome.

Feelings after three months

I've mentioned a bit recently that I'm feeling pretty weary. This is partly due to the project, it's just hard to remain so focused on changing or identifying very fundamental parts of my behaviour. But I think it also has a lot to do with not having had a real holiday for over 18 months now.

I hope Activity 7 helps me recharge my batteries a little, or more appropriately, gives me some direction as to how I might find ways to slow my life down so I have the opportunity to recharge.

Having said that, I'm feeling positive about how it's going. I certainly feel I've grown in the last three months, and understand a lot more about myself than I did starting the project. I also feel it's provided me with a platform to start being authentic, and to hopefully inspire other people along the way.

As mentioned in an earlier post, my three words for this year are Do Share Inspire, and I feel that I am living the intent of these words. There is still a very long way to go, another 17 '30 day' activities, and some small project activities to be exact, but I am very happy and proud of the project so far.

Day 93: Slowing down and speeding up

Day one went pretty well, although I've come to expect that. It's how day 15 goes that will give me some indication of whether this is something I feel can and should be part of my life, or has had any impact on me. Having said that, below is a little bit of day one.

An open plan office does me no favours

Slowing down is going to be a huge challenge, particularly the whole 'not multi-tasking'. I've become so used to email alerts and working on multiple tasks at the same time, it just feels like second nature. I do know it's not productive though, and have had periods in my working life where I've moved away from being a slave to my email and tried to become more focused on my tasks; it's not like I've never tried this before.

One of the main issues is I work in an open plan office, with a lot of distractions; or distracting people to be more accurate.[4] This is why creating my own soundscape from 30 days of Better Listening was such a powerful realisation for me. I do have my iPod at work, and regularly use it when I need to focus; the concept of a soundscape enhances that idea, making me more aware of my surroundings, and when they have taken control.

I think this will negatively impact slowing down because it's difficult to focus on a single task in this sort of environment. The conversations around me, as well as people popping into my cubicle, are distracting and impact on my focus. I find once I've been distracted that's when I start checking emails and flitting through other things. I have to remain disciplined this month.

Meditation win

I did take the time to do a guided meditation last night, the first time I have meditated in just over a week – so that's how well Activity 5 went. It was nice and helped me to relax a little, but my brain was still whirring a lot.

And yes, I feel I should mention that I get the idea of meditation and I know it takes years to truly quieten your brain while meditating. I understand the principles of meditation and know to acknowledge and set aside the thoughts that come up. But when I say my brain is whirring, for me it means I have all of this energy running through my body and I can't even sit still to properly try. I can't quieten myself down enough to focus on my breathing, to start calming anything – and then my internal critic starts in about how useless I am.

I usually push through for a little bit, but eventually that cacophony of noise in my head is only increasing my stress levels – so I stop.

---

[4] I also include myself in this. It is by no means a judgemental comment on the people I work with; simply a comment that the people in the space and their conversations are distracting.

Speeding up Activity 6

The problem I have at the moment is I feel like I need to pick up 30 days of Drive with a little more energy, but I feel like this would go against slowing down. I know it's probably not the case but I feel like there's a conflict there.

I'm a little stuck on this activity at the moment. I'm reading Simon's book, which is great; I'm learning about my limbic brain, and how hard it is to explain my WHY because of how it works. It's actually a very annoying thing to know. There is part of my brain that probably understands all of this, but it has no access to language and can't help the rest of my brain get it – and people claim we are the product of intelligent design!

I have made some progress with all of this though, I will post something up in the next few days to explain this in more detail. Interestingly some of this became a little clearer after watching one of the new TED Talks yesterday *Peter van Uhm: Why I chose a gun*. It's very inspirational and well worth a watch.

February 2012 – Huge leaps ahead

REFLECTION – 30 DAYS OF AN ASIAN DIET

If this activity simply revolved around sticking to an Asian diet for 30 days then I did really well. Alas that is not the case, and so I need to reflect on the things that didn't go so well.

The food

But let's start with the fun stuff – the food. You already know I struggled with this a little, mainly the lack of bread and chocolate – not combined of course, although a nutella sandwich does sound good… but I digress.

I consumed very little red meat during this 30 days. There were dishes of beef and lamb, but they were few and far between. The one thing I did finally manage to acquire a taste for was tofu. In the past this has never been something I've enjoyed, but we had a number of tofu meals and it was a staple on the rice paper rolls.

The change in diet did affect how I felt physically. I generally felt less bloated than I usually do, even when we had a few banquet type meals. But I felt my diet had a lot more salt in it than usual. Derek and I don't eat a lot of processed food generally, and we don't use a lot of salt in cooking, or to season after the fact. With the Asian diet, I think it was all of the soy sauce and fish sauce; I just felt like I was consuming more salt than usual.

The meditation

Again, you know the outcome for this wasn't great. I did pretty well in the first week but could not get into the swing of it. I started forgetting and then, if I'm truly honest, I remembered but couldn't motivate myself to do it.

I feel this is partly because I don't like doing things I don't do well, and there is so much going on internally at the moment that I could not sit still for five minutes, let alone even attempt to focus on my breath and clear my mind. But that's an excuse, it does not mean that I shouldn't have persevered.

Fortunately, meditation is part of 30 days of Slowing Down, so I get to try this again. I will try to find some more guided meditation podcasts, they seemed to work a little better than trying it myself.

The exercise

I'm afraid this was another fail. I did take Lily for some extra walks, and I did go out at lunch a couple of times, but on the whole I didn't increase my physical activity that much. For the last week I probably did less than usual.

To be honest, this does not surprise me. I'm not entirely sure what has motivated me to be fit and active in the past, but it certainly isn't here now. I need to do something about this though, since we will hopefully start baling the house (we're building with strawbales) in the next couple of months, and I will need to be a little fitter for that process.

And so generally...

This was definitely an interesting activity to do, but I don't feel I did it justice during the 30 days. I did feel quite good from the dietary changes alone; I've also been taking fish oil tablets regularly again, which I think contributes to that overall wellbeing.

Some of the dietary changes will remain, particularly less red meat, but it won't be as restrictive as it has been. Hopefully I can get into meditation in the current activity, and I know that the exercise has to improve, I just need to find a motivator.

Living in the grey

I recently mentioned the talk by *Peter van Uhm: Why I chose a gun*. This made me reflect a lot about my time in the military, particularly for working out my Why. I haven't put a lot of comments onto the TED site, it may surprise you all to know that I don't usually open myself up to criticism from strangers, but for this talk I couldn't help myself. This was my comment:

> At one point in time I chose a gun as well. I joined the Australian Defence Force at a time where our only (openly acknowledged) overseas deployments were peace keeping. I joined because I felt that I could contribute to something important, the safety of our country and our region. I will never regret that decision or the time that I spent in uniform.
>
> I did have moral crises around Iraq and Afghanistan. This was mainly because I had to send my young troops along and I wasn't sure of the cause. But I did my job because it helped inform decision making and keep our troops safe. We also supported planning the evacuation of Australians injured in the Bali bombings, and the deployment of a significant and substantial assistance mission after the tsunami in Indonesia. What I did helped keep people safe at the same time that it helped conflict to advance.
>
> This is the duality of most things in our society. I got to do things that I was incredibly proud of, but that meant that I also was involved in

> other things that I questioned. I guess what I'm saying is that the world is not simple, it is not black and white – violence or non-violence – there is a lot of grey and we live in the grey.
>
> Thank you Gen. van Uhm for the talk, and the soldier for her sacrifice.
>
> This is always going to be controversial, just look at some of the comments below to see that. For me the most important thing that people should take from this is that the people who choose the gun are not mindless, violent humans who want war –because if you choose to put yourself in harm's way to fight/assist something/someone it is usually due to a belief that things can be better or that the people deserve better. It might seem misguided to some of you, but I think that the courage to do this deserves to be acknowledged and respected.

In particular, this has made me think about why I joined the military and what it gave me, what need it satisfied in my life. It has also made me think about the things I didn't like, the things I had issues with in the military, and ultimately the reason I decided to leave.

This is the third time I've rewritten this post, there is so much I can and probably should say about all of this, and trying to get it into a blog post has been challenging. What I wanted to say, is I think what drives us changes at different points in our lives.

Life is not black and white, it is a varying shade of grey based around the compromises we have made at any given point in time. My time in the Royal Australian Air Force (RAAF) was a classic example of this, and the compromises made during this time helped me realise my important values. The funny thing is, I never thought about it this way before. I'd never realised that there were all of these conclusions my brain had reached about the situation – which is why I'm having trouble writing it.

Best job ever

I should point out the Command Systems Information Manager (CSIM) position I held for almost five years was the most fulfilled I have ever been in a job, so far. There were a lot of positives; things that made me feel proud of what I was doing; respected in my contributions; and like I was part of something larger than myself.

Even when I had to send my troops to set up systems in the Middle East, I did so with a sense of confidence we were helping the decision making processes; helping keep our troops safe. I wasn't happy about our involvement in the war, I had joined the Australian **Defence** Force; war was not something we did when I joined. But the world changed, and I was a committed part of the team. In the murky greyness of the competing emotions (otherwise known as life), I felt staying and supporting our troops was the most important factor.

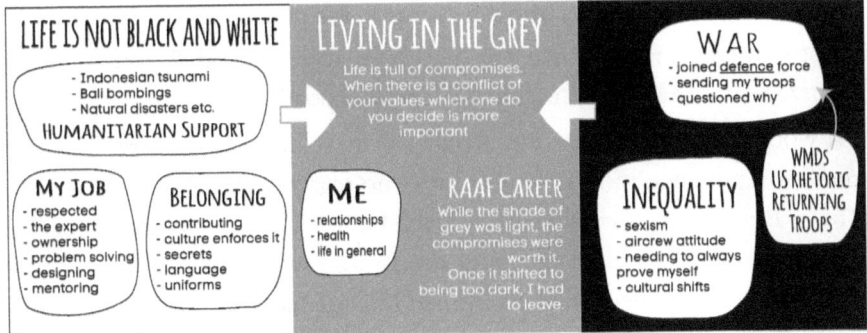

But on the flip side

So if it was so good, why did I leave? Well, I had a very strange RAAF career. My posting to the CSIM position was only my second posting, and I stayed in the role for almost five years. They were *willing* to let me stay in the position for longer if I wanted to, but at the end of my six year short service appointment I decided not to extend.

The reasons for leaving are simple and boil down to one thing – life became the wrong shade of grey. This was mainly due to a shift in the culture within my section.

I was used to being the only woman in the room, and as a junior officer I had to earn respect; this didn't worry me. Once people worked out I knew what I was talking about, my experience and knowledge were generally respected – until one posting cycle changed enough key people that culture shifted. For some reason, my knowledge was suddenly not as good, it was regularly questioned, and I was marginalised from all decision making around training, which I had solely designed and delivered since implementing the system about 18 months prior.

Once the culture shift started I began to notice other inequities and subtle discrimination. The staffing change started a process that made remaining in the military no longer an option for me. I no longer felt like I was a valued and contributing member of a team with a positive impact on the operations of the RAAF. I no longer felt I had a voice, and could effect change.

I guess, seeing this in writing, I can see how that made it unpalatable for me to remain in uniform as we continued to send our members off to war. While I felt like a valued and contributing member of the team it was important for me to stay to support that team. As those feelings were undermined, I felt less commitment to remaining part of the organisation. Did it matter if I wasn't there, when I wasn't listened to anyway?

If you are a female thinking about a career in the military…

A last comment about some the negativity above — and if you think it's negative you should read the first draft of this post!

I would never discourage any females from joining the military. It was an amazing experience and I have absolutely no regrets about being an air force officer. But you need to remember it will be hard, and be willing to leave if it gets too bad. Above all else, you need to be willing to speak out about actions that are not acceptable. I learned this the hard way, as I didn't speak out about an incident that I continue to carry around with me — but that's another story altogether.

Day 98: Successfully slowing down

It's been almost a week of slowing down now, so I thought it was time for a quick post about the progress. I also need something a little light-hearted after writing the previous post over the weekend.

I'm feeling pretty happy with the progress so far.

- I have caught and stopped myself multi-tasking on a few occasions, but I'm not totally weaned off grabbing the iPad when watching TV.
- I left the office at lunchtime every day last week, even if only for 15 minutes. The one day I ate lunch at my desk I didn't use the computer.
- We took Lily to the beach twice on the weekend, which was very relaxing.
- I took time out for myself on Saturday morning to do some op shopping, just a nice slow meander through a couple of op shops. Then I joined Derek up at the house build for lunch, savouring our lovely view.
- I've meditated twice, using the 15 minute guided meditations. I think this is a little more practical for me to set a goal of meditating for a little longer a couple of times a week, rather than a daily five minutes.

The big news – for me anyway

The huge thing that happened last week is my boss has approved my request to start working part time! I've been thinking about this for the last month. It's not just for this activity, but doing this activity gave me the push to make the change. I'm going to 0.9, so one day off a fortnight. I think it will make a real difference.

The important thing is my brain has kicked into this quite well; maybe the recent activities have prepared me for it. I'm quite vigilant about when I'm not following the 'slow' principles, and while I there have been a few times I didn't correct myself, the compromises have occurred for a reason.

The only thing we haven't practiced is slow food, but there is still plenty of time to get into that side of things; I think we needed a week off from thinking about food at all after 30 days of an Asian Diet.

A side note

The only other thing is that I'm now not sure how to fit everything into my days if I can't multi-task. So I've decided that housework will go by the wayside at the moment. Seriously though I do find myself having to think a little harder around scheduling things, which means I don't get as much down time but does that defeat the purpose?? Something to ponder.

Day 100: That has to be a milestone

I only realised as I went to write this post that today is Day 100 of My Year of TED. I'm actually pretty chuffed about finally hitting triple figures, a pretty good milestone. Added to that, today I will be writing two posts. This one is about Activity 6 and the second one I'll do tonight about a project I have been doing based on another TED Talk.

But about my drive

I've done a lot of deep thinking in the last 25 days about my drive and my Why. Little things have been popping in and out of my head, as well as not so little things evidenced by the post on *Living in the grey*.

Importantly, I'm starting to get more of an idea about my values and my drive. I feel like I am starting to really make some progress towards the answer I've never been able to find.

A few statements to ponder further

I've been writing these things down in a number of ways over the last couple of weeks but this is probably the easiest way to share it all. It's still a work in progress, but this is what I have come up with so far.

- I want to make a career writing, designing and helping others understand their world.
- I want to create simple, practical, elegant and easy to understand resources to aid this purpose.
- It is important to me that people are not discriminated against in any capacity, whether that discrimination is intentional or not.

- It is important to me that everyone has the opportunity to reach their potential, especially as children.
- It is important to me that, as much as possible, life is fair.

What does this mean about my Why? I'm not entirely sure yet but I think this is the clearest picture I have had about this in my life. I don't yet know my purpose, I don't have a fully defined list of values, but I am getting there.

Launching the Do-Pad – a notepad for doodlers

I mentioned there were a couple of different ways I would use TED Talks in this year-long project. One of those categories was Project Talks, for something that was a discreet project rather than a month long activity.

The first of these is probably the most exciting for me, because it ticks so many boxes. I have a mild obsession with stationery; I love creating beautiful and practical things; and, I am somewhat addicted to doodling.

It is the creation of a notepad designed particularly for doodlers. The project is inspired by Sunni Brown's wonderful *Doodlers, unite!* talk, which resonated strongly with me. As a doodler, I know I am more focused when I am filling the margins of my pages with drawings about what's being discussed, or simply colouring in all of shapes made by the letters on the meetings papers. I have always known it helps me focus, and Sunni has provided me with evidence of that.

I've probably mentioned this talk 10 times in the last couple of months when people commented on my doodling; definitely an idea worth sharing.

The notepad

Which brings me to the project. I think I got the idea for this when I did the Letterpress course last year. It included a cool garden design for the notebook covers and I thought it would be nice to have a notebook with that design so I had something to colour in or patternise during meetings (I love making up words).

This evolved into an idea for a notebook with a few different designs that could be traced, coloured in, added to and generally used as a catalyst for doodling.

I added to this the need to have pages that could be used for visual note taking, sort of like mind mapping where you draw out the concepts being discussed in a visual/diagrammatic manner to help you understand it better. I love doing this sort of conceptualisation of ideas, so having some pages dedicated to that purpose would be great as well.

Importantly this works in with my three words for 2012:
- Do – I created the notepad and published it.
- Share – I'm telling you all about it.
- Inspire – hopefully if anyone buys it they will be inspired to doodle more, or start doodling.

The Doodle Revolutionary's Manifesto

Looking through Sunni Brown's website I came across *The Doodle Revolution* pages. I thought this was a brilliant idea, so I signed the manifesto and contacted Sunni to get permission to use it in the Do-Pad. Sunni has kindly agreed to allow this, so everyone who buys a Do-Pad also gets a copy of the case for doodling, and how useful it is in developing understanding. Which is great if people start nagging you about paying attention while you are doodling in the notepad.

Available through Lulu

This is available print on demand through Lulu.com. Since creating the first Do-Pad, I have updated it a number of times. It is now 200 pages and includes: lined and blank note pages with patterns; mind mapping pages; and a variety of list pages. It is still print-on-demand, but I am hoping to do a large print run, which will make it more affordable. Check kyliedunn.com for details.

How do we judge our value?

I love the internet. I love the freedom it has given us to find information but mostly I love the ability it gives us to share and connect with like-minded people.

The need to feel valued

I've spent a lot of time thinking about what drives me and what my Why might be in the last 27 days; yes, Activity 6 is nearly over. This thought process has allowed me to realise another of life's little truths. We all like to feel valuable to others, we all like to feel we have something to share. This has a lot to do with some of Brené Brown's words around connection and belonging, but I think that 'valued' is probably the best word for it.

The thing is, we all have something to share. Each of us has some knowledge or wisdom we can share with other people to make their lives easier/better/fuller etc. For some people, what they share can inspire and change the world; for the majority of us the results are much smaller, and closer to home.

This realisation struck me the other day when one of the women at work came back from shopping in her lunch break. She was having a bit of a laugh because when she was out looking at baby stuff in one of the department stores (she's pregnant with her first child) these two young *bogan* women started talking to her and offering advice.

> Quick explanation, for all non-Australians – a bogan is the derogatory slang term we use in Australia for a particular type of people who are perceived as less educated and in a lower socio-economic situation. It's a little like redneck, trailer trash, chav terms in other countries.

Anyway, back to the story. She wasn't being mean about these girls, she thought it was quite nice of them to offer her all of this advice. Things like which products to buy, where to get the best price, and even down to the best way to deal with sore breasts when breast feeding (apparently freezing a damp cloth nappy – don't say this isn't educational). They barrelled her up in the store for about 20 minutes imparting all this hard earned knowledge.

It occurred to me, and I mentioned this to her, that these girls (they were quite young apparently) probably felt elated by the fact they had taught her something. The wisdom and knowledge they have about babies might be the only thing they feel they have any expertise in, and they just wanted to be able to share that with someone.

And sometimes it's not knowledge

We all like to feel valuable to other people, and for me it's I can help people understand something or see the world in a different way. Other people might get this value more from physically doing things for others; providing emotional support to others; or by contributing to organisations that provide these sort of support services to others.

Partly this post is another rambling one about something else I have realised about myself during 30 days of Drive. At another level this post is about sharing something I had never thought about in this way before, sharing a new piece of knowledge I've come to understand.

It doesn't surprise me that I feel connected in sharing my knowledge; I value my intelligence, and I've already mentioned how much I live inside my head. Now it's not like I don't enjoy connecting on the physical and emotional side of things – I'm not talking in absolutes, just preferences.

Something for me to remember

I think I need to be more aware of this when I am dealing with other people. I need to remember that everyone needs to feel valued, and so when people are trying to connect with me or help me out in some way I should let them – because I think if everyone in our society felt valued, or valuable, then the world would be a very different place.

ACTIVITY 8 • 30 DAYS OF SIMPLICITY

As mentioned when talking about my drive, I love design and simplicity in design. Therefore, this activity was always going to be included in the project at some point. It's something that's very important to me, and something I would like to do a lot better.

The talks

I think this activity has the largest number of talks associated. The talks that have inspired this, and will be included in some way are:

- *Rory Sutherland: Sweat the small stuff* – this is one of my favourite TED Talks. The concept of a Chief Design Officer is something I truly believe government would benefit from. I will be taking the concepts around focusing on the small things that can improve our services and make it easier for people to engage with us. I'm not sure how this might apply to my personal life at the moment, I think it is more work related for me.
- *John Maeda: Designing for simplicity* – John's talk is much more focused on making changes in your personal life to embrace simplicity. John's book *The Laws of Simplicity (Simplicity: Design, Technology, Business, Life)* and his website Laws of Simplicity outline the 10 Laws and 3 Keys for living a life of simplicity, which is about living life with more enjoyment and less pain. I haven't read the book yet, but I have read through the website.
- *Alan Siegel: Let's simplify legal jargon!* – Alan's talk is about using plain English as an empathetic way of communicating and gathering information. It's about changing the content, making it simple and intelligible. This would be another one to apply to work.

- *Sandra Fisher-Martins: The right to understand* – this is the first non-English TED Talk I've watched, and I was extremely glad I did. It is much like Alan's, about using plain language in official documents, but this one resonated with me a little more; Sandra talks about writing and designing documents to make it easier for people with low literacy to understand them.

The challenge – trying to introduce more simplicity into my life and my work

I work in government, so there are many processes and information sources that could benefit from a simplicity focus. I've been doing this with the work I'm involved in at the moment, but I could probably take this further.

The main work challenge is to simplify our processes; I have already identified a couple that could be made simpler. The main issue is I don't have much control over these processes. This means my role will be making suggestions during this time to try to influence other areas of our business.

In my personal life, I could certainly benefit from renewed focus on Laws 1, 2 and 3: Reduce, Organise and Time. I find it interesting that in my work life people think that I am a very organised person, but in my personal life I don't appear to be that organised at all. This is partly due to the fact that we are living in a 'temporary' house which is too small for us, combined with our busy lives of building the house, hobbies and this project. But I'm sure there are things I can do to feel more organised in the house, and I think this is an important challenge for me to take on at the moment.

The activity

Rather than detailing all of the things that may or may not be included in this activity I am going to outline this activity in a different way. At least once a day I will focus on simplicity. Whether that's when I'm writing something for work; redesigning something for work; or making changes in my own life, and simplifying an activity or process that I go through.

I figure this should align nicely with 30 days of Slowing Down. I am anticipating that introducing simplicity into my life should make things easier, and thus less time consuming.

This means I should blog every day with this activity, to capture the simplicity application of the day. So I guess factoring the writing process into my day is probably one of the things I need to focus on first.

While it might seem, from this post, this activity is less structured than some of the more recent ones, I think it's because I'm carrying a pretty strong idea of this in my head, which doesn't necessarily transfer into writing. Hopefully you will all see what I am doing/achieving as this progresses.

Day 105: Last day of drive

I can't believe it's been 30 days of Drive already. Maybe that's because I don't feel like I achieved enough, or maybe because I can't believe it is the middle of February already.

The reflection post for this one will be quite long, as I plan on detailing more of the processes I completed to reach this point. But for the final day I think I will share my Why, or what I *think* my Why is at this point in time.

I've decided to use Simon Sinek's terminology for this, because I think it works better for me than anything I came across in Tony Robbins material – so here goes.

My (draft) Why
- **Purpose** – to create items that make the world a simpler/easier place for people to live.
- **Beliefs** – life should be as fair as possible, with everyone having the opportunity to realise their potential.
- **Cause** – trying to make society more equal and letting people understand their abilities/strengths/value.

I've called this my 'draft why' because I think I need to test drive it a little to see whether I got it right.

I also know why I've never done this sort of thing before, because it looks incredibly wanky to write it out this way. Don't get me wrong, I don't think these are things I have achieved, I don't even know if I am capable of them, but I think of all the things I've learned about myself during this process, these statements capture the things that drive me.

Activity 7 update
I'm still relatively happy with the progress on slowing down. We experienced a bit of slow food over the weekend. We went to the grower's market in town and bought some lovely local produce, enjoying some of it as a very simple dinner last night.

I've still been meditating, cutting it down to a couple of times a week has made it a lot more achievable. I have also been doing more exercise, focusing on taking a little extra time for me.

Not multi-tasking is probably the hardest thing. After so many years of doing this it is second nature for my brain to flick between tasks – I find it particularly difficult to just watch TV without surfing the web. I am focused on doing this though, and have made some very definitive changes towards single tasking. I still catch myself doing things I probably shouldn't, but I simply acknowledge it and try to be more focused.

Honestly, slowing down is a very difficult thing to achieve in the modern world – but I am happy so far with the attempts I am making. I'm particularly impressed with how dedicated I have been about making sure I take a break at work and not sit at my computer during lunch; I guess it's the little things.

Day 106: Simplicity Day 1

Yesterday I simplified one of our internal web pages, instructing people how to update their phone details at work. The original page was written by the IT folks, which meant it was full of jargon and explanation the staff didn't require. A few of the staff had mentioned they couldn't understand the page, so they hadn't tried to update their information.

I will send the page to a couple of people today to check whether it's now a simple enough instruction for them to follow.

I'm afraid this is likely to be the sort of earth shattering change I will be making as part of 30 days of Simplicity, but as Rory Sutherland points out in his talk, it's often these small changes that can make a world of difference.

Day 107: Simplifying complexity

Late last year we had to produce a diagram of the committee structure we operate in. This is a convoluted structure of National, State and Regional committees. The diagram was meant to try to simplify this and finally provide a picture for the executive about what exists and our commitments.

Today, thinking about what I could do for simplification, I realised that while we may have simplified this picture for the executive we had failed to provide it to the rest of the organisation. So in the guise of simplicity, today I published this diagram on our internal knowledgebase and publicised it to staff. This required a few changes, because even after two months it was no longer accurate – got to love government!

Tomorrow may be a little difficult in simplicity, I'm spending five hours of my workday in Aboriginal Cultural Competence training, which I'm really looking forward to. But it means I won't have a lot of time to work on anything. So I will be looking for any chance I can find. Maybe I need to think about something more personal... we'll see.

Slowing down took a little bit of a backseat today, unfortunately. Work was just too busy at the wrong times for me to be able to have a quiet lunch away from my computer. However, this was the first lunch I've missed in that way, so not too bad.

Day 109: Rome wasn't built in a day

Unfortunately, the majority of things I want to tackle in this month in my workplace are not going to take a day. Yesterday I started making some changes to client fact sheets I want to rewrite into plain English. Getting the old ones replaced will require some negotiations with the area that is actually responsible for the material, but I'm hoping they appreciate not having to update the material themselves.

I also have to craft a kindly worded email for another part of the business I was engaged with yesterday. A training session which is more like a conversation should not consist of 125 powerpoint slides in anyone's reality. The content of the course was great, we just didn't need it on slides.

I will also be working on some fact sheets for a rapidly approaching information session we are running with the community sector in early March. So a lot of work related simplicity at the moment.

Slowing down update

Slowing down has unfortunately taken a back seat in the last couple of days. Work has been hectic, and I feel quite harried – definitely not what slowing down should feel like. This is a great reality check in the project though, because it shows I have not come to terms with how to do this when things are busy.

So this is obviously something I need to be aware of and spend a bit of time considering; how I still feel centred and not pulled in all directions when my environment is busy. Maybe it just has to fall by the wayside during these times, but that would be a shame.

REFLECTION – 30 DAYS OF DRIVE

I mentioned at the end of the activity that the reflection post would include more detail around the process. I thought I would do that through a visualisation of the process, because I obviously have too much spare time.

But first a little history

This is not the first time I've tried to work out what drives me, or what my Why is. I think that in many ways this is something I've been thinking about on and off from high school. I was never lucky enough to be the kid who knew what I wanted from my future. I knew some of the things I didn't want; I was never interested in being a mother, and I was never interested in just having a 'job'. Interestingly, I refer to all of the roles in my career as jobs, I wonder if that says something?

I have also known that nothing I've been doing has hit the spot. It's not that I haven't enjoyed many of the roles I've had in my working life so far, it's just that I've felt like something was missing. The easiest way to explain it is, I've always felt like I should be doing something more, that I haven't been living up to my potential.

So I didn't start this process from scratch, but I have never made such a sustained and focused effort on trying to answer this question for myself. I think there was always a little part of me that was afraid to find out the answer to the question; once you know you must to do something about it.

The process

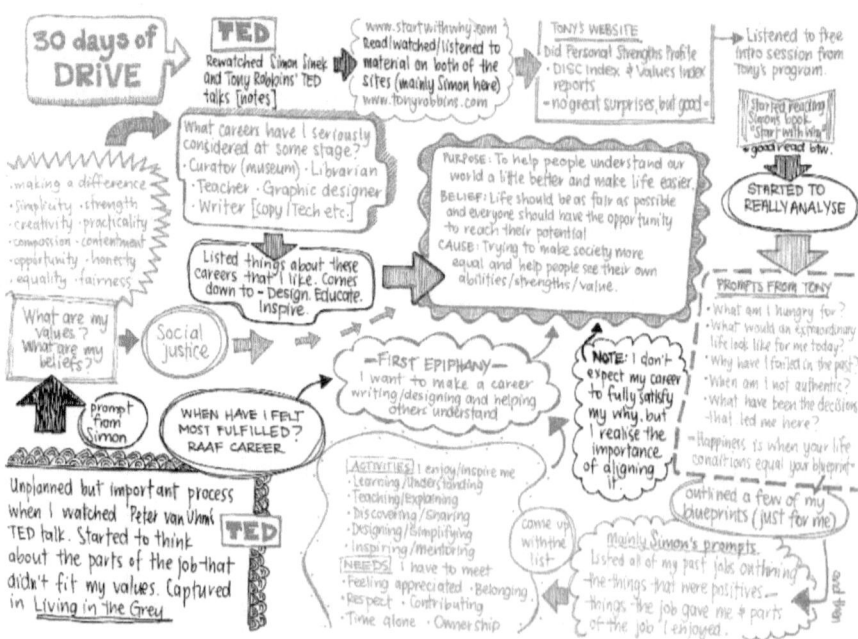

The steps to my Why

In simpler detail the steps I took were:

1. Re-watching Simon and Tony's TED Talks.
2. Going through both of the websites and reading/watching more.
3. Getting my DISC and Values Indexes from Tony's website.
4. Reading Simon's book and listening to Tony's introductory audio.

5. Considering a lot of prompts from Tony's talk, especially outlining a couple of my blueprints.
6. From Simon, and a little bit of Tony, I listed all of my past jobs and the things that worked – bits I liked and things they gave me.
7. Came up with the list that was in the *Starting to outline my drive* post.
8. Spent time considering when I have been most fulfilled in my life – my RAAF career.
9. From this I had my first clear epiphany, which wasn't a huge surprise – I want to make a career out of writing and designing things that help others understand.
10. Serendipity stepped in with Peter van Uhm's talk, which made me think a lot about the parts of my RAAF job that didn't fit my values – outlined in my *Living in the grey* post.
11. Combined with step 10, Simon prompted me to think about my values and beliefs. I came up with a list of my values and realised that a very big driver for me is social justice.
12. Last list was the careers that I have thought about pursuing at some stage (curator, librarian, teacher, graphic designer, copywriter, technical writer, any sort of writer). I listed from this the reasons why I've considered them in the past. I came up with three words – Design. Educate. Inspire.
13. From all of this work I sat down and went through all of the notes to came up with a draft Why (Purpose, Belief, Cause).
    a. The Purpose has been slightly refined in the past few days – *To help people understand our world a little better and make life easier.*
    b. The Belief – *Life should be as fair as possible and everyone should have the opportunity to reach their potential.*
    c. The Cause – *Trying to make society more equal and help people see their own abilities/strengths/value* have remained pretty much the same.

This did not happen in a vacuum; the realisations I have already made about myself through this project as a whole and my three words for 2012 [Do. Share. Inspire.] definitely contributed to the outcome of this process.

Final reflection

If you have always struggled to work out what you think your purpose or direction should be in the world, I would recommend this sort of process. In the end, I found Simon's approach to be more in sync with what I was trying to achieve; although Tony's talk and the content from his site did definitely provide some things for me to consider.

I feel like this is pretty much there. It may not be perfect but it feels right, so while I could probably play around with the semantics for months, the general meaning and how it feels in my head is right.

One of the things that came out of all of this was that I had never consciously thought about how my career needs to align with my Why (well everything does really). I've always known I don't expect my career to fully satisfy my purpose, but I had never thought about how misaligned some of my roles have been. Then again, without knowing my Why before now it's probably not surprising. I also realised that this explains why my two marriages were destined for failure... but we won't get into that here.

I guess I understand a bit more about why I'm doing this project, and a lot of the activities I have done/plan to do. It seems I'm doing this just as much for all of you as I am for me; maybe on some level, I knew that anyway.

> If you want to do this for yourself, the *Living with Intent: The 10 Steps to Defining Your Why from My Year of TED* ebook and workbook will guide you through the process. Check it out on kyliedunn.com.

Day 111: Reduce and Organise
Applying John's Laws 1 and 2

Not all of the simplification activities relate to work; and not all of it has to do with design. The reason I included John Maeda's talk was because his laws are around simplifying your life, and my life could use a little simplification at the moment.

So this weekend I decided to tackle the study. I don't know why Derek and I insist on putting a desk and chair in our study, we never use it as a working space; it is more of a storage area, and not a well organised one at that. It amuses me when people at work say I'm well organised, maybe at work but not at home.

The main problem with the room here is the same as the rest of the house, it is too small. Now this isn't a major life issue since we bought a house that was too small for us, as an incentive to get our new house built. It was a sound theory, it's just a pity the house build is taking longer than we had planned – but this isn't the place to vent my frustrations about that.

I have just finished reorganising the shelves and reducing the number of books we have stored in the room. Hopefully this means I can move some stuff out of the lounge/dining room to fill up the gaps.

The aim for this small piece of simplification is to reduce the general stress levels I feel when I'm trying to relax at night. Having a cluttered living space does have a significant negative affect on me – a fact I am fully aware of and yet I still don't keep it neat and tidy. What is that about?

Activity 7 update

We've also had quite a slow weekend. Today we took a long drive exploring the coastline near us and going to local markets. I'm two-thirds of the way through this activity and I think it's certainly had an impact. Nothing mind-shattering or life-altering at the moment, but I am feeling more relaxed and a little more focused on what I'm doing.

I keep reminding myself that none of these activities occurs in a vacuum, so some of this may have to do with flow on impacts from previous activities. Potentially some of the relaxation comes from ceasing the incredibly introspective activities that have dominated the project so far.

Either way, I'm enjoying my 30 days of Slowing Down and will be sorry to see it end in 10 days.

Day 115: Simplifying the story

I've been fortunate in my current position that I seldom take work home, but the last couple of days were exceptions to the rule. This meant I didn't have a lot of time for either of the activities I'm currently doing, but that's okay because that's life.

Designing to tell a story

But it's not like they've gone by the wayside. As part of the work I was doing I had to put a spreadsheet together to model the impact of a decision over time. I hate spreadsheets at the best of times, so I put a bit of effort into thinking about how to put this together. The aim was for it to stand alone as an explanation of the model we developed. This took a couple of versions before I felt it flowed well as an explanation, and my boss agreed.

I think this is one of the hardest things in designing documents, particularly ones without a lot of words. For people to be able to pick them up and see the story they are trying to tell, without you having to lead them through it.

John Maeda's Law 4 is Learn – because *Knowledge makes everything simpler*. Unfortunately for most of my work, when I'm designing to tell a story I have to assume my audience knows nothing. At the same time, the stories have to be as brief as possible, hence the difficulty in crafting them.

It's particularly hard because to design a document you already know the story, so it makes complete sense to you since you know what you mean to say. This is often the bit where I have to take a step back and give it to a small number of people to find out where the story falls short, because it more often than not does fall short in the first draft.

Overcoming my ego

It used to upset me when I worked hard on something I thought did the job, but other people couldn't see the vision I had created, or the story I was telling. Nowadays, I realise I shouldn't be upset about it because it means I haven't made it simple enough yet. The story is not giving the reader enough knowledge to understand it fully yet, and my job is to give them those pieces.

So now I don't wait for it to be polished before I show it to a few other people and, more importantly, I realise I shouldn't be annoyed at them for not seeing the genius in what I have given them (yep, sarcasm font is definitely needed). All it means is my job isn't done yet, since it is my job to help them understand it.

I'm not entirely sure what this post says, maybe I'm still suffering a little fatigue from the last couple of days. But I think this is the first time I have consciously acknowledged that a big part of my job is storytelling. They may not be riveting stories, and most of them would put children to sleep from boredom, but they are stories nonetheless. Maybe it will help me to think of them in this way – if nothing else it might make them feel more interesting.

ACTIVITY 9 • 30 DAYS WITH LESS MEAT

This will be the shortest launch post yet, because the concept is so simple I could just put the talk title down and I think you would all work it out.

The talk

I first listened to *Graham Hill: Why I'm a weekday vegetarian* in late 2010, and it's an idea that has intrigued me ever since. The concept is exactly as the talk says, limiting your consumption of meat by only eating it on weekends.

The idea is this will give you many of the environmental and health benefits of being a vegetarian, without requiring you to completely give up meat. So it's more achievable for those of us who enjoy meat.

This appeals to me because I'm a fan of pragmatism. This concept is a very simple, yet powerful way, that we could all make a big difference, without the all or nothing approach.

The challenge
The challenge is pretty self-explanatory; it's one of the nice, practical talks. I will limit my meat intake by becoming a weekday vegetarian. It's a good thing I finally developed a taste for tofu during 30 days of an Asian Diet. There are a few vegetarian recipes we had during that activity which will make a resurgence in this one.

The activity
This section is probably a little redundant for this talk but I'll go through it anyway. For this activity I will become a vegetarian during the week. That means I will not eat any meat, chicken or fish, from Monday to Friday. This will be a vegetarian diet, not vegan, so dairy and eggs are still allowed.

And a special nod to my artist, for this activity – I love the evil chicken turning into a lettuce in the artwork.

Day 118: Where is the time going?
A difficult week for slowing down
I can't believe 30 days of Slowing Down is almost over; I feel like it should only be halfway through. I'm not entirely sure whether that's a good sign, but on with the update.

This week has been very up and down as far as slowing down is concerned. There were a couple of days during the week where I had very little downtime, including taking work home one night. During this time it was impossible not to multi-task, and I didn't take time for myself over lunch or to meditate. I did notice my stress levels increase during this time, maybe a combination of the hectic pace, and not following my slow actions.

Once the work was finished, by lunchtime on Thursday, I took control back and started to reapply the activity parameters. This meant taking time for myself, being single-task focused and a few other things.

Hopefully in the last few days of slowing down I can continue all of the tasks of the activity.

And what about simplicity?

I've been following these principles with the work I've been doing. Unfortunately the documents I was writing earlier in the week couldn't have the plain English principles applied; they were internal, and at a level where that's not deemed appropriate. I did try to simplify them as much as possible, and I did take some time to simplify other supporting information.

Thursday and Friday gave me more of a chance to develop simplified documents, which I tried very hard to achieve with a couple of communication pieces I was responsible for on Thursday.

Friday was an interesting day since I had to present information to the Southern office about our recordkeeping project, and the wiki we've implemented for the organisation. Even though I'm usually very careful when explaining technical/system concepts to non-technical people, I realised I do have to try harder to simplify the explanation of these systems. There were a few questions seeking clarification on some of the terms, and one of the staff queried whether there was a page on the wiki that explained some of the technical terms.

This is probably a very good idea and something I will start on next week.

Day 121: Last day of slowing down

Today is the final day of slowing down. As always, there will be a reflection post done in a few days with a more considered analysis of how this activity has gone for me, what did and did not work and what I felt I achieved.

Overall though, as I start my last morning of slow, I feel energised by this activity. Did I do everything as I planned? Not at all. But the things I did manage to change in the 30 days – the mindfulness around trying to single-task, and be more in the moment – were enough for me to feel relaxed and renewed by this one.

There were some periods of heightened activity at work during these 30 days that I think would have been more stressful for me had I not been focused on slowing down. So there are certainly aspects of Carl Honoré's talk I intend to keep in my day-to-day life.

More on that over the weekend.

Simplicity is never simple

I have started working on a number of things I haven't been capturing in the blog. Partly because the weekend was so hot and I was not inspired to write, and partly because I've gotten into this mindset that what I write here should be about what I have done and not what I intend to do.

I realised after my last post that this concept is a little crazy because, as I mentioned before, a lot of these things can't be done in a day. I long ago came to an understanding about the aspects of my nature that make me do this sort of thing. They are some of the more broken and insecure parts of myself, some I've previously discussed here; most tied to my perfectionism and need to never fail. So, I decided to break that habit with the list below. These are actions I have started or plan to start for simplicity; the things I would like to be able to have an impact on and make changes in:

- I have made the jargon and acronyms page for the wiki, as discussed in Day 118. Now I need to promote it and get other people contributing.
- I have been placed in charge of a project at work that has the potential to be very complex and time consuming. I am currently working on the project plan, with a focus on how we might simplify the tasks.
- I have given the Housing area my amended fact sheet, in plain English, and have offered to help with rewriting more of these if they wish.
- I've been looking at our websites, and am developing a brief on how to simplify them; their purpose, navigation and content.

With all of these I'm trying to keep John Maeda's Laws of Simplicity in mind, particularly those around Trust, Organise, Reduce and Failure.

Now look at all of this in relation to the Why I have worked out for myself and you can see that this activity was an inevitable addition to the project.

March 2012 – Grateful for the recharge

REFLECTION – 30 DAYS OF SLOWING DOWN

Activity 7 came and went in a blur, which is a little ironic given it was slowing down. I don't feel like I did this for 30 days, and maybe that is the power of slowing down.

There were a couple of very simple things I wanted to try to do in this activity, but the underlying concept was to apply the general principle of Slow that Carl Honoré outlined in his talk – savouring time instead of counting it.

The things I had listed for this activity were:
- meditating
- stop multi-tasking
- stop eating lunch at my desk at work
- enjoying slow food
- relaxing
- giving up StumbleUpon.

How did each of these tasks work for me?

From the outset I will say that I didn't do as well in this activity as I had hoped, but I'm getting used to that feeling. However, I am very happy with the things I did achieve; overall I do feel like I was more present and considered in the activities I was undertaking in these 30 days.

Meditation – I think I've made enough comments about how this hasn't been working so well for me in previous activities. It was a little better during slow for two reasons. First, I didn't plan to do this every day, which was significantly more realistic. Second, and more important, I stopped trying to meditate properly. By this I mean that I remembered meditation is a mindfulness exercise, and while it requires quiet so you can focus on trying to focus on nothing, it doesn't require me to be in a darkened room shut away from everything.

So meditation has become something I do while walking from the car to work; washing the dishes; or hanging out the laundry. I've tried to make it more about focusing attention on clearing the endless chatter in my mind, and less about where and how I do that. Yes, I have still done some standard meditation as well, but incorporating the process into some of the mundane, daily rituals of life has made it easier for me to practice. I'm calling it pragmatic meditation – not the ideal way to do it, but it works for me.

Stop multi-tasking – this was always going to be the hardest action, and I could have done better. Probably the biggest achievement was gaining control over email interruptions, by turning off all my email alerts at work. This meant it was completely up to me to check for email, rather than being interrupted during other work. It took a bit to get used to, as I was writing a document my brain would automatically stop and think about email and every couple of minutes. However, after 30 days of this activity I can honestly say sometimes I forget to check email for a couple of hours, if I'm in the zone with the work I'm doing. This is certainly something I'm keeping.

As for other multi-tasking, well I still had the iPad and laptop with me while watching TV at times, but this was usually when I wasn't actually watching TV. I was quite disciplined at not having them if it was a show I wanted to watch. What this shows is how often the TV is on as habit/background noise, and we need to just turn it off more often.

As for not watching TV during dinner, this is always hard because of the time we eat dinner, which is at ABC News time. So we usually still had the news on, but then again there is a lot of news I ignore so we were only partially attentive, if that counts?

Stop eating lunch at my desk – I was pretty successful at making time in my day to leave the office and get some fresh air, and time for myself. Sometimes this meant I did come back and eat lunch at my desk, but I seldom did that while looking at the computer. Usually it was looking out the window and just being in the moment.

I've found this was an extremely positive change. During the crazy week I had recently, I missed being able to take time for myself, and I felt the impact of not slowing down a little in my work day. I know this might seem like an obvious requirement for many of you, but sometimes common sense isn't! So this is definitely something I aim to keep.

Slow Food – we did this a couple of times on the weekends. We went shopping at the farmers' market twice during the 30 days and had a couple of lovely meals, practising the principles of slow food. We had done this a little with 30 days of an Asian Diet as well, and it is something that we need to remember to do more regularly. It's nice to be mindful about preparing and consuming food, rather than the usual 'quickly cook and eat' we do during the week.

Relaxing – this was generally achieved with the other tasks I was doing, but there were some days I had to focus a little more on making time to relax. I would generally think about this as I was driving home from work in the afternoon, whether I felt I had taken time to relax during the day, or if I had to do something in the evening. Having that little bit of focus on making time to relax does shift your thinking, and I think this is something I will try to keep in mind as well.

Giving up StumbleUpon – this would have to be a fail but, you knew there was a but in here, I did do this for the first 10 days. After that it was probably only about five or six times during the whole activity. So I don't think I did too badly, given it's something of an addiction.

Overall analysis

I mentioned on the last day that I do feel more relaxed after this one. I know this doesn't happen in a vacuum, and outside influences, as well as the stresses I'm putting myself under, all play a part in those feelings. But I do feel more centred, and generally relaxed after these 30 days; this activity has definitely contributed to that. Maybe it was simply well placed amongst the other activities, but it has revitalised and re-energised me.

Like 30 days of Living the 3 A's, I think this is the sort of activity that everyone should do. Even if there are only a couple of things I'm able to take forward into my daily life, taking 30 days to actively think about your actions and focusing on individual tasks, is very powerful. Thank you for helping me understand that Carl.

Forgot one thing: the other thing this activity prompted me to finally organise for myself is the reduction of hours to a nine-day fortnight. I should hopefully get to start this shortly, and I can't wait to have an extra day a fortnight just for me, and the things I want to achieve. I'm thinking of dedicating most of that time to something that will support the outcome of Activity 6, but I'll post more about that when I know what I'm doing.

Day 125: Activity updates and Introversion

There hasn't been a lot going on in simplicity in the last couple of days; there have been a few other things consuming my time and energy. You know the old saying 'life is what happens when you're busy making other plans' – well we have had some very sad news about Derek's dad's health, so our focus has shifted. The initial shock is over though, and we're sorting things out for how we deal with the next few months, so next week the activities should start up again with renewed focus.

Weekday vegetarian

I have been following Activity 9 very well, but it was only two days last week so there isn't a lot to talk about yet. I've just come back from grocery shopping and tonight we will be making a vegetarian lasagna that will give us quite a few meals (this thing is huge). Hopefully this will be an easy activity to follow, although Derek is not compelled to undertake this with me. Given how much manual labour goes into building a house, I don't expect him to give meat up during the week for my project.

A huge thank you to Susan Cain

What did happen yesterday was that TED kindly loaded Susan Cain's talk up on their site, which was better than I had even hoped for.

For those you who aren't aware, TED2012 was held last week in Long Beach; it consumed some of my time with the tweets and blog comments.

One of the speakers this year was Susan Cain, the author of *Quiet: The Power of Introverts in a World That Can't Stop Talking*. Being an introvert, I couldn't wait for this talk, and I have ordered the book as well.

Her talk, *The power of introverts*, has been viewed over 328,000 in less than 48 hours; it's certainly a topic of interest in the TED community. There have been a few extroverts who have made comments about how the talk is anti-extrovert and makes the case that introverts are better, which I find fascinating.

For any extroverts out there, it's not all about you. Try to turn the filter off and listen to her talk, because that is not what she is saying at all.

My experience

I've grown up thinking there is something wrong with me because I am introverted; that the need I have to spend time alone with reduced stimulation is somehow not 'normal.' I was held back a year at school because I was 'too shy' to progress to senior primary, and since I started school a year early they felt it would be better to keep me back to build my confidence.

Seriously! How is telling a child who was at the top of their class academically, and had as many friends as they actually wanted, that they weren't fitting in and had to stay back a year (losing all said friends) going to build confidence!!! And that's just one of many times I was told, or got the message I was broken.

But I digress. Susan's talk is not anti-extrovert, it is simply espousing the benefits of introversion in society. She suggests that we need a little more acknowledgement of the power of time alone, and being quiet so you can contemplate yourself and your ideas. Susan makes it very clear that we need extroverts and introverts need to display extroversion at times too. I heard it as a simple request for extroverts to stop pushing their way of thinking, creating and operating in the world onto everybody else – a plea for balance if you will.

Please watch her talk, whether you are an introvert who needs to know there is nothing wrong with you, or an extrovert who needs to understand that what you perceive as 'shyness' is actually just our innate need for time alone. I think there is something in this talk for everyone.

Day 128: All about reducing something at the moment
Thoughtfully reducing content

Simplicity is moving along fairly well. I'm still trying to be mindful of keeping my written work language simple. Yesterday I started crafting a survey we're asking the community sector to take. I started about five times trying to explain the process, what we needed to get and why, before I ended up with a simple flow chart of the process. This allowed me to remove a considerable amount of the explanation, making it easier to follow.

I've been trying to keep John Maeda's *Laws of Simplicity* in my mind when doing this sort of work, I have them printed and stuck up in my cubicle. The summarising of this information came through *Law 1: Reduce – the simplest way to achieve simplicity is through thoughtful reduction.* I realised I had fallen into the trap of trying to tell them everything in this survey, when it isn't the right channel for that story. So I culled it back to 'what do I need to remind them about when they start taking the survey?' since there will be many other communication mechanisms on the detail of the project.

What I've come up with is a simple graphic explaining why we can't progress without this information, and a reminder of which elements of data are essential to the process. This hasn't been reviewed yet, but I know what I have at the moment is a lot clearer and simpler to interpret than what I started with.

Not missing meat

The heading is a little misleading, since we are still eating meat on the weekend so I don't think I have much of an opportunity to miss it in some ways. But I think that's the value of weekday vegetarian; being able to reduce meat for health and environmental benefits without being totally restrictive.

Last night we had the Corn Pancake Stacks that a good friend sent me the recipe for – the bonus of having vegetarian friends is getting some great recipes. It's a yummy and simple recipe; if all of our meals are like that, this month won't be a stretch at all.

Day 131: Not good enough people!

A chance meeting...

I've just had a man at the door asking for donations for the *Relay for Life*, a fundraising event we do for cancer research here. He had his two small children with him, a girl of about six and a young boy about 10 months old.

As he was writing out my receipt I asked him if he'd been out long getting donations this morning, just innocuous small talk. He said that he hadn't been out for very long today, but thought he'd take the opportunity. He didn't get to do much with the team at the moment because he is busy looking after his wife, who is still receiving treatment for her cancer. She was having a nap, so he got the kids out of the house to let her sleep, and to get some donations for the relay.

In the couple of minutes we spoke about it I discovered she had throat and mouth cancer; she found the radiation therapy hard; she had a feeding tube as she was unable to eat at the moment; and she got cancer while pregnant with their young son.

I shared a little bit about the situation we are going through with Derek's dad at the moment, as he has liver cancer which can no longer be treated.

What shocked me most was they had no idea what sort of cancer she had, 'they didn't really tell us anything'. He has no idea whether her treatments are working and they don't have any sort of idea of her prognosis, 'we just turn up for appointments when they tell us to'.

...can sometimes give you a focus

I work in the Department of Health and Human Services, in the Human Services side, and I have recently joined a steering committee that is about working in health-promoting ways and improving health literacy.

I have been writing a lot about simplicity in the last month, and how we need to simplify the information we provide as the government. Maybe they have been told exactly what's going on, but they couldn't work out what was being said. Or maybe the doctors haven't wanted to scare them or adversely impact her mental state during treatment. And yes, if they didn't understand or feel they had enough information they could ask, but it has been proven time and time again that people don't like to question their doctors.

Whatever the case is, they should know about her treatment and exactly what they can expect. They should know what they're fighting; be given some idea of the journey they're on; and what the anticipated outcome is.

I am not just condemning the Tasmanian health system here. I know that Derek's dad has had to deal with large voids of information about what they can expect, treatment pathways, what they mean etc.

This boils my blood, and you can bet that I won't be quiet about it when I get back to work. The way we work with the public needs to change. The information we provide needs to improve. We need to be better public servants than we are currently being.

I don't usually rant very much in this space, but this obviously hit a nerve. Now to do something about it.

ACTIVITY 10 • 30 DAYS OF MORE HAPPINESS

The talks

A few weeks ago I watched the TED Talk, *Shawn Achor: The happy secret to better work*. Apart from being one of the funniest talks I think I've seen on TED; Shawn tied his theory up in a neat little five step process, which means it was a shoe in for inclusion in my project.

While I have selected and scheduled the majority of the activities so far, I had left some gaps for talks that inspired me during the project. There have also been a small number of planned activities I've felt won't work as a full

30 day activity, now I understand the project. That means I had a spare slot, so what better way to fill it than with more happiness.

There are many talks on TED that are about improving happiness, including some of the talks used in earlier activities. For that reason I struggled with what to call this activity, and what other talks might complement Shawn's.

I decided to include two others in this activity, *Nic Marks: The Happy Planet Index* (a concept talk) and *Ric Elias: 3 things I learned while my plane crashed*.

The challenge

I already feel like I've increased my general happiness and contentment with life. Many of the activities I have done so far have left me feeling happier and more confident. But who couldn't use more happiness in their life?

The challenge with this activity is to do the exercises Shawn outlines, and be more mindful of the things that Nic and Ric both talk about; to see if I can achieve an even greater positive focus and maybe even more happiness.

The activity

Shawn lists five daily activities to help people improve their happiness:
1. Write down three gratitudes each day – this should only take two minutes and is three new things I am grateful for.
2. Journaling one positive experience in the last 24 hours.
3. Exercise – I love setting myself up to fail.
4. Meditation – and I am a glutton for punishment.
5. Random act of kindness – taking me all the way back to the focus of Activity 2. Shawn recommends sending a positive email thanking or praising someone in your network every morning.

Ric's three life lessons are:
1. Don't postpone anything.
2. Eliminate negative energy – that one is easier said than done in my work environment.
3. Be the best parent you can be – since I'm not a parent, I'm taking this to being the best whatever role I'm performing with Derek, my family and friends.

Lastly, Nic's Happy Planet Index lists five ways to wellbeing, and it's well worth visiting the website for more information about them:
1. Connect – with the people around you.
2. Be active – can you see the alignment here?
3. Take notice – be aware, appreciate simple things and reflect on life.

4. Keep learning – try/learn something new; challenge yourself.
5. Give – do something nice for a friend or a stranger.

While this may look like a long list of things to achieve, I think it is quite clear that there is significant alignment between Nic and Shawn. It is also cheating a little as I have continued doing some of these things from previous activities. But some continue to elude me; not so surprisingly the physical ones like meditation and exercise.

Importantly, I hope to have the time to journal and write my three gratitudes on the blog, which will hopefully hold me more accountable for doing the work.

By the way, don't you love the artwork for this one? Nothing says more happiness like armfuls of puppies, thanks Matt.

Day 135: Last day of simplicity

Last day of Activity 8

And so another activity comes to an end. I can't believe I've already completed eight of them. At the same time, I seem to have been doing this project forever.

I've learned a lot by focusing on simplicity over the last 30 days, the detailed reflection will cover all of that. The main thing is that this is already a big part of how I think about the world, and how I approach some parts of my work and my life. As with most of these activities, I could do it so much better by maintaining more focus.

For my final day of simplicity I'm trying to complete some of the work I started earlier in the activity. I'm pretty happy with my achievements so far, there's only so much I have the ability to influence in such a short time.

As for weekday vegetarian...

This activity is going extremely well; we've had some wonderful food so far. I don't miss meat during the week; to be honest, I haven't thought about it. Maybe if I had a craving it would be different, but meat isn't something I usually crave. Although I don't think that I could give it up altogether.

Old habits

I noticed last night that it hasn't taken me long to get back to some of my pre-slowing down habits around multi-tasking. I'm trying to reassert some of the rules I had in place for the activity, because they were extremely beneficial. So that means I need to stop Stumbling while watching television; either it's a time to relax or a time to do things, it can't be both.

Day 136: Starting more happiness

Three gratitudes for today
1. The inane conversation of teenage girls behind me at lunch 'but you didn't want to be a pole dancer because you're too virginy' – gold!
2. My photos were printed in 10 minutes, so I didn't have to go back.
3. The lolly jar at work (this may appear a few times within the 30 days).

Today's positive experience

This is a nice easy one for today since we pretty much got the engineering sign-off on the house frame, just two minor things to fix.

This means when Derek makes the fixes we are right to get the roof on – finally! I know this probably excites Derek more than me, because it was his hard work that built the house frame (well him and Glenn the builder). But sometimes I feel like we'll never finish our house, so this is a huge deal.

It also means we should be ready to start building the strawbale walls after Easter, which is exceptionally exciting. Not only because we will have walls, but because I'm intending on taking some time off to help with this process. So I get to be more involved in the house build, and I get a break from the office, which I haven't had for far too long.

Day 137: Kylie Dunn's Day Off

Today's three gratitudes
1. Derek driving himself to the airport at 4:20am.
2. Finding a perfectly coloured cardigan for $4 at Vinnies.
3. Having a yummy reheat so I didn't have to cook dinner tonight.

Today's positive experience

The entire day was my positive experience. This is the first day of my new part-time working hours, where I'm having one day off a fortnight. It's taken long enough to get this sorted through HR and payroll processes, but that's all water under the bridge now that it's finally started.

I didn't have anything planned for today, except trying to get some more reading/research done for this project, and getting some creative time for myself. As it turns out, I have the whole weekend to myself. Derek is visiting his parents, so I didn't feel as much urgency in spending the time alone wisely today. That will of course change for future days off, I need to start getting some plans in place for that.

And some of the other things?

- It's only Day 2 of Activity 10 but I have exercised each day and, assuming I do meditate tonight as planned, I will have done that both days as well.
- I didn't do a random act of kindness, like Shawn suggests, today. But I did do a quick cleanse of my wardrobe and donated a bagful of clothes to charity.
- I tried to be a good mum to Lily (yes she is our dog) by spending some time playing this afternoon. She still doesn't think it's enough, as her sad eyes and huffing next to me on the lounge indicates, but I'm happy with the time she got today.

Day 138: TED put Brené Brown's talk up today

Today's three gratitudes

1. Lily let me sleep in until 8am this morning – usually she is up and wanting to go out a little earlier.
2. We still had paper towels in the back of the car – Lily rolled in something bad when we went for a walk this morning so I got to clean her up before getting back in the car.
3. Rediscovering the *Hyperbole and a Half* blog through a random tweet about its creator. I had been Stumbled onto her 'How a fish almost destroyed my childhood' post a while ago and hadn't thought about the site since. The rediscovery made me smile today.

Today's positive experience

This is so easy, today's positive experience was TED putting up *Brené Brown: Listening to shame*. This is the only talk from TED2012 that I was anticipating more than Susan Cain, although it was an extremely close call. I wasn't sure what she would say in this talk that could differentiate it from the first one, but the focus on shame was great. I'm not going to go on about it, suffice to say I think that should all watch it and I don't think you'll be disappointed.

Day 139: Four crazy dogs and good friends

Today's three gratitudes

1. Lily was quite well behaved at the beach, even without a squeaky ball to get her attention.
2. Derek came home from visiting his parents (yay!)
3. Derek came home with takeaway, so I didn't have to cook (double yay!)

Today's positive experience

Today's positive experience was the wonderful day shared with friends. We took the dogs down the beach, to have a laugh as they insanely ran around and harassed the other dogs. After wearing them out for about an hour we all came back to my place for lunch and a catch up.

There is nothing quite like spending a quiet Sunday afternoon good friends, except maybe doing it in the company of four insane dogs.

And as for the other things...

The exercise has been going well, as has the meditation (surprisingly). I haven't been doing the random act of kindness, although as I write that I realise I have been regularly praising people in the TED community (speakers and contributors to the conversations).

The TED community has also challenged me in eliminating negative energy. I don't know why but there are too many trolls on there at the moment. While constructive criticism is a beneficial part of this sort of community, some of it is less than constructive. At the same time I am reading Kathryn Schulz's *Being Wrong: Adventures in the Margin of Error*, which is making me acutely aware of my beliefs and the potential to be wrong. So I am trying to keep an open mind about some of the opinions that do not align with what I feel is right. More about that in a later activity.

REFLECTION – 30 DAYS OF SIMPLICITY

This activity included a lot of TED Talks, but that wasn't a problem because there was a strong focus on communications and language (Alan Siegel, Sandra Fisher-Martins, and Rory Sutherland) whether directly or indirectly. John Maeda's talk is about overall simplicity, so I was able to use it more in my personal life as well. All in all, quite a focused combination.

So what are the main things I discovered/rediscovered during this process and where to from here with the simplicity journey?

Language is not simple

This is particularly true in government and government communications. We seem to take a lot of words to say things that should be, in theory, very simple to explain. To understand why, you need to understand some of the issues around this. I think the following characteristics are to blame:

Avoiding misinterpretation (or covering our arses) – we over-explain everything, and provide too much detail to reduce the chances of people misinterpreting the message. A lot of what we do is so complex there is no way to ensure people don't read what they want into the policy or information. All we end up doing is making what should be 'simple' communication complex, often by introducing details and issues to explain that they don't apply.

One-size fits all – often times we work from the concept that one communication should suit everyone, rather than having multiple pieces in varied formats, targeted at each audience. This is not always the case but we often decide the same document should be used internally with all levels of staff, and externally with stakeholders, organisations and the general public.

We don't want to offend – there is a push in many government organisations to introduce plain English rules into our written work. I think it's a great initiative that would benefit everyone. But there are some people who believe this level of communication is too simplistic, and the people using the material will be offended by how simple we have made it. Seriously?! While some people may initially think 'this has been dumbed down', as long as it tells them what they need I'm pretty sure they won't care.

History of formality and waffling – we have spent so long being taught to write in a non-committal, passive voice. My career in government started when I joined the Royal Australian Air Force, where we learned 'defence writing', there is an art in it apparently. The main thing I remember is it had to be formal and always in the third person; this writer sees a problem with that. Even though there was a push for us to learn plain English writing about four years into my career, my senior managers would always change the language back, and I was told that my style wasn't correct defence writing – it will be hard to break this tradition.

The conventions weren't as strict in the other government departments I've worked, but there is still a tendency to not use 'I' and 'we'. This complicates the writing, you need to create convoluted constructs to avoid using these particular pronouns. As a result, there is often an overuse of the passive voice, making content even harder to understand. I continue to struggle with this one regularly, because I slide into the passive voice without noticing – and once I'm there I find it hard to step back out. Due to our non-committal communication style, the passive voice seems to be the preferred way of writing in government (there it is again, unplanned).

I don't know how to resolve all of this, maybe focus and training is the only answer, but it has to improve. Simply put, I am well educated and have good comprehension skills, but I struggle with some government content; I don't know how some of the general public deal with it.

For me, I will continue to push along with incorporating plain English rules into my writing, as much as I can. I will also continue to push this with others where it is appropriate to do so.

Structuring information is seldom simple

I'm an information manager and have had many jobs designing web structures, setting up shared drive folder structures, and designing file structures for recordkeeping. So this one is not news to me, but I did have a few painful reminders of just how complex it can be.

Not only do different people have different ways of approaching information, but a single person can have different ways of doing it at different times. It comes down to the main focus of the day, or your current task focus. Sadly, information has no innate classification within it, it's all about hierarchy and what the author thinks are the important elements. Is it a finance/logistics document or logistics/finance?

This gets incredibly complicated in web structures, particularly on sites with poor search engines (like our intranet). There were a few things I started trying to sort out during the 30 days that I will continue to push along; this is one area that's been annoying me for well over 18 months now.

Simplicity in my everyday life

It was beneficial to apply John Maeda's laws of simplicity to some aspects of my daily life. Some of this will come back in a later activity as well, but for now I found the laws of Context, Learn, Organise and Reduce to be particularly powerful during the activity.

I felt much more comfortable when I organised the study to reduce the amount of clutter in our house. These are not epiphanies, I know I always feel more settled when things have a home and there is less clutter, but we tend to forget these truisms on a daily basis.

The one other law I tried very hard to remember was Failure; some things can never be made simple. This came in handy on a number of occasions, when I couldn't make something any simpler, and it still required a considerable amount of explanation so the content was understandable.

And in summation...

Again, like many of the previous activities, the power in this has been giving it a focus for 30 days. Making sure that before I began tasks, I put the simplicity filter on to see how I could potentially improve things. Overall, I found using that filter has made me more considered in my approach, and has improved some of the work I've produced.

In some ways it might have been cheating to include something I am very passionate about and have already tried to incorporate into my career. But I had not made a concerted effort to push plain English in my work before, and with the web design I feel I should have done something about it by now but haven't. Then there is the application of the laws in my everyday life, which I hadn't attempted previously. So while I am passionate about it, I haven't been conscientious about applying it practically.

That has now changed, and this is an activity I will keep. There is such a long way to go to improve government communication and information for the general public. Now I know my Why it makes a lot of sense that this is part of my How.

Thank you to all four speakers for such inspiring calls to action.

Day 140: When is potential humiliation positive?

Today's three gratitudes
1. The weather was lovely today.
2. Funny work colleagues taking the piss out of each other.
3. A good initial meeting about a way forward with my project.

Today's positive experience

I've thought a lot in the last few hours about whether I would mention this on the blog. I know I've said My Year of TED is a vulnerability exercise but I'm not sure how vulnerable I'm willing to make myself, even after watching Brené's new talk on the weekend.

But then I thought about two things, what harm will it actually do? And, it's probably not that surprising anyway.

So, what was the positive experience today? Applications opened for the Sydney auditions for TED2013 speakers. That's right, I'm going for the ultimate vulnerability, rejection from TED – or if I make the shortlist, rejection by the TED community.

So if I am worried about, and pretty certain of, rejection, why am I going to apply? Well I can list a number of reasons, the ability to talk at TED; the ability to attend TED; it would be the ultimate Share and Inspire for my 2012 three words; and it would be the perfect ending to My Year of TED. Basically, the benefits outweigh the potential for mass humiliation, and given some of the things I've already said in this blog, how much more potential humiliation can this cause? Don't answer that.

I will keep you informed of the progress of the application. I have been thinking what I would talk about since they announced the crowdsourcing method for speakers for 2013. I have it narrowed down to two things at the moment, so we'll see how that goes.

Day 141: Thank you for reading

Today's three gratitudes
1. A very nice compliment from my boss today.
2. Very grateful the women I work with are such good cooks – great afternoon tea.
3. Woke up with a very clear vision of my TED application talk, way to go sub-conscious.

Today's positive experience
This morning my Blogger stats hit 5,004 pageviews, it's now 5,036. This might not seem like a lot, and of course it isn't, but it's still a milestone for me. For the last five days the pageviews have been in triple digits, which is an exciting shift. There is little point in all of this writing and sharing if people aren't reading it, and although it does unsettle me sometimes that I don't know who is reading it, at least someone is.

So I would like to take this chance to thank you all for letting me consume your time, and ask a favour. If you like the blog then consider sharing it with one other person in your life you think might enjoy or learn something from it; I'd appreciate it.

Random acts of kindness
I've been enjoying the renewed focus on saying and doing things for others again. I'm trying to keep this as part of my daily routine, but when work gets very hectic I do tend to forget. I find it's a nice way to take myself out of my own head, and how I'm experiencing the day. It helps me appreciate others more, but also keeps me more connected to the people around me.

Day 142: Not an overly positive day

Today's three gratitudes
1. This morning's sunrise, an absolutely glorious series of colours changing through clouds of the slightly overcast sky.

2. People who understand my frustrations and allow me to bleat about the stupidity of other people.
3. Learning that someone I have been concerned about is doing okay.

Today's positive experience

It's a bit of a challenge today to come up with a positive experience, not that it was a particularly horrendous day but it was draining. It is a requirement to come up with a positive experience, so we'll see how we go.

Probably the best thing that I can come up with is that I shared my TED audition talk with two people and they both thought that it was good. Now I have to work up the nerve to actually record it and apply, yikes!

Day 143: My 100th post and other events

Today's three gratitudes

1. Derek, who I'm always grateful for and probably don't tell enough.
2. Finding good resources for the work I'm doing at the moment – thank you UK government.
3. Lily being so incredibly excited I fixed her bunny and she was able to play with it – she's so cute.

Today's positive experience

The positive experience for today is that this is my 100th post on the blog. I actually feel this is a pretty impressive feat considering the best I've managed previously is 31 posts over a much longer period of time on my information and records management blog.

So now I have over 5,000 views and 100 posts, but I still only have 11 comments. And while I enjoy talking to all of you I'd love you to talk back as well. So how about it? What's been your favourite activity? If you were doing this what talk would you base a 30 day activity on? Is there anything I haven't mentioned you would like to know about the things I've done so far? And as always, feel free to be anonymous if you would like.

Day 144: Nothing like the sound of rain

Today's three gratitudes

1. Good friends, and a lovely lunch.
2. Fantastic new vegetarian recipe cooked for me for dinner (I'm telling you, Derek is a gem).
3. Serendipitous discovery of information while I was doing research today. I love it when you go down a rabbit hole and end up

somewhere you need to be, for an entirely unrelated topic than you started with.

Today's positive experience

Oddly enough I would say the weather was the positive experience for today. I say oddly enough because it has been cold and rainy, with even a small hailstorm in the middle of the day. But I had to spend very little time outside, instead I got to enjoy watching the weather from my nice warm cubicle.

It's not that I love bad weather, it's simply this is the first really cold day of the year, which included some snow on Mt Wellington. It means that we have a fire going for the first time this year, and in all likelihood we will go to sleep and wake up to the sound of rain, which I also love.

The other reason it is positive today is I know I'll be over it by the end of the weekend, so I'm trying to make the most of it early on.

Day 145: Everyone loves a good buy

Today's three gratitudes
1. Sleeping in this morning.
2. Another wonderful talk made available on TED this morning – *Billy Collins: Everyday moments, caught in time*.
3. Derek's perseverance to tether my phone to his laptop, so I can blog while we are visiting his parents.

Today's positive experience

We're building a house, and we are probably not the greatest bargain hunters in the world. Neither of us is good at haggling and we don't pay much attention to sales happening around us. So today we happened to be in Moonah, by a series of confusion and error, but we won't go into that. While we were there we decided to just drop into Harvey Norman and check out the rangehoods; this is the sort of random thing we do.

I should explain, about 12 months ago we happened to go into the same store when it was changing ownership and purchased our stove. This was a Belling stove I had fallen in love with but could not bring myself to spend $8,000 on. We got it just under half price in the changeover sale, but that was a different positive experience.

Anyway, today we went in and we were looking around at the rangehoods. We came across the clearance section and they had a 110cm Belling rangehood (that is the size of the stove we bought) for less than half price; it was only $647. It was black, which I think will work better than the silver ones we had been looking at. So given that we had budgeted $2,000 for the rangehood, I think that rates as a very positive experience for the day.

Day 146: When negativity hits

Today's three gratitudes
1. Fluffy pancakes for breakfast.
2. Lily being exceptionally well behaved when we went out today.
3. I finished my application video, after about 32 tries (seriously!).

Today's positive experience

I think today in general was a positive experience. Last night was spent in a pretty negative spiral, not worth getting into in too much detail, suffice to say I think I battered my self-esteem into total submission.

I'm not sure why these moods come over me, but last night was a particularly severe bout of self-loathing and negativity.

So the fact I woke up this morning feeling okay, and had a lovely day with Derek and Lily is enough of a positive experience. That's probably more than enough sharing from me.

Other parts of Activity 10

I have definitely not been doing enough exercise as part of this activity. Meditation has been going fairly well though. The trick I learned during Slowing Down is working for me, being less formal about how and when I meditate allows me to do it more successfully.

Given the comment above, I'm obviously not that successful in removing negative energy from my life. But given that the worst negative energy comes from inside my own head at the moment, this isn't as easy as it sounded when I put the activity together.

Other things are ebbing and flowing; as always some days I'm better at doing these things than others. On the whole I feel I'm achieving the intent of the exercise, even with the meltdown last night. But I don't know whether I would say this is bringing me more happiness than the other activities so far. I'm only 10 days in though, so a lot could happen before the end.

Day 147: Overcoming writer's block

Today's three gratitudes
1. Lovely, complimentary friends.
2. Finding a great site from StumbleUpon.
3. Finding out how to put a StumbleUpon button on my blog.

Today's positive experience

You know how sometimes you get given a task to do at work and you just can't find a way to make a start with it. You try to start the document but it's like writer's block, but the worst kind of writer's block because it's not even for something you want to write (most of the time anyway).

I was given a task last week to write a document about our performance indicators and how we might redevelop them. I'm sure it will end up being a riveting read in the end (can you guys tell when I'm being sarcastic yet?), but I just couldn't work out how I might pull it together.

So I started all of the research and conceptualisation, as you should; then today it all started to come together. I've still got a way to go with the document, but at least it has form and a big chunk of content now.

Day 148: I'm out of titles

Today's three gratitudes

1. Builders who put a smile on my face this morning as they giggled like school girls about a rat in the building they're renovating.
2. Conversations about good food and slow food.
3. Another little epiphany from Kathryn Schulz's book *Being Wrong: Adventures in the Margin of Error*, loving this book.

Today's positive experience

For today this would have to be that the presentation of my paper at the meeting this afternoon went well.

I wasn't overly concerned, it wasn't a controversial paper. But there was the chance it would cause some angst with the forum members, mainly because we don't have enough information on the topic at the moment.

Final week of vegetarian

This week is the last week of 30 days with Less Meat. We've both been enjoying this activity quite a lot, so the reflection will be very easy to do.

Day 149: How I feel about living in Tassie

Today's three gratitudes

1. Derek – I know that I've mentioned him in this before but I am grateful for him and everything he does for me every day.
2. Nurofen.
3. Equip sale where I scored a very cool fish necklace for $5.

Today's positive experience

This was a rather serendipitous positive experience. It started with a response to one of my speaker emails. I've mentioned that I try to contact every speaker before using their talks. One of the speakers emailed back today and asked me if I liked living in Tasmania, which is something I haven't thought about for a little while.

Drafting the response was a wonderful experience as it reminded me how I do feel about our new home. I thought I would include it here:

> In short I love it! We've only been here for a little under two years now, but it's a little like stepping back in time, and a lot like living in a big country town. I love how slow it is down here, the natural beauty of everything, the two degrees of separation between you and everything else, the lack of queues and crowds pretty much everywhere and, I think most of all, I love how many stars I can see in the night sky.
>
> I'm sure that there are limitations to being so 'isolated' from the rest of the country, but we are still only a couple of hours flying time away from family and friends that we left behind. We are limited in the stores that we have and even the hours they are open. But I haven't found any of these things to be restrictive at this point.

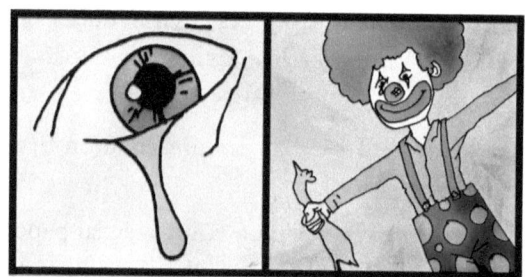

ACTIVITY 11 • 30 DAYS OF PRECONCEPTIONS

As human beings it's part of our nature to classify everything – animals, plants, books and of course people. The problem is that in our haste to classify things we often only see one part of a person/event, and make snap judgements, which create stereotypes. As well, the media pushes stereotypes down our throats – current affairs programs show us that all lower socio-economic people are slackers; all 'boat people' are terrorists and queue jumpers; and all elderly people are gullible pensioners waiting to be duped.

This is why, when I heard Chimamanda Ngozi Adichie's talk I knew it would be the basis of an activity for the project.

The talks

There are actually three talks that have informed this activity, which seems to be a trend at the moment. The first talk is *Chimamanda Ngozi Adichie: The danger of a single story*, which is about how we limit the way we think of others and even ourselves if we limit ourselves to a single story of cultures, races and people.

The second talk is *Bill Strickland: Rebuilding a neighbourhood with beauty, dignity, hope* which is an incredibly inspirational talk about not believing the stereotypes around poor people, and the power of treating them like they deserve more.

The third talk is from *Derek Sivers: Weird, or just different?*, which is the simple idea that something obvious to our culture may be completely different in another culture, but just as valid.

The challenge

The focus of this activity is to challenge my own preconceptions of people and events based around their story, and what I think I might know. I'm just as guilty of this as everyone else. I have my own preconceptions about cultures, races, countries, politics, as well as lesser characteristics. While I might try not to think of the world, and the people of it, in a black and white/stereotype way – well I'm human and that's how we function.

To focus on those preconceptions/stereotypes, and even prejudices, for 30 days; to try to acknowledge and overcome them will be a huge challenge.

The activity

There are two main parts of this activity:

1. Maintain awareness of when I am judging people or thinking of them based on a single story or preconception. When I catch myself doing this I need to think about whether the assumptions I am making about them alter the way I treat them, as opposed to other people in the same situation – and yes I know part of this is fundamental to practising compassion.
2. This is the more time consuming part of the activity. I will make a concerted effort to find out more than the single story that the media might be pushing about a person, event, incident etc.

A great example of the latter part of this activity is Kony2012. I watched the YouTube video, along with millions of other people, and was moved in a very emotional way about their cause, and what they were trying to do. But

I didn't think about the other stories that might exist around this, which have come out in a very big way since the launch of Kony2012.

When I heard the first lot of criticism I was a bit closed-minded to it, after all I had emotionally invested myself in the cause through the movie. But then I realised I should find out more about it, that there were passionate people speaking out against it and they must have a reason why. So I read quite a few articles about the issues people have with the Invisible Children, and I think that some of the criticisms are legitimate. So now I am sort of Kony neutral. I hope that they find him and prosecute him, but I am not willing to put my time, effort or money into it.

It will be a difficult 30 days, since I intend on challenging my beliefs, which is never an easy thing. However, I feel this is an incredibly important activity to do.

Day 150: Fashion pops up again

Today's three gratitudes
1. Brioche. Soft, melty brioche.
2. Lovely, wonderful, supportive friends at work who make the day go quicker.
3. Last day of my work week, yeah 0.9!

Today's positive experience

I haven't spoken about op shopping and clothing for a while now. The change in clothing is something I have adjusted to quite well. So much so this morning I found myself changing, because I was in black, white and grey, and felt plain.

That was a weird feeling, to find that my old 'uniform' was no longer entirely comfortable for me. It was very positive as well, because it shows this one has been a real change in the way I see myself in the world.

To top that off I found a very cool, red jacket for $8 at the Salvation Army today. So I guess clothing was my positive experience for the day.

Day 151: Last day of Activity 9

Today's three gratitudes
1. A little bit of a sleep in.
2. Making a new friend.
3. Lily being a pork chop.

Today's positive experience

Today I finished Kathryn Schulz's book *Being Wrong: Adventures in the Margin of Error*. This was an interesting read that has given me a lot to ponder. I am considering doing an activity based around both of her talks – *Kathryn Schulz: On being wrong* and *Kathryn Schulz: Don't regret regret* – but I need to formulate it a little more in my head.

Last day of weekday vegetarian

I will do a full reflection post on this activity on the weekend. I don't think I have to spend too much time considering the implications of this and its contribution to my life.

Day 152: Making connections

Today's three gratitudes

1. Tartan wellingtons on sale.
2. That Derek didn't get *three* tonnes of firewood delivered (sore arms).
3. Lily killed the squeaky toy quite quickly – it was one of the high pitch squeaky toys she loves, but they're not very hardy.

Today's positive experience

We were in town today and decided to have lunch somewhere nice. We had planned on doing a tea tasting at Chado for Derek's birthday, but they don't do tastings while the MONA markets are on.

Anyway, we thought we would go to lunch at Chado to try some tea out, and have something a little different. We had bento boxes and green tea, which were very yummy, and a nice change from the sort of lunches we usually have on the weekend.

Can't wait to go back in April though and do the full tea tasting. We haven't done a tasting since the two hours we spent sampling teas in Tibet.

A note on sharing

I've been doing a lot of connecting of late, or to be more accurate a lot of social networking. It's part of a process to get the blog a little more out there, but it's also part of the connection side of things. It's not that easy because I am crap at pushing or selling myself, and my default position with this sort of thing is 'why would they be interested in what I have to say?'

Yeah, so you can all understand why I'm writing a blog now?!? This is one of the myriad of self-doubts I'm trying to overcome through My Year of TED, and one of the many things I can't believe I have written down for the world to see – go excruciating vulnerability.

I've been connecting with other people who talk about TED Talks and a couple of blogs with a broader audience. This has given me a slight increase in traffic to the blog, which I am very grateful for as well.

But I would love to have more people reading the blog (even though it's an extremely scary concept for me). So if you are enjoying this please share it with others.

REFLECTION – 30 DAYS WITH LESS MEAT

As I mentioned in the launch post for this one, the concept of being a weekday vegetarian intrigued me when I watched Graham Hill's talk in late 2010. It's such a simple concept, and yet it is so powerful. Imagine the impact on our environment if we all became weekday vegetarians.

It's not that hard

Let's start with this point, for the last four weeks I've been a weekday vegetarian, and it was not difficult to achieve. The only time I had a problem was when we went out for a pub lunch one Friday. The closest thing to vegetarian was a caesar salad; I did eat some of the bacon bits because I felt it wasn't right to waste them when they had already been used on the dish.

On the whole, we ate some wonderful food during the 30 days, and I didn't feel deprived of anything in the process. If anything, I think I enjoyed my carnivore meals on the weekend more than usual, because I wasn't eating meat every day of the week.

It's good for the wallet as well

I can't tell you exactly how much money we saved during this activity, but I do know it was at least $20 a week cheaper for us to eat this way. It could have been even cheaper if we planned our menus better.

It's not just cheaper to do, but there is the added bonus that for most of the meals we didn't need to be as concerned about refrigerating the leftovers quickly, or eating them within a couple of days. Removing the issues around meat safety added a layer of simplicity to cooking and keeping food – and we all know how much I love simplicity.

I am an omnivore

It's important for me to note that I could not give up meat entirely. As much as I enjoyed the weekday break from meat, it will continue to be part of my life. Some people may find this disappointing, but I can't imagine not being able to have lamb roast, peri peri chicken or even bangers and mash.

The bonus is that if we're eating less meat then we can become even more conscious about choosing sustainably farmed animals, improving the quality of the food for us, but also the quality of life for the animals we are consuming. This also aligns with the slow food concept, so it keeps another activity in my focus as well.

I know this will not be enough for the true vegetarians/vegans out there, but be happy with a partial convert.

So where to from here?
I'm sure you can all guess that this one is going to stay. I feel healthy, I've enjoyed the food, it's been financially beneficial, and I think that it is a socially conscious thing to do.

Having said all of that, I am going to make a slight amendment to the rules that Friday can be flexible. The reason for this is two-fold: Friday is usually when I go out for lunch with friends, and it can be a little limiting to not have meat; and, while Derek has been wonderfully supportive with all of this I know that he would have appreciated being able to have meat one more night a week than we did.

So, I will remain vegetarian from Monday to Thursday, and will probably stay vegetarian on Friday more often than not. And if anyone else has any great vegetarian recipes they would like to share please let me know. The recipes I got from friends for this activity were well used during the 30 days.

Thank you Graham for an incredibly simple, but very powerful idea.

April 2012 – Hard to be happy

Day 153: Filling in the gaps

Today's three gratitudes
1. An extra hour with daylight savings ending.
2. My icons came out pretty well for new Do-Pad.
3. Derek looking after me today (I haven't been very well).

Today's positive experience

Filling in a few holes that have appeared in the My Year of TED schedule of activities. I did have all of the activities planned, but as I've mentioned there are a few I realised wouldn't work as 30 day activities. This has left some gaps in the schedule that I've been filling by moving activities up. There are still a number of gaps that now need to be filled, so I've been back on a TED Talk kick to try develop a couple of activities.

A word on preconceptions

While a large part of this activity is about challenging my own preconceptions, I also want to take the opportunity to challenge some of the stereotypes and preconceptions in the media. This weekend a new debate has sparked over applying a 90 day limit on detaining asylum seekers, which gives me a prime topic to focus on.

So today I started doing some research into this topic, which I already have a bit of knowledge about, with the aim of presenting a simplified take on both sides of the story. Last year there was a fantastic show on SBS, *Go back to where you came from*, which should have provided mainstream media with a more even-handed approach to this complex issue. However, just doing a quick search on 'illegal immigrants' has saddened me with some of the vitriolic rhetoric espoused, by what I sincerely hope is a very vocal minority of our society. My in-laws listen to talkback radio, and I hear other people at work talk about these issues, so I realise there is still a popular mainstream story about the evil, queue-jumping, boat people.

Importantly, even though it should be clear which side of this debate I sit on, I need to make sure I am clear about the other side of the story. I know some of the arguments, and some do have a little validity to them. But like so many other complex issues in the world, there is no black and white in these arguments; it is very grey, and murky. More on this later in the week.

Day 154: Nothing like a good April Fools' joke
Today's three gratitudes
1. Google's Gmail Tap promo – very funny.
2. Crazy work friends who made it even funnier.
3. A good day on blog stats.

Today's positive experience
I struggle with these some days, which I'm assuming is pretty obvious for anyone reading them. I've managed to find something positive each day, it's just that some days don't have a stand out experience.

I understand this is the basic concept, it makes you find something positive in your day thereby allowing you to realise your day wasn't all bad. But it's not that days like today have been negative and I need to find something positive, it's simply that the whole day has been fairly neutral, apart from the gratitudes mentioned. I'm just saying it might be better to do gratitudes *or* positive experience, but maybe not both.

All of that aside, my positive experience for today is that two of my friends, who I run a lot of my creative things past, both like the concept of the lists pages in the Do-Pad. Yes, I am doing a Version 2 of the Do-Pad which will include a variety of list pages and extra notes pages to make it about twice the size of the original.

Day 155: Bittersweet positive experience today
Today's three gratitudes
1. Lovely weather.
2. Cute Easter egg from my boss.
3. Interesting post on Raptitude.com that ties in with last activity.

Today's positive experience
Tonight was the final episode of *The Green Wing* (I know it is an old series but this is the first time I've seen it), and why is that a positive thing I hear you ask? As much as I have been enjoying this it also does my head in. It's one of those shows that I enjoy a lot, but it has this underlying level of insanity and annoying characters that also make it frustrating to watch.

At one point I considered buying it on DVD so I didn't have to wait to see how the insanity would unfold each week. But as it went on I became extremely glad I didn't do that, because quite frankly I think if I watched more than one episode at a time I would have lost my mind.

Only English comedy shows have that insane cringey/crazy element that make it difficult to watch multiple episodes at a time. Shows like the *The Office*, *Extras*, and the *IT Crowd* all come to mind.

So it's a positive experience that it's finally finished and everything has been somewhat resolved, but I'm also quite sad that it's over. As the post title says, a bittersweet positive experience today.

Random acts of kindness

I thought I would do an update on the random acts of kindness. This is one of the parts of more happiness I've been enjoying. I have tried to keep up thanks and praise since Activity 2, but some days are far more successful than others. Having it as a focus again for this activity has helped me bring this back as a daily action.

Day 156: Short post today

Today's three gratitudes
1. Have to be grateful for the lovely weather.
2. Photos were quickly processed at lunch today.
3. Wonderful dinner, of course made by Derek.

Today's positive experience

Today I completed Version 2 of the A5 Do-Pad. It is still private at the moment, I want to get a copy to check it all before I make it public.

The new version is 200 pages and includes new pages for a variety of lists. I'm quite excited about the evolution of this and I think that this version is much more complete. I'll be launching it soon, after I check it out of course.

The danger of stereotypes in the 'boat people' debate

I'm going to start this with a caveat, which I shouldn't but... I don't often publicly enter debates around such volatile topics as the refugee debate in Australia. I have a very keen self-preservation gene, and don't like to open myself up for attack on my personal beliefs, in case you haven't gathered that for yourselves. But 30 days of Preconceptions is a little different, so below is a description of the two stereotypes as I see them in the public space. I know many people believe something in between but this is about the dangers of these two extremes, and how the issue can never progress while these are the two public stories.

There are two stereotypes in the 'boat people' debate inside Australia – or I should say in the 'people who arrive by boat from our northern neighbours' debate. They are the right-wing 'they're all illegal immigrants' and the left-wing 'they're all refugees escaping persecution'. I mentioned earlier that this was the first stereotype I want to tackle, as it has come back up in the media, and I personally feel it's important for us as a nation.

The right-wing illegal immigrant

For right-wing commentators, boat people are all illegal immigrants who are paying to jump the queue to get to Australia. Worse still, many are criminals who would never get into the country if they tried to do it by legal means.

They destroy all of their papers when the boats near Australia, so that our government can't verify their identities, or the stories they tell about where they come from and their 'supposed' refugee status. This is why they should all be in detention, because they are 'illegal immigrants'.

The use of that phrase is extremely important. When a commentator uses that phrase to describe people arriving by boat you know which side they're on. It is an emotive descriptor meant to provoke the response of 'well they're criminals,' 'they're queue jumpers,' or 'they're doing something wrong'.

One of the far more vitriolic claims in recent times, that of the illegal immigrant as receiving more government money than Australian pensioners, is a great example of what this stereotype is meant to do. This was circulated around as an email that even had air time on current affairs programs. It adds to the negative image of these people as 'spongers' who are taking from our society, getting more money from the government than the aged pensioners who have worked hard their entire lives for this country – yes that is how this story went. By the way, complete lies!

SANITY WARNING: If you want to be appalled by the interesting 'facts' and rhetoric of this debate try menzieshouse.com.au or hothead.com.au, there are many more out there. Sometimes I am ashamed to be Australian.

The problem with this stereotype

This is a stereotype that depicts the scary, evil foreigners who come here by illegal means and are taking the food from our mouths. By the way, it is not illegal to seek asylum in Australia by boat – it simply is not illegal to do what they are doing! Over the last decade it is more common for this to be followed by rhetoric around Muslim beliefs and wanting to turn our country into an Islamic state, just adding to the hype.

It's an awful argument that creates a culture of fear and loathing around refugees in Australia. And the big problem is, how do we distinguish people who have immigrated here 'legally' when they are of the same ethnic background as the *evil* illegal immigrants? Well quite frankly we don't, do we!

It feeds on the fear and concern that people might already have about the 'other'; the different cultures, religions and ethnicities that are coming into our country. This is nothing new, the same thing happened when we turned away from the *White Australia* policy (yes that was a thing) and again when we took Vietnamese refugees in the 70s-80s.

The main problem is that it doesn't allow people to consider the individuality of the humans involved. They are all judged the same, and that judgement is of criminals out to suck our country dry, and take over our way of life. It's dangerous because it spreads insidious lies and half-truths to a population that is already concerned about not having enough for the future.

The left-wing asylum seekers

To the left-wing commentators, the boat people are all asylum seekers. They are all people who are fleeing from situations that are impossible to exist within, and they all deserve our sympathy and support. Every one of the asylum seekers is a legitimate refugee who is willing to make the ultimate sacrifice and risk their lives to make it to Australia; to have a better life.

For this group, there is no legitimate reason to keep these asylum seekers in detention, and they should all be brought into the community and processed in quick time, so they have a level of certainty about their future here. Moreover, keeping them detained leads to mental illness, suicide attempts and riots, that will cause all of them further harm.

This rhetoric makes a big deal of the right-wing hatred, and paints anyone not in their corner as being nasty people who have no concern for other human lives. At this far left side of the scale you are either totally in or inhumane, there is no middle ground.

The problems with this stereotype

A major problem about this stereotype is it generally becomes more about the people promoting the stereotype, and less about the people they're trying to protect. This is probably due to the mainstream media depictions of the left-wing group – you know, 'tree hugging hippies' and the like. So, the arguments they put forward are usually countered with personal attacks on their naivety, or questioning their patriotism; standard right-wing arguments.

There is a real problem with the stereotype though, it does not allow for any discussion or possibility that the asylum seekers might not be what they claim to be. This stereotype promotes the single story that all asylum seekers are nice, honest people who are fleeing persecution, and there needs to be an acknowledgement that this might not always be the case.

What this stereotype fails to take into account are the two minority groups of asylum seekers. The people that may not actually be seeking refuge from persecution (those subsequently not found to be legitimate refugees); and, more importantly, the refugees who aren't necessarily nice, honest people, or aren't of the right 'character'. And as long as this group fails to acknowledge the fears of the right-wing, there can never be a middle ground.

What does all of this mean?
The left-wing accuse the right of promoting inhumane treatment (UNHCR do much the same I should add), and the right-wing accuse the left of being naive tree huggers who are blind to the reality that we are being overrun by criminals and terrorists.

The major issue is that the stereotype debate stops people from thinking about the individual refugees and their own stories. This was why the SBS show, *Go back to where you came from*, was such a powerful interjection into the refugee debate. It shifted the conversation from the faceless 'boat person', humanised it with individual stories, and helped us understand that the average refugee story is more than the stereotypes we see in the media. Rather, they are personal stories of loss, fear, pain and isolation; they are stories that break the stereotypes and humanise refugees for us.

And personally, once that veneer is broken down, I don't believe the majority of Australians would support mandatory detention or offshore processing. We need to discuss the real stories, the complex mix of issues around these people, and allow the people leaning to the right to see the large number of positive refugee stories that exist in our culturally diverse country.

What is still missing?
The biggest issue with this stereotype, and the fearmongering around us being overtaken by boat people, is that the vast majority of our asylum seekers do not come on the boats! This is probably the most shocking fact that does not get enough air time in the media. And yet, it is the most important fact that could shatter the stereotypes of 'illegal immigration', and destroy to constant political debate in this country about the absolute importance and priority to stop the boats.

The fact is, the vast majority of our asylum seekers come on planes; on average 95% fly into the country on legitimate visas. They come into the country on visitor, business or student visas and they claim asylum once they are in the country. According to a number of sources, asylum seekers arriving by boat are considerably more successful in their claims for refugee status than the ones arriving by plane.

So the fuss made over people arriving by boat from our northern neighbours would seem to be blown out of all proportion. They constitute an incredibly small percentage of the number of asylum seekers we get, and they are often found to be genuine refugees (well over 80% in my research).

To paraphrase FDR, we have nothing to fear but fear itself people. There are far more pressing issues in our country than the small number of people willing to risk their lives in a boat to come here. The likelihood of them not being what they claim to be, or not being of sound character is extremely low, so we need to come up with a better way of dealing with them.

The processes aren't working, and a lot of people are hurting because of it. Do I think we just open the borders? Of course not. But we need a real debate about the issues that is not based on the single stories currently dominating the media. Maybe the outcomes of the recent federal inquiry into our detention centres will lead a more balanced debate about this topic, who knows. [Spoiler alert: it made it worse, a lot worse.]

Factual sources about immigration, refugees and asylum seekers in Australia can be found on these sites, among many others: Refugee Council of Australia; Australian Human Rights Commission; and Refugee Action Coalition Sydney. The Australian Human Rights Commission is a particularly good resource.

Day 157: Fantastic Indian food

Today's three gratitudes
1. Nice catch up with people at morning tea.
2. Derek bringing Lily by to say goodbye – she's at the kennel.
3. Supportive friends around my boat people post – needed a bit of support before I had the courage to post.

Today's positive experience

Derek and I don't go out very often, quite honestly we aren't overly sociable people. It's not that we don't enjoy catching up with friends, it's just we're very comfortable with our own company and we're homebodies. Derek is probably a little more introverted than I am, so this should make sense.

Anyway, with Lily going off to the kennel yesterday we took the opportunity to stay in town and go out to dinner with friends. So the positive experience was good food and good company, combining to make a lovely night out.

And yes, I did break weekday vegetarian for this, but there has to be a level of pragmatism around the application of these rules.

Day 158: Wow my life can be boring

Today's three gratitudes
1. Slow start to the day.
2. Starting Susan Cain's book, I'm going to enjoy it.
3. Hot cross buns, need I say more.

Today's positive experience
Probably the most positive thing today is that we managed to get some spring cleaning done in the house (it's spring somewhere in the world). It certainly beat spending three hours trying to stop my computer from blue screening; I still haven't resolved that one.

As much as we are looking forward to seeing Derek's family tonight, it is going to be a very challenging trip as well. So spring cleaning it is – ever get the feeling your life is really sad sometimes?

Day 159: My father-in-law

Today's three gratitudes
1. Our flight last night was uneventful.
2. Derek's dad had a good day.
3. A brief break at the shops.

Today's positive experience
We're with Derek's family for Easter, and while it is a very challenging and sad time (his dad is not going very well) it is also a very positive thing that we are all here, and he had a good day today. I haven't gone into a lot of detail about all of this, because in many ways it's not my story to tell.

But now that I am here, well this is about my experiences after all. So, I was shocked when I saw him this morning, he looks a lot older and sicker than I had anticipated. He was so happy to see us though; he had a very alert and active day chatting with us, and listening to us all talking.

I think it will be the last time we are all together with him, so it is a very important weekend. I'm enjoying myself in one way in particular, he seems to have adopted me as his co-conspirator. He's in that interesting stage where he's being extremely cheeky, saying things he usually wouldn't say – my favourite comment tonight was 'chicken, you'd think it was the only meat ever invented – bleh'. The thing is, he looks at me when he saying it; then he smiles this weak, cheeky smile, so I can't help but smile back.

We have another day and a half up here, so you can expect much the same sort of post tomorrow night. I have a feeling I'm going to get in trouble for encouraging him before we leave, but to hell with it! He doesn't have long on this planet; he is obviously very tired of being sick, and not being able to do anything for himself.

Don't get me wrong, I feel extremely sorry for Derek's mum as well, it is difficult for her in completely different ways to be looking after him and putting up with his outbursts. I have also spent time talking with her today about how she's feeling, and listening to her talk about the situation. It's just that he's the one who is dying and so he has more right than any of us to be annoyed about the situation. So if a few smiles and chats from me help him deal with it, then I'll be a co-conspirator as much as he wants for the next day and a half.

Day 160: Hidden treasures

Today's three gratitudes
1. Wonderful morning spent with family.
2. Easter egg hunt.
3. Another good day for my father-in-law (Norm).

Today's positive experience

We had a wonderful morning going through some of Norm's stuff, there were quite a few things he wanted to explain and talk about. The best part was going through his old camera collection.

Norm is a bit of a bower bird. Like a lot of men, he has a shed full of some useful things and a lot of random stuff. He has been collecting cameras for a very long time; he was a very keen photographer. But no one was prepared for just how much stuff came out of the camera cupboard.

To top it off there were some very special old cameras, not only because they have sentimental value for Derek, but because they are exceptionally cool. Not just cameras either, there were funky flashes and tripods as well.

The very positive thing was how happy Norm was that I was keen to take all of this gear home with us and create a display area for it. He was expecting me to be less than enthusiastic for Derek to bring it home, but I think that there are a good dozen pieces (maybe a few more) that would make a wonderful display in the new house. So we got some funky, sentimental camera gear; and made Norm's day – two bonuses.

A small note on preconceptions

I've had a few moments on this trip where I've had to shoot down stereotypes. This is not unusual when we are with Derek's parents (or mine for that matter). I'm being a little more mindful about it at the moment, partly because there are some issues it is not worth getting into because of the circumstances, but partly because I'm thinking more about the stereotype involved, and why they would only have that single story.

As usual, I don't feel like I've made any progress in changing their minds, but I can be very patient at times, and I've found that changing minds requires a lot of patience.

Day 161: Ric's three things take on new meaning

Today's three gratitudes
1. Playing with one of our nieces.
2. Connecting through conversation.
3. Our flight left on time.

Today's positive experience

We're back home, that would have to be the positive experience for today, hands down! We had a lovely time with Derek's family, but it was also stressful, emotional, draining and frustrating. It was very sad to say goodbye to Norm. I am pretty certain I will never see him again, but Derek might see him when he heads back up in early May, we hope.

Ric Elias' three things

It's very pertinent for me to reflect a little on Ric's talk, partially from our experiences with Derek's dad being terminally ill, but mainly from some of the things he talked about over the weekend.

As a reminder, Ric's three things were: 1) Don't put things off, 2) Remove negativity, and 3) Be the best parent you can be. It seems a near death experience, or terminal illness are the events that prompt us to say and do what's in our hearts. So below are a couple of my observations:
 1. Norm mentioned a number of regrets he had, things he wished he had done when he was still strong enough to do so. None of them were earth shattering, they were things that should have been simple

enough for him to achieve; they just didn't seem like a priority until he realised he was no longer able to do them.
2. This is probably the hardest part of Ric's advice to follow, since there is so much negativity in our lives. And when you get to the situation Norm is now in, removing negativity becomes more important, but more complicated. He's carrying resentment about needing to rely on other people, since he's too weak to do much for himself. There is also negativity around him, which makes the situation worse. It is an unenviable situation for everyone involved, it is difficult to say goodbye, and I imagine facing your own mortality adds to that. So the sadness, fear, anger and resentment means it takes a strong group of people to remain positive.
3. I doubt anyone ever feels like they reach this, being the best parent or even the best offspring they can be. I know there have been a lot of comments from the family over the last couple of days about regrets – not being closer to help out, not taking the time to do things they might have, and other things that are not for me to discuss here.

The moral of the story

I've realised more than ever that we shouldn't wait to say and do things, because we never know what is going to happen. Derek's family is fortunate in some ways, they've been given the time and opportunity to say the things they have put off – we have all had a chance to say goodbye. So while watching Norm in this condition is hard, at least a terminal illness has these benefits (among the many drawbacks).

I will be using this lesson when I start my next activity on Sunday.

Day 162: The start of a roof over our heads
Today's three gratitudes
1. Sleeping in, in our own bed.
2. Picking up Lily from the kennel; apparently she had very little sleep over the last five days.
3. A quiet day to recharge the batteries.

Today's positive experience

This one's easy, the roofers started on the house today. They managed to get all of the tin sheets across the front of the house; we're hopeful they will come close to finishing this week, assuming the rain stays away. This is massive, since we can't start the walls until we have a roof. It's a positive step towards getting the house built, so it has to be today's positive experience.

I can be so judgemental, how about you?

I've been realising over the last couple of weeks how often I think in stereotypes, and as a result how much I judge people. Just watching the news tonight I found myself judging the people in the stories, one person in particular really irritated me. It's not like this surprises me, I know I'm just as susceptible to this as everyone else, but being aware of it has made me see exactly how much I do this.

The bonus is that most of it is simply my immediate reaction, a Pavlovian response if you like. The initial response is usually tempered with a consideration of the other circumstances may not have been mentioned, the hidden stories.

For example, Matthew Newton's recent arrest in the US. Don't get me wrong here, I'm not about to start defending a man who has assaulted two of his girlfriends and conducted himself in questionable ways in other forums. When I heard the news I thought 'he's screwed up again, he obviously needs help'. But Derek's mum made the comment 'I don't get it, he's throwing his life away and yet he had everything. Just look at his parents.'

I couldn't help myself, I just said 'yeah born to famous parents who both had extremely busy careers; that must have been such an easy childhood'. She just looked at me like she usually does whenever I attempt to contradict her vision of the world.

I don't want any of you to be under the misconception that I think his upbringing excuses his domestic violence or other behaviours. I'm just saying it would be naive to believe that he had a great upbringing or should have a perfect life just because his parents are famous and seem to be nice (the *A Current Affair* interview they did in 2010 seemed to be a bit calculated and protectionist – or is that just my preconceptions coming out again?).

There is the hope that I will learn to be less judgemental during this activity. I've been working on compassion, but I know I can still be very judgemental – I don't think I'm alone in this trait.

Day 163: Last few days of more happiness

Today's three gratitudes
1. Another day off to make a six day holiday. Even with all the emotional stress visiting Derek's parents it has been a good break.
2. Lovely weather, not too warm and not too cold.

3. Susan Cain's book *Quiet: The Power of Introverts in a World That Can't Stop Talking*. I'm about halfway through and it's already amazing.

Today's positive experience

I received an email today to say the order of Do-Pad version 2 notepad has been shipped. As with the first version, seeing the new pages actually in print and all bound together will be an exciting thing.

It'll be a few days until they arrive, but given that today was a pretty slow day this was probably the stand-out event.

ACTIVITY 12 • 30 DAYS OF LETTERS

I knew I would include an activity based around *Lakshmi Pratury: The lost art of letter-writing*. This was partly because it is such a simple and practical concept that lends itself to the project, and partly because it allows me to indulge in my passion for fancy paper and handwriting.

The talk

In her talk on letter-writing, Lakshmi Pratury explains that there is a beauty and personal nature to writing a letter that is being lost with electronic communication. It forms a physical connection between two people, no matter how much time or distance has gone by – it can even bridge a gap between the living and the dead.

The challenge

This is a seemingly simple challenge, although I'm sure it will be inherently more complicated to write important letters. The challenge will be to capture my thoughts and feelings about the important people in my life as letters – beautiful and personal letters. Possibly the more difficult part of the challenge will be mailing the letters.

This is a timely reminder for me about the value of writing letters for a deeper connection. Our friends and family seem so far away since we moved to Tasmania; emails, text messages and phone calls don't always cut it.

The activity

Quite simply, this activity will consist of writing letters to my family and friends. Some of these letters will be simple descriptions of how things are going, so just updating people through a letter. The majority of the letters will be very personal, capturing my feelings and letting them know things I might not have articulated in the past. To make these letters even more special I will source beautiful paper that helps me tell the story of the letter.

Blog posts during this time will be more like reflections about the process, and letters I have found particularly difficult – I expect most to be difficult.

Day 164: My meditation practice isn't crazy after all

Today's three gratitudes

1. Living in Hobart – got in to see my doctor on 90 minutes notice.
2. Living in Hobart – only had to wait five minutes to get into the pathologist.
3. Wonderful friends who listened to me explain a very tiring weekend.

Today's positive experience

Retail therapy and a good chat with one of my friends at work. This resulted in new brown boots, a gorgeous scarf and cute earrings; only the earrings were full price.

I've been looking for brown boots for a few weeks now. Given my misfortune with shoe shopping; finding a pair that fit, were the right type of brown, and 40% off was a plus.

Meditation and exercise

I'm sure it will continue to surprise you that this part of the activity is a little hit and miss. Exercise is the bit I have been missing most, although I have been well disciplined with not parking at work, so I walk more each day.

Stumbled across a great post on Zen Habits today entitled *How to meditate daily*. This reinforced my approach to meditation as being a mindfulness exercise that does not require me to be in a certain place, sit a certain way or take a certain amount of time. It has given me a nudge to start increasing the time I take each day. So meditation is going fairly well, in my style.

Day 165: Last day of more happiness

Today's three gratitudes

1. Finally got a system issue resolved at work.

2. Presentation at steering committee meeting went well.
3. Lily being a complete pork chop when I came home, always makes me smile.

Today's positive experience

This is the last day of more happiness. I think it's been very interesting to be focused on this, especially during the very difficult time around Derek's dad's illness. But I'm a little over doing the daily work, so I'm rather glad that today is the last day.

Fighting the stereotype of the 'typical' public servant

I've mentioned a few times that I am a public servant. Over the years I have copped a fair amount of grief about this, due to the common preconception that public servants have a cushy existence and don't work very hard. This drives me crazy, because I don't believe I fit this stereotype at all. At the same time I have worked with people who do fit into this mould, so I get where it might come from.

In the 'good old days' there was a lot of nepotism and waste in the public service – go on people try to deny it! It was still the minority of people that gave the public service this reputation; it's just not possible for government to have achieved so much if everyone was sitting around doing nothing. This has been reinforced by the power of the unions in the public sector, with the 'they can't sack you anyway' view many people have.

This judgement doesn't work so well in the current era:
1. Lifelong job security is a thing of the past – Tasmania is in the process of downsizing their public service (like many other governments around the country). We no longer have long term job security; it is no longer a job for life. Although as I say this I am acutely aware that we have more job protection than some people in private industry.
2. It is possible to sack a public servant – It might be incredibly difficult, it takes considerable time and effort, but it is possible in most Australian governments.
3. Many people don't consider the public sector as an option for their entire career – I personally believe this is a very positive change. It means that people are increasingly interested in achieving so they can use that experience to move into private enterprise.
4. Following on from point 3, there is no longer a public service exam – this used to get you into government straight out of school. The

change means a growing number of employees have already been in private enterprise when they come into the public sector, so they have a different appreciation of 'business' (you know the whole profit and loss concept government doesn't tend to have).
5. I won't get a pension for life – unlike many retiring public servants are still receiving. Instead I will have superannuation like everyone else. That means I will have to work through to 65 (or whatever random age is set by the government by the time I reach it) before I can get a pension. That's a lot different to many current retirees, eligible to retire on a good pension at 55 from government jobs.
6. We are increasingly accountable and having to perform more tasks with less staff – there is a huge push for transparency in government, which means waste and inaction is not easily hidden from the public. Added to this, many areas of the public service are under the threat of job outsourced to the community sector.

There are probably as many lazy, unproductive people in public service as there are in other large industries and organisations. There are always people who try to do the least amount of work they can, see how far they can push certain rules, or act belligerently. Furthermore, sacking people from private enterprise can also be extremely difficult, especially very large businesses. And this is the point; I believe these sort of people can only thrive in organisations of a certain size, where there are enough other staff (dedicated and hard-working) to make up for the laziness of the few.

Now, I'm not saying I'm the best employee in the world, but I work hard, I am very task focused, and I get results. I also get very irritated when there are people around me who don't work hard. I hate the fact that as an entire workforce we get judged by the behaviour of an ever decreasing minority.

I am a public servant. I have chosen a career serving the public's interests and, like many public servants, I take that role seriously. The majority of public servants could get higher paying jobs in private enterprise, but they choose not to. Okay, there are a percentage of people who are completely institutionalised, that bitch and moan about things that don't matter (you'd be surprised, or maybe not), but they're in private enterprise too.

So, when you meet a public servant don't assume they are lazy, paper shuffling bureaucrats who wouldn't work in an iron lung. Many of us are hard working, passionate people trying to do the best we can to achieve inside very broken systems that need a massive overhaul.

If you know a public servant who you might have made fun of in the past, the next time you see them take the opportunity to thank them. Because while there are aspects of the work that are not overly taxing, there is a very schizophrenic nature of working in a government department. Being accountable to multiple masters can make it a quite stressful job – especially for hard working public servants, and no, that is not an oxymoron people!

Day 166: The power of sharing stories

Okay, so for the last 30 days I have regularly posted gratitudes and positive experiences, and now I find myself sitting here thinking 'I need to post, why haven't I written anything today?' It would seem that the legacy of this particular activity is that I now feel the need to post daily. I'm assuming this will wane as things progress, but for now I'll humour the OCD thoughts in my head – what have I got to lose?!

But I'm not doing the usual posting, so I was wondering what I could share, and then I remembered a story someone recently shared with me. This friend, Stephen, told us about an amazing experience he was fortunate enough to have, thanks to his company.

I'm not sure how many of you might know about the *Reach* organisation in Australia? It was established by an amazing man named Jim Stynes, who has sadly recently lost his battle with cancer. This is part of their About Us blurb on their website:

> Reach believes that every young person should have the support and self-belief they need to fulfill their potential and dare to dream.

One of the events that they run is called 'Camp Maasai', and this is the event that Stephen was fortunate enough to participate in. The basic structure of 'Camp Maasai' is they get together a group of teenagers from their programs, and a group of people from corporate Australia. During the camp they pair individuals from the two different groups together and do a number of activities focused on sharing and trust. These aim to *promote empathy, understanding and awareness.*

An activity of preconceptions

So you can see why I was interested in this activity, and what Stephen thought about it. This is about removing the stereotypes these groups have of each other. The adults from the corporate group start understanding the difficult lives some of these kids have. Through sharing their stories, the adults develop an appreciation for why these kids are in the situations they are in – and after you understand these stories surely it's difficult to not apply that understanding to other teenagers?

Of course, the adults share their stories with the teenagers as well. They share their histories, the things in their lives they have had to overcome, their failures and their successes. This helps the teenagers understand there is hope for them, because there is little likelihood that all the adults had 'perfect' lives – personally, I would say that nobody ever has a perfect life, we all have obstacles we have had to overcome. It also helps the kids adjust their stereotypes about business people, and even adults in general.

As Stephen spoke about it you could see how he was affected by the experience. His concepts about youth, and youth issues have changed, and that's only a small part of the overall impact from the camp.

The pieces are coming together

This has strengthened a thought that has already been running through my head since before this project started. This thought is about the amazing power of sharing our stories with others, as Brené Brown would say making ourselves 'excruciatingly vulnerable'. This has been churning away inside my head, and hearing about 'Camp Maasai' has solidified some of the thoughts, now I just have to think of what action I might be able to take.

This thought is to be continued…

Day 167: Sad news

We were woken this morning with a phone call from Derek's mum. His father had been admitted to hospital on Friday and passed away about 7am this morning. He had obviously used every ounce of energy to hold on to say goodbye to all of us at Easter.

This has delayed my reflection post on more happiness, for obvious reasons – ***Farewell Norm, you will be missed.***

REFLECTION – 30 DAYS OF MORE HAPPINESS

In some ways this was a wonderfully timed activity, in the last week of the activity I desperately needed more happiness. But I still struggled with some aspects of this activity, and I think the only way to explain it is to tackle each of the talks and what I was trying to do with them.

Ric's three life lessons

This part was based on *Ric Elias: 3 things I learned while my plane crashed.* So how did I feel I went against his three life lessons?

Don't postpone anything – as I mentioned in a post, this took on a whole new meaning with the weekend spent with Norm. Do is one of my three words for 2012, and this is a big part of not postponing things. But I know there are things that I have planned for the project that have to be put off until the right time. There were a small number of actions I took during the 30 days that I was putting off, but most of these were more procrastination than anything else.

More than anything, this part of the activity, and the situation with Norm, were probably the deciding factor to bring forward 30 days of Letters. There are things I think I should say to some important people in my life, things I have never been brave enough to put into words.

Eliminate negative energy – I predicted this would be difficult in my current working environment, and I wasn't wrong. Although I did catch myself being more compassionate to people who would ordinarily have annoyed me, so I guess I did manage to do this a little. This is always something I could be better with.

Be the best parent (partner) you can be – I tried very hard to be a better parent to our puppy during this time, and she did get more playtime into the process. Although I'm sure that trying to keep her ear infection under control wasn't perceived to be a good thing on her behalf. I was also very conscious about being a better partner; cooking and cleaning more than usual, but also trying to be completely selfless about the situation Derek is in with his dad at the moment. Again, always something I could be more attentive to – couldn't we all.

Shawn's five daily exercises

Shawn Achor: The happy secret to better work was the catalyst for this activity. So how did I go with his daily exercises?

Write down three gratitudes each day and **Journaling one positive experience in the last 24 hours** – I'm going to write about these together, since they are basically the same sort of task. I get the concept behind this, it makes you reflect back on your day and find at least a couple of things for which you are thankful. The main issue I had with this was that some days I struggled to think of them, and when that happened I felt sad about my day – even if I wasn't feeling sad before I started the task.

Maybe I thought about the gratitudes a little too much since I was writing them so publicly, and maybe I expected too much from my positive experiences for that reason as well. I did do it every day, and some days it made me smile thinking about the good things from the day, but there were at least five days in the activity where I struggled and felt worse as a result.

Exercise – I was very disciplined in not parking close to work during this time, so I at least had the incidental exercise of walking to and from work. There was definitely an increase in physical activity during this time but I do not believe I focused on exercise during the activity; sadly as predicted.

Meditation – I think this is the fourth time meditation has been part of an activity now, and I can honestly say that I did do this as a daily exercise. Mainly, this was by turning meditation into a mindfulness exercise that doesn't require me to do it a certain way for a certain time. Then there was the serendipity of finding a supportive blog post from a blogger I really enjoy *How to meditate daily*.

Random act of kindness – I should have tried to do this the way Shawn suggested, but it felt too false/forced to do a morning email to someone. Instead, I renewed the focus on something that has been hanging around since Activity 2. I am far better at giving praise and thanks to people in my life now, I still hesitate at times but I'm much better than I was. So this part was a success for me.

Nic's Happy Planet

The last part of the activity was part I didn't talk about during the 30 days, but that doesn't mean I wasn't thinking about it or using it as a focal point; after all it is a concept talk. It was based on *Nic Marks: The Happy Planet Index* and this is how I went.

Connect – in the not postponing and the random acts of kindness, there were a number of times throughout this exercise where I focused on connecting with people. This has been a very powerful aspect of the project as a whole, so it wasn't hard for it to be a successful part of this activity.

Be active – I've already talked about the failure to properly exercise more in the activity, but I was more physically active and practised mindfulness. So this was successful as well.

Take notice – the daily gratitudes and positive experience were a complete reflection of my everyday life. As hard as they were at times, they were a chance to stop and take notice of my life.

Keep learning – having to write a daily reflection with this activity was a challenge in itself, and allowed me to learn a little more about the ways in which I continue to be broken. During this activity I also spent time learning about asylum seekers in Australia, interesting facts I hadn't realised before.

Give – the random acts of kindness and time spent with Derek's family over Easter have involved a large amount of giving – both in time, friendship and emotion.

So how do I feel about the whole activity?

I don't know that this made me feel any happier than I was before commencing it. Having said that, it is not very fair of me to assert whether that was solely down to this activity. It's been a very emotional month in so many ways. Maybe it would have been harder without this activity, who knows. What I do know is that not having to do the daily work has been a relief, but then there were many days I really enjoyed it.

Like everything in life, there is a time and place for the exercises in this activity. So these will become part of a growing repertoire of skills I can use when they seem appropriate; when I need more happiness or a jolt about how I am living my life.

Thank you to Shawn, Ric and Nic for your wonderful ideas.

I have an idea, just go with it

This might be crazy but… I've had an idea running through my head for a while. There are many internet sites where people share their stories – one of personal favourites is *postsecret.com*; check out its creator's recent TED Talk *Frank Warren: Half a million secrets*.

So I'm setting up a new blog called *'I am not just a…'* as part of my 30 days of Preconceptions activity, which is focused around trying to understand the other stories that might exist – not just the stereotypes.

Purpose of the blog

There are two intentions for the blog:
1. A place for me to refute some of the single stories that come out in the media, or even within my own social environment.
2. An interactive site where people can send me their own stories of being misjudged, labelled and undervalued; or how they have broken out of the stereotype that was restricting them.

And why am I doing this?

I have long believed that one of the biggest problems in our society today are the stereotypes that dominate our media, and therefore society. You know the sort of thing I'm talking about. Ever since 9/11 all Muslims are terrorists waiting to blow something up; all gay men are sexual predators waiting to turn heterosexual men; all Gen Y'ers have short attention spans, are lazy and technologically savvy; all welfare recipients are lazy and shiftless, and out to get everything they can from the taxpayers; and all atheists are hateful, soulless people without any morals.

The thing is that society, and in particular the media, feed on these single images as an easy way to tell a story. We are so well versed in their imagery that they only need mention someone's religion, culture, age, sexual orientation, or a myriad of other characteristics for us to form a very quick value judgement of that individual. For instance, in Australian society if someone is a Christian we are supposed to judge them as good, but if someone is a Muslim or Atheist then we are supposed to think 'bad'. And whether we like it or not, there is a small part of us that does this without even noticing most of the time.

It sets up a fear of otherness
As well as allowing us to quickly form a value judgement of an individual, it ensures that the person or people being discussed are considered different to us – it enhances their otherness. What I mean by this term is that it creates a barrier between us and the group/individual being discussed, which I believe reduces our capacity for empathy and compassion.

By classifying someone as belonging to a group we don't belong to, it creates this feeling that we don't understand them, and they don't understand us. It also allows us to judge on a macro scale, removing the individual from the story and resorting to the stereotypes.

> Men often hate each other because they fear each other; they fear each other because they don't know each other; they don't know each other because they cannot communicate; they cannot communicate because they are separated.
> – Martin Luther King Jr.

Or 'You can't hate someone whose story you know'
Think about how often you have heard someone talking about 'them' – be that an ethnic group, cultural group, religious group, etc. When people talk about the stereotype of a group they use all-encompassing statements like 'they are X' or 'they all Y', and more often than not these are negative.

But then someone will say something like 'well our Indian grocer is the exception to that' or 'but the Muslim guy at work is not like that'. Because when we know an individual it conflicts with the stereotypes – because none of us are just the stereotypes that society creates. Knowing an individual helps us understand that everyone else is like us, they are a complex set of stories that cannot be summed up in a stereotype. When we know the stories we understand each other, and when we understand each other there is less chance we will fear each other.

It sets up a hatred of ourselves (reinforced by others)
Worse still is when the very public negativity around a particular stereotype affects the way individuals think about themselves. It's bad enough when other people hate us because of our otherness, but it must be horrid to hate yourself because of it. Since stereotypes and preconceptions usually support the negative aspects of a culture, religion, sexuality, race, gender etc, it is easy to see how this might occur. We need only look at some of the research around teenage suicide rates in lesbian, gay, bisexual, trans-gender and intersex youth (LGBTI) to see the negative impact this has (Wikipedia).

A lot of these negative concepts are also reinforced by bullying. Most bullies rely on the stereotypes as a way of targeting and harassing individuals. They might also be reinforced by our own families, who only have the 'single story' about a particular group, and cannot open themselves to the concept that someone they love might be in fact an 'other'.

Sharing is becoming the definitive characteristic of the 21st century
The evolution of the internet has given so many people in the world voices they never had before. Some of these voices are anonymous, and they share painful details of lives that people have never been able to share. But many of these voices are sharing their individuality, or advocating for their groups or societies. We have the capacity to learn more about each other than at any point in history. We can break down the walls of stereotyping, of pushing preconceptions, of fostering single stories of fear and hatred.

The more we share, the more we realise we are not alone in this world. The more we share, the more we understand that someone from another country, who speaks another language, believes in other gods (or none at all); well that someone might actually have more in common with us than the person next door, or members of our own family.

By sharing we break the preconceptions of the traditional media, we challenge the way we view the world and the people in it. By sharing we make the world a smaller place, and we make it less fearful. We judge people less on random characteristics of birth and more on the actions and contributions they bring into the world.

Sharing allows us to develop understanding, and I believe that once we truly understand we can develop acceptance of the other – not just tolerance of a stereotypical existence.

The site will launch next week, I'd love to include a story from you in it.

Day 175: Halfway mark rapidly approaching

I'm sure that you all understand why there have been no posts in the last few days, as I've been in far Northern NSW with Derek's family for his father's funeral. It has been a very difficult time and has made me reflect on a few things in my life, including this project; that's a post for a later date though.

Writing letters

I scheduled this activity before Norm passed away, but I think it was a good choice to be doing at a time when loss and our mortality is so prominent in my life. I have drafted my first letter, I will be writing it up tonight and sending it off tomorrow. The first one is for a very dear friend who has had a huge impact in my life, although she has only been in it for a few years. It includes many things I've never said to her in person. I want to make sure she understands her influence in my life.

I have made notes for a number of other letters over the last week as well. I know the majority of the letters I want to write, now I just have to write them; then, most importantly, send them.

It is probably worthwhile for me to mention I did something like this previously, but the letters were never sent. In early 2003 I was diagnosed with a cyst in my pituitary gland; it was larger than the gland and squishing it. This meant I had to undergo neurosurgery to have it removed. The surgery was not overly scary, they went up through my right nostril, drilled a hole into my skull, and aspirated the cyst through that hole. So they weren't taking my skull apart or going anywhere near my brain, but I was terrified by the concept nonetheless.

So I wrote a letter for each member of my family, for my best friend, for my (then) husband and for another good friend who had also agreed to give the letters to people if anything went wrong. As a footnote, that friend was Derek, my current partner; he has always kicked himself for not sneaking a look at his letter when he had the chance.

When I recovered from the surgery Derek gave the letters back to me, and I shredded them, so no one would ever know what I wrote. I don't think I fully remember what I wrote given the number of years between now and then. But I know those letters were more courageous than the ones I am writing this time; there is a freedom in writing something you know won't be read unless you are no longer here to deal with the consequences.

All of this is to say that I am terrified about this process in many ways. I am a people pleaser who has grown up in a family that tended to embrace denial of the major problems in our relationships. While I don't want the letters to offend, I do want them to contain an element of honesty that might upset the people reading them. This is going to be a challenging activity.

New preconceptions/stereotype blog

Today I also put the first post onto my *I am not just a…* blog. The new blog is located at this web address iamnotjusta.blogspot.com. The initial post is my post about the purpose of the site. In the next day or so I will be telling part of my story, how I am not just a… I'm also trying to entice a couple of people I know to write their story, a way to get the thing moving along. I'm thinking about other things that could be done for this as well, any advice or recommendations are always greatly appreciated.

And how is Activity 11 going?

I've been very vigilant about not judging by a single story in the last few days. I'm still amazed how often I do this, and how quickly I categorise people just on their appearance. I know we all do it, but that doesn't make it any better.

The danger of a preconception when diagnosing

There was a rather shocking thing I realised the other day about the medical profession, which should not have come as a surprise but sort of did.

We often joke about my mother being a medical anomaly, she's had a very interesting medical history which includes a messed up carpal tunnel operation resulting in her wrist joint being replaced with part of her hip bone; the sweat glands in her armpits becoming infected, resulting in their removal; and suffering toxemia during her pregnancy with my younger brother, resulting in a complete hysterectomy at the age of 25.

Toxemia is a condition of having extremely high blood pressure during pregnancy, which is an important point to note. Because my mother has always had very high blood pressure, and has been on various medications for it over the last decade, if not a little longer.

Recently she saw a different doctor at the medical clinic she goes to. While this woman's bedside manner apparently leaves a lot to be desired, she is the first doctor to say that Mum's ongoing high blood pressure is unacceptable. So she sent her to a cardiologist to try sort it out. Also, the cardiologist is the first doctor to sit down with Mum to try to understand all of the reasons why Mum might have high blood pressure, rather than attributing it to her weight.

Yes, Mum is overweight, she has been to varying degrees throughout our entire lives. I'm not talking about seriously overweight, but anywhere between 15-35kgs above her 'ideal weight'.

But the cardiologist was appalled that she has never had hormone tests, more appalled when he found out about the toxemia and hysterectomy. It was when she was telling me this I realised that, in all likelihood, Mum's doctors have always treated her with the preconception that her weight is the reason for her health issues, and that is an extremely dangerous thing to do. Because while her weight may be a contributing factor to her high blood pressure, they shouldn't presume it's the only, or indeed, main explanation.

Personally, I feel bad that I had never even thought about this as a potential problem and there is the distinct chance I've been doing the same thing. But I am not a healthcare professional, and we should expect better care from them. So we're waiting for test results to come back to see if there is an underlying story that has never been considered for Mum, to see if she can finally get any relief from the constant symptoms of her high blood pressure. In the meantime I think we've all learnt a valuable lesson, not only for managing our own medical treatment but also for any healthcare professionals out there; make sure you keep a more open mind when considering diagnoses.

Day 180: Challenging preconceptions a-plenty

You know the sensation, that when you are focusing on something it seems to be all around you? Well that has been happening more and more with the 30 days of Preconceptions. Here are a few examples:

Images of Africa

I came across a tweet from TED's Chris Anderson about a YouTube video called *African Men. Hollywood Stereotypes*. This is a great video showing that African men can be so much more than the stereotypes that we see in movies – mainly mean, over-the-top warmongers.

The video is done by an organisation called *Mama Hope*, which is an organisation that works with people in various African countries to help unlock their potential and transform their communities.

When I watched it I thought it was great, although I was really ticked off with the subtitles which I do not think were required. But regardless I thought it was nice to see something to even out the Kony imagery.

Then I remembered one of the things this activity is all about, which is not accepting the single story of the media and looking into it further. So while I think this video and the sentiment associated with it (Stop the pity. Unlock the potential.) is far better than Kony2012; I can see that there is still warranted criticism about the push for positive images. There is still a very patronising aspect to doing this, but it is better than nothing. We have to start somewhere, and the aspect of Elliott Ross' piece is the comment 'By the way, what is this obsession with proving Africa has a middle class?'.

I think this it's important to show the complexity of African society to the world. So people understand that Africa is not a continent of completely impoverished nations and people. That they have communities and aspects of their societies that are the same as ours. This is the basis of the talk by Chimamanda Ngozi Adichie, and even though the new story may not be perfect, it is better to have positive imperfect stories to counteract the negative ones than to not have them at all.

The climate change debate

The other one this week was a documentary on ABC TV called *I can change your mind about climate*. The concept of this documentary was to take two people on opposite sides of the climate change debate and allow them to traipse around the world talking to 'specialists' to try to convince each other about their side. I found this to be extremely unsatisfying, only partially redeemed by the Q&A episode shown afterwards.

My main problem was way too much time and energy was wasted on the debate about the science, which is a comment supported by one person from the UK in the documentary. But the majority of the documentary is taken up with people arguing about how many degrees the earth has warmed; the location of the weather sensors and how they alter the actual situation; and a whole heap of malarkey about whether we are speeding it up or not.

The thing is that the real debate was about whether we should be changing our lives; whether we should have a carbon tax; or whether this is some sort of conspiracy by, well I'm still not entirely sure who they are blaming the conspiracy on.

You see, I'm all for us taking the approach that we have only finite resources on the planet, and we are polluting it way too much as it is. So if we can find more sustainable and less pollution-creating ways of doing things then we should, end of story. This is actually a very popular opinion but it had very little airtime in the documentary. At least the airtime it did have outlined that focusing on the debate is the way climate deniers stop us from moving forward with the changes that need to be made.

And yes, I do believe humans are hastening the natural process of climate change. But as I said, for me this isn't about saving the planet from climate change, it's about saving the planet from overconsumption and pollution.

So while it was nice to have a forum that allowed some for some reasonable arguments and discussions, I felt the amount of money that was spent on the documentary could have been better spent on other things – maybe presenting a more positive and even handed message about what we can do, what the carbon tax is all about, and how it might actually benefit us. The Q&A episode probably would have been enough.

Activity 13 will be delayed

Activity 13 was due to start on 1 May and would have represented the beginning of the second half of My Year of TED. I was having a lot of problems deciding which activity I would tackle for number 13, and that was bothering me.

Taking a chance on myself – hard work

Last Thursday I had an extremely vulnerable day. I mailed off my first two letters, which took much longer to finish than I would have hoped, and I put myself out there with the Do-Pad. I've mentioned before that I am an introvert, and although I may not have mentioned this in so many words I also lack a lot of confidence when it comes to my creative work.

It's not that I don't like it myself, it's that I have pretty big doubts about other people being willing to spend money on it. But, as part of My Year of TED I am pushing my vulnerability, which includes creating uncomfortable situations as part of putting myself out into the world more.

What I did was a seemingly simple task, approach a local store who stock a cool range of somewhat eclectic bits and pieces and see if they were interested in the Do-Pad. I had prepared for it, but I should have written the things down I knew they would want to see. Instead, in the stress of the moment I did my usual talk too fast and made it all too confusing. She was nice and asked me to email through the proposal and she would talk to her business partner about it. I was proud of myself for even having the conversation, but at this point in time I haven't had the courage to put the proposal together; that is a job for next week.

I was somewhat bolstered when I returned to work and read an entry on David Seah's blog called 'Facing the blankness'. It made me feel a lot better that someone I respect creatively also has these sorts of concerns and issues in the world. But I digress…

Just plain overloaded

After this incident I had this dread of doing the launch post on Sunday. I had chosen to do one of the big activities out of the schedule, but it took another day for this to sink in, and almost finishing Susan Cain's book for me to work this all out in my head.

I tweeted on Thursday after the incident that I was in vulnerability overload; I was actually in introversion overload. Over the last couple of months I haven't had a lot of time for me, to kick back and recharge my batteries. I've always known this is just part of who I am, Susan's book has helped me understand this better, and be more accepting of it.

I've realised that I'm feeling very exposed. The preconceptions writing has been particularly challenging, since I'm not usually that big on putting some of my opinions out into very public spaces; and letter writing, which is so much harder than I had expected. Add to this Derek being away a bit, the last weekend we spent with Derek's dad, and then the funeral – well quite frankly, I'm completely wiped out at the moment.

What's 15 days amongst friends

So, I've decided that the best thing to do is to take a break. I will continue letter writing, there are at least six more I intend to write, and I've only managed three so far. I will also be doing the reflection on preconceptions, and I will be doing the second quarter reflection as well. But I won't start Activity 13 until the 15th of the month.

This also gives me a little more time to prepare for Activity 13 – solidify the concept and process it in my mind and start some conversations with people who I think might like to be involved. The break might also help me get on top of all of the physical crap my body has been going through in the past month; don't ask.

May 2012 – A little off track

Day 183: End of preconceptions (yesterday)
Activity 11

30 days of Preconceptions ended yesterday, and I can't say that I am sorry. This one has been a real challenge, and not just because there were so many things that happened in the media, and my immediate world that brought this to a head. It showed me just how many preconceptions I carry around with me, and how quick I am to apply them.

The reflection post for this will be in a few days. It will be very interesting to reflect on everything from these 30 days, and what I can carry forward.

Writing letters

I have still only written three letters, and only two of them have made it into the post. The third is a letter for my sister, and I'm in a bit of a dilemma about rewriting it or not at the moment. It's not like I haven't done anything for the other letters, there are dot points for all of the remaining letters, covering the things I want to include. I'm just finding it incredibly difficult to get into the mindset to do them.

This would be easy if I were only writing gumpf, but since I decreed they should all be meaningful and special, well that makes it all a lot harder to do.

My aim is to get another five letters written and into the post by the end of the activity, and I don't think that's unrealistic. I know there are two of them that should flow pretty well once I start writing, I just have to start. There are another two that will be a real challenge in not saying the things I really want to say – I know those relationships couldn't survive the honesty of my emotions, I've tried and failed too many times.

I also have a letter in my head I want to write to one of my best friends from school, but I have no way of getting in contact with him. He was one of those people who you don't realise how special and important they were until later in your life, and by the time I had done that I'd pretty much lost the chance of finding him again. Maybe I'll write it anyway and hope that the universe gives me the chance to send it one day, who knows.

I will also be starting the second quarter reflection post in the coming days, and aim to have this up over the weekend. Still a very busy time, even with the delay to Activity 13.

REFLECTION – 30 DAYS OF PRECONCEPTIONS

I spoke a little about this during the 30 days, it was a very confronting activity at times. Having said that, I will start this reflection by saying I think this is something everyone should do regularly. Like most of the activities I've been doing, making something a focal point in your life gives you a different perspective of how you operate day-to-day. When it's as important as potentially making snap judgements that impact how you treat, work with, interact with or simply think about other people, then it is worthwhile understanding your preconceptions, prejudices and stereotypes.

My preconceptions

I mentioned during the activity I was somewhat surprised just how much I 'rapidly categorised' people on their appearance alone. It's not like I had no idea that this was something I do, like everyone else, but until I focused on doing it I didn't realise how instinctual it truly is.

I've been thinking about this in the last week and I've realised that, while I may have been categorising people quite rapidly, I don't feel I was judging them; more that my brain was doing a basic grouping exercise. This might be naive of me to think that I wasn't always negatively judging people by categorising them, but I guess I say this because the majority of the categories were associated with identifying potential risks, and I saw very few of these.

At the same time, it was very challenging for me to realise this part of my nature, and to be more aware of some of the prejudices I have. For instance, Ford drivers have been something I've picked on for a number of years, partly because my father-in-law was such a Ford devotee, and it was a joke. What I've realised is I do have a prejudice about them now. It's not entirely baseless, but there are enough other crap drivers on the road that it's an unfair judgement. I realise that I need to find ways to address some of these prejudices, which is something for me to think about further.

Challenging the media

I have a pretty active cynicism of the mainstream media and the way they feed us information, so I was always going to enjoy this part a bit. However, it was confronting putting forward my views and knowledge of a situation into such a public forum.

As well as the items that were included in the blog posts about asylum seekers, African images and climate change, there were a few other things I looked into. For example, there was a recent judgement by a NSW court that a young girl should receive a multi-million dollar compensation payout after she became a quadriplegic with severe brain damage from eating a KFC Twister. The way they said it on the news my brain immediately went to the 'well that just sounds dodgy', and I wasn't the only one in the room who had that reaction either. So I looked into it and found out that she got salmonella, and that this can go to your brain and cause all of the medical issues she has – so completely legitimate, and incredibly tragic.

But why didn't the news say, after suffering 'salmonella encephalopathy – a brain injury linked to food poisoning that also left her with a blood infection and septic shock'? [*Inquirer News*] It's not like this would have taken much longer to say, and it may have raised awareness of the real dangers of salmonella. Or do they cater so much to the lowest common denominator now that technical explanations have no place in the news?

I have my opinions, like everyone else, and they do impact the way I view the world and the information I'm told. This activity helped me realise just how set in some of my opinions I am. While I don't generally feel bad about that, since I do bend further to the social justice, liberal side of opinion – I have realised I should keep a slightly more open mind about things.

And in relation to the talks

This was always more about Chimamanda Ngozi Adichie's talk than the others, and I feel I did that talk justice in the activity. I educated myself on a number of issues and thought about the multiple stories that might be involved in people's lives – and of course I launched the *I am not just a...* stereotype/preconception blog.

In relation to Bill Strickland's talk, I didn't have much of an opportunity to apply his points during the 30 days. I had planned to spend some time thinking about how I might be able to make suggestions for our service delivery areas around Bill's talk, but there was a rather significant personal event that occurred in our lives that diverted attention.

For Derek Siver's talk I did make an effort to be aware of any thoughts around considering something odd/strange/crazy. What I did find was I spent more time bringing this up with other people's opinions. This is not an incredibly unusual role for me, especially around my in-laws, but I did try to be a little more considered around putting forward the case for different cultures, attitudes and actions.

So where to from here?

I think it's very important for me to maintain more awareness of my preconceptions, and when I might be adversely judging people by considering only one aspect of them.

I'll let the cat out the bag a little here and state that Activity 13 is going to be 30 days to Start a Movement. For the 30 days of this activity I will be trying to find ways to promote the *I am not just a…* blog and trying to make people more aware of their preconceptions and stereotypes.

I've got a few target demographics I'm going to try promoting this with, but I would love to hear from any of you about how/where you think this might be promoted. And let me know if you would like to share your story to challenge a stereotype you face.

To all three of the speakers, thank you for the inspiration.

Day 189: Enjoying my slight break

I started to relax the minute I made the decision to have a two week break in the schedule, but I haven't been completely idle.

Letter writing

I completed two more letters over the weekend, and they made it into the post today along with my sister's letter from last week. It has been incredibly difficult to write these letters, as I keep saying, but I think it's worthwhile.

This has been particularly important for someone like me, who has not been overly good at expressing gratitude and praise. The freedom of writing it into a letter allows me to say more than face to face, but it has an added difficulty that I am very aware what I've written down is forever.

Since I have a few days to myself over the weekend I aim to finish the last three letters and maybe take on one other one; we'll see.

Six month reflection

I still can't believe I'm halfway through the project. In some ways it feels like I've been doing this for years, in other ways I feel like I've just started.

The reflection post is progressing, there just seem to be a lot of activities to include in this one so it is taking a little longer than I anticipated. That and I've been enjoying the break, so I haven't been pushing myself too hard.

Post refuting the 'immorality of atheists'

I've put another post up on the *I am not just a…* blog entitled Atheism does not equal immoral. This was prompted from finally watching the Q&A 'Easter' special with Richard Dawkins and Cardinal Pell. This is something I am a bit sensitive about, because I think I'm a pretty good person, and I know a few religious people who I would not consider good people. Anyway, the post explains it all in more detail.

I am also preparing for the launch of Activity 13, lucky for some.

QUARTERLY REFLECTION 2 – HALFWAY THERE

I've completed 11 activities so far in the project, and I have to say that I am slightly exhausted by the whole thing, hence the current break. Like last time, this reflection won't include Activity 11, since it's only just finished.

30 days of an Asian Diet

I learned that a reduction in bread, pasta and red meat does have an impact on how I feel.

The food part of this activity was a total success and very enjoyable. We've found a couple of dishes that have become part of our standard recipe mix, which has been great. It also helped me finally develop a taste for tofu, which became very important for weekday vegetarian.

The common theme for me in a lot of these activities though, is that the physical aspect of this was less successful, both meditation and exercise. I started off quite well, but physical activities will always go by the wayside when my life gets busy.

Thank you Dean Ornish for an inspiring talk that contributed to some positive changes in my life.

30 days of Drive

I finally found a way of working out some of the important things around my Why, and how I want to contribute to the world.

Like many people, this is something I've struggled with for a very long time – what is my purpose in life, and what can I be doing to satisfy that nagging feeling inside me that I should be doing more. By focusing on this, using expert advice and direction, I drafted a purpose, cause, belief and values.

I'm continuing to validate these as I go through the remainder of the project; I know there are more activities to come that will help me understand this further.

The process was quite arduous, and there were some things I went through about my past that I probably could have lived without revisiting. But it got me to the point I wanted to reach, so all worth it in the end.

Thank you Simon and Tony for the TED Talks, web content and Simon's book. You have helped me reach a greater understanding about what drives me and what my Why may be. Now I just need to work out the how and what, and I'll be set.

30 days of Slowing Down

Slowing down helped me recharge my batteries and taught me not to underestimate the power of savouring time instead of counting it.

This is such a simple concept and makes so much sense, slow your life down; you will enjoy it more, and be less stressed. It's one of those things that in theory seems so simple it can't work. There are two things wrong with that statement: it is not simple, but it does work.

I did well at ceasing the multi-tasking during this 30 days, as well as taking time away from my desk and even enjoying more slow food. But as usual the meditation and exercise aspects could have been a lot better.

I did come to a happy compromise with meditation in this activity though, where it became a mindfulness exercise I would do for short periods while doing mundane tasks – I call it pragmatic meditation.

Thank you Carl for the wonderful talk, and the tweets I should add. This activity was much like the 3 A's, something everybody should take time out of their lives to try. It does change things, and right now I feel like I need to refocus on it for a bit so I can regain some of that peace and relaxation.

30 days of Simplicity

Simplicity is seldom simple, especially when you work in government.

I was really looking forward to this activity, since I seem to have made a career for myself in simplifying and explaining things to people. Combined with that, I love design; I struggle with it at times but love it all the same.

In the reflection post I spent a bit of space explaining why I think this is so hard to do in government, and my opinion about all of that hasn't changed. If anything, the highly political budget estimates process we're going through at the moment, has reinforced all of those musings.

I'm trying to maintain the principles of simplicity at work, as much as I'm allowed. I continue to have some wins, particularly around a recent task explaining rather complex modelling to senior staff. I am also trying to keep John's laws in mind, and have recently ordered his book to learn more about these. Hopefully it will help me apply them more successfully in the future.

Thank you to all of the speakers (John, Rory, Alan and Sandra). Your talks all contained a spark of inspiration for me, and I hope to one day feel like I'm achieving the simplicity in my life and my work that you espouse.

30 days with Less Meat

It's very possible, and quite enjoyable, to be a weekday vegetarian.

This is probably the most simplistic activity so far, being a weekday vegetarian. The concept being that for many people it's not possible to give up meat entirely, but if you give it up during the week then you significantly reduce your impact on the environment, and improve your overall health.

I enjoyed this activity a lot, so much so that I have kept it – well pretty much kept it. I am a Monday to Thursday vegetarian, and sometimes that goes over to Friday but sometimes it doesn't.

This change has also been beneficial to our bank balance; wins all round.

Thank you for such an inspirational, yet very short, talk Graham. It proves that sometimes the simplest suggestions can be the most powerful.

30 days of More Happiness

This reinforced that focusing on something is often the key to bringing about change, but that sometimes the focus can have an adverse effect.

I haven't got much more to say about this activity since the initial reflection post. As you know, during this activity we went to visit my father-in-law who was dying of cancer; six days after we left he passed away. So I don't feel I can evaluate this fairly given the circumstances. I will say this was a well timed activity, and maybe it was another sub-conscious choice to make an exceptionally difficult time a little easier.

I did struggle a bit with the daily gratitudes and journalling, but in hindsight I think this did have a lot to do with the fact I was doing that online – and while I am being pretty honest and open about this whole process, there has to be some sort of filter.

Thank you Shawn, Ric and Nic for very practical talks that had insightful points to focus on. While I didn't do them all equally as well, they have certainly been added to my growing repertoire of skills and tasks.

Feelings after six months

If you've been following along at home you know I took a two week break after finishing 30 days of Preconceptions. I think that's probably evidence enough about how I am feeling at the halfway mark in the project.

But let's break that down a little more, because it isn't a very fair assessment of the first six months. It's probably more indicative of some poor activity choices around an already emotionally draining time.

I don't think I can put into words how different I feel at this stage in the process to how I felt before I started. I certainly have a renewed confidence in myself and feel quietly optimistic for where the entire project will lead me in the end. There have been so many good points, so many things I have learned about myself – major and minor epiphanies.

There is a lot more to do, and in many ways the second part of this project will be more intense and challenging than the first. I made the comment that I needed the break because I was feeling overloaded, and in particular I was feeling introversion overload (which reminds me I still want to write a review of Susan Cain's brilliant and life changing book.) Following on from the last two activities – preconceptions and letters – I plan to try promoting something quite hard. This will be draining, since one of the things I am least comfortable doing is putting myself out there.

At the same time I feel prepared for the next lot of challenges because of everything I have learned over the last six months. It's been difficult and tiring, but it has been a rewarding and satisfying process to go through so far. Let's see if I can't keep the enthusiasm to step it up a notch for the last six months.

ACTIVITY 13 • 30 DAYS OF STARTING A MOVEMENT

The talks

Activity 13 is the culmination of a few previous activities, but it has been mainly inspired by Activity 11. There are two talks that have influenced the development of this activity: *Derek Sivers: How to start a movement*, and *Seth Godin: The tribes we lead*.

Derek's talk is about the importance of the first follower, and how they can be more important than the 'lone nut' who starts the movement; they transform the lone nut into a leader. Seth talks about the fact that leaders need to find something worth changing, and assemble tribes to spread the idea, and create the movement.

There have been two more recent talks that have provided me with inspiration to really pursue the *I am not just a...* blog as my movement. The first is *Frank Warren: Half a million secrets* which is about the creation of one of my favourite websites, PostSecret. The second was a recent talk from *Tavi Gevinson: A teen just trying to figure it out* about her Rookie website, which I've only recently discovered but love the concept of.

The challenge

This one should be pretty clear, my challenge is to start a movement. By now it should be fairly obvious why this is a pretty extreme challenge for me. I am an introvert and I'm not at all comfortable putting myself out there, and less comfortable with causing controversy.

With that in mind, I'm hoping that as the 'lone nut' I find a couple of first followers (probably extroverts) who see the value in this activity. These people will then hopefully pass it onto their tribes, growing the movement.

According to Seth, in order to be the leader of the movement I need to: challenge the status quo; build a culture; develop curiosity; connect people to each other; have charisma (apparently the movement will provide that); and show commitment to the task. I'm not entirely sure how I can/will do all of this, but I'm up for the challenge.

If it fails? – since I am likely to be asked this by some people in my life. Well the process of starting something is part of the TED challenge, a successful movement would just be a bonus as far as I'm concerned.

The activity

My *something*, or my movement if you like, is called 'Challenge your preconceptions'. It's not just about the *I am not just a...* blog. It is about getting people to focus on at least one of their stereotypes; to acknowledge that stereotype; learn more about the condition of people in the group; and be aware of just how their judgement impacts the way they deal with people they believe fit into the stereotype.

In 30 days of Preconceptions I learned a lot about just how quickly and often I judge people in my daily life. I've commented that the majority of this wasn't necessarily negative, but there were times I felt myself acting differently with people because of my preconceptions about them. Although I identified many of these preconceptions, I didn't challenge them that much.

So this activity is to try to start a movement around the concept of 'Challenge your preconceptions' and give people a chance to engage with each other on the topic.

This activity will commence on 15 May – I hope I can inspire you to be a part of the movement.

Day 196: Last day of letter writing

Today is the last day of 30 days of Letters and I feel I need another 30 days to do this justice.

The letters I didn't write

I will go into a lot more detail in the reflection about the letters I did write, and how I felt about writing them. I just feel the need to mention that I didn't get all of the letters done I wanted.

The two I missed out doing were the ones for my mum and dad. I will write these at a later date, it wasn't a good time to do it over the last week. I haven't spoken all that much about my family in the blog, but I will say my relationship with my parents can be somewhat complex due to a lot of things that happened in the past. There is little point writing about any of that in a letter to them, and it's not what I wanted their letters to be anyway.

Unfortunately, I've been struggling through a very blue fortnight, so I felt it was better for everyone concerned if I just stayed away from their letters.

There will be a complete reflection post in the next couple of days, but for now I will say that it was a very worthwhile activity to do and I will finish the last two letters at some stage.

Challenging your preconceptions

Tomorrow I start a movement, why not I have a few spare minutes. Below is the explanation of the activity; the concept and the methods for sharing your stories. More information will be available on the *I am not just a...* blog about sharing.

> Preconceptions, we all have them. Whether they are seemingly innocuous, 'Oh you work in IT; can you fix my printer?', or extremely negative judgements that affect how we interact with others, 'Oh you're an atheist, that means you must have questionable morals'. They exist within all of us.
>
> It is a very natural thing for humans to do, classify things in our world so we can analyse their potential threat or benefit to us. It is something we have evolved to do, and do very well. It is a skill our ancestors used to keep them alive – that sound is likely to be a cheetah that can kill you; that person by the river is from an enemy tribe so may hurt you; that tree has leaves so there must be water nearby, etc.
>
> But we can get stuck in our preconceptions, judging people through stereotypes that are only one potential facet of that person. They are often very simplistic, and regularly untrue. And yet they will alter the way we interact with people, both in good and bad ways.
>
> Challenging our preconceptions is something that we should all take the time to do. Not only does the process help us understand how much we actually do this and the effect it is having on our interactions, but importantly it helps us see some of the preconceptions that we might not even be aware of.
>
> The real aim of challenging your preconceptions is that you might learn more about a stereotype that you use, and hopefully stop judging people you think fit into that stereotype in such a limited way.
>
> What does that all mean? It means rejecting the single story that the media might be telling you about asylum seekers, young people, old people, people of different faiths, people from different cultures, climate change, the occupy movement, people on welfare, and a myriad of other stories. It means looking deeper, reading more, listening to a different source of information or even talking to someone from the group that you have preconceptions about.
>
>> Men often hate each other because they fear each other; they fear each other because they don't know each other; they don't know each other because they cannot communicate; they cannot communicate because they are separated. Martin Luther King Jr.

Challenge your preconceptions is a concept, it is a simple thought, that if everyone in the world focused on understanding the preconceptions they have, and made an effort to challenge just one of those preconceptions; it could be a step towards making the world a more accepting and equitable place to live.

Join with us in June 2012 to understand your preconceptions – the stereotypes that you judge others by – and select one to challenge. Take a small step to developing a better understanding of yourself and the people around you.

Day 197: Starting a movement

Today is the first day for 30 days of Starting a Movement. I'm excited and completely petrified of this activity – excited that it might achieve something, but petrified of the work I will have to do to make that happen.

Please remember that I'm encouraging you all to share stories on the *I am not just a...* blog. You can have your story posted up anonymously if you would like, simply mention that when you email the address in the blog to submit your story.

We all have stories we can share about how people misjudge us by the stereotypes they ascribe to us, and we all have stories about doing the same to others. This is a chance for your stories to potentially help and educate others.

REFLECTION – 30 DAYS OF LETTERS

This activity was always going to be a challenge for me. As you might remember, Activity 2 was about trying to make me more comfortable giving and receiving thanks and praise. Extrapolating from this, you would be correct in guessing that I haven't been very forthcoming about letting people in my life know how important and influential they have been.

That is the reason I wanted the letters associated with the activity to be meaningful and important. It was also what made them more challenging.

During the 30 days I wrote six letters: three to friends; one each for my brother and sister; and one for my partner Derek. All of the letters included something I had never said before; some included a lot of somethings. Some of the messages in the letters were just a formalisation of things that had previously been said.

I tried to make them all a little special as well. They were all made into handbound booklets, illustrating that they were more special than a standard letter.

It was even more difficult to write some of these than I had thought it would be. There is something about committing thoughts to paper, that someone will read without you being there to explain, that is extremely daunting. I was particularly concerned about my sister's letter, since I was raising many things I had never discussed with her.

As I mentioned on the post for the last day, I had also planned to write letters to my parents. But since I was feeling a bit depressed during the last week or so of this activity I decided that wasn't a good idea. I love my parents, but there is a lot of negative history I wanted to avoid including in these letters, and being depressed was going to make that hard to achieve. I still intend on writing these letters down the track, I just need to be in the right place for that to happen.

So how did it go?
As hard as this activity was, I did enjoy it and felt I got a lot out of it. It helped me say things I had always struggled to say to people. It was also a great creative process to make these booklets, with these special messages for important people in my life.

The feedback I have received has also been very positive. So all in all I think this one has been a pretty successful. I will write my parents' letters in the coming months, and may even write a few other letters that I considered for this activity, but didn't have enough time to execute.

I would actively encourage everyone to have a go at this one. It is so rare for people to receive written correspondence these days; just think about how much you would appreciate receiving a handwritten letter from someone special letting you know how special you are to them.

Thank you Lakshmi for lovely TED Talk and idea worth spreading.

Day 204: Adding a talk to Activity 13

Practising extroversion
I've realised I missed a talk that should be included in starting a movement; *Susan Cain: The power of introverts*. I've mentioned previously how much I loved this talk, and it has probably become one of the concept talks of the project. The part of the talk, and Susan's book *Quiet: The Power of Introverts in a World That Can't Stop Talking*, I am trying to apply is the bit about embracing extroverted traits.

Like many people, I'm very uncomfortable putting myself in positions where I am open to rejection. This means that for starting a movement I don't have a lot of active experience in putting a message out there. I also don't feel comfortable in asking people for assistance. I have been doing a few things that are out of my comfort zone in a big way, but I need to do more to try and get the movement out in the public space.

What do you think?

So I'm going to crowdsource this. What else do you think I could do to promote this? Are there any websites you think I should approach or any articles you've read that might align to Challenge your preconceptions?

And while we're at it, what do you think about the movement? Is this worthwhile pursuing? Are any of you willing to undertake the activity in June? What preconceptions would you challenge?

Day 207: Why Susan Cain's book is so important

I have been quite remiss in actually writing about Susan Cain's fantastic book *Quiet: The Power of Introverts in a World That Can't Stop Talking* and how much it has resonated with me. Since I am including it as part of the current activity I thought I should probably talk about it a little.

I've probably said this enough in the blog already, but I am an introvert. I briefly spoke about all of this when Susan's TED Talk came out, but I thought I should expand on this a little more, and the value of Susan's book. What introversion has meant throughout my life is an underlying feeling that something is wrong with me; unfortunately, this was a feeling that many people reinforced. This is why Susan's TED Talk and book are so incredibly important. They validate the inner me, the part of me I have actively tried to hide around others, because for so many years that part of me was 'wrong'.

This was reinforced from a young age. It began in primary school which, like my sister, I had started a year earlier than usual – I briefly mentioned this a little earlier, but here is the longer story. During second class, so when I was seven years old, my teacher started the rhetoric I would hear and read on reports for the rest of my school years. Basically it went, *Kylie does well academically but she needs to be more actively involved in class and overcome her shyness* (paraphrased of course). The thing is that I can't remember feeling shy. Yes, I had some social anxiety, still do. Yes, I could be self-conscious answering questions in class, but I think that is fairly normal for a child, and probably had more to do with my perfectionism trait than shyness.

But I digress, we're at the end of second class and apparently my teacher felt I was too shy to progress to third class (the distinction was junior primary to senior primary, so I'd be with the older kids). Since I was a year younger than the norm, it was recommended I repeat second class, to give me a chance to 'build my confidence'. Now let's take a step back here and think rationally. If I was a shy child surely the worst thing you could do is destroy my self-confidence by making me repeat a year and taking me away from the friends I had made!!!

My parents, not ones to challenge people in authority, agreed that I would repeat. The most bizarre thing was the school actually put me in a composite second/third class and put me in senior primary anyway; the damage was done, and I wasn't raised to question authority. Instead I think I started to believe that I was too shy, didn't speak out enough, and wasn't social enough.

I have tried, for so many years, not to be that person. I felt like a failure every time a report card said I was shy or not outgoing enough, but at the same time I never felt like I was taking a back seat. I was a school councillor, I was the lead in a couple of school plays, I sang in the choir, I played netball and softball for the school, I was on the debate team, and as an adult I have even presented at a small number of conferences and seminars. *Postscript: and now I speak about My Year of TED.*

I enjoyed all of these things, I didn't do them to fit in or please others, I did them for myself. I found them to be taxing, and they certainly weren't parts of my daily routine, but I wasn't a complete loner who didn't join in on any activities, like some of the feedback from school would suggest.

There are other things though that made me feel like there was something wrong with me. For example, I've never had 'a lot' of friends. I mean, I get along fine with people but at any given time in my life there have only been a couple of people who I've felt I could call upon as friends. I think that at this point in time I have more friends than any time in my life, which is an odd experience for me. The thing is that I had friends, and good friends too, but until I was in my 30s I always felt I wasn't social enough and there was something wrong with me (I was too shy and lacked confidence), that's why I didn't have many friends. I blame the media portrayal of school and shows like *Friends*, well that and the people who rampantly bullied me for years at school; these all reinforced the notion I was somehow wrong.

What Quiet has helped me understand

Having a wonderfully supportive partner and rapidly approaching my 40s, I have come to accept who I am, my limitations, and my need for 'me' time in the last few years. But if I had the knowledge from Susan's talk and book

when I was a child, teenager or even young adult, my life may have been very different. I would have understood that:
- it was perfectly fine for me to be comfortable one-on-one or in very small groups, and that my contributions in those forums was enough
- spending my school holidays reading, listening to music and catching up with only one or two friends a few times was the way I recharged my batteries to deal with the social nature of school – and that's okay
- just because I don't enjoy small talk doesn't make me socially inept
- there are many other people in the world like me, I'm not abnormal or wrong in some way
- not wanting to speak up in class or take a leadership role does not mean I'm shy
- other people's expectations about how I should behave are just that 'other people's expectations'; they are not reality and do not take into account what I want
- there are so many exceptional people in the world who feel just like I do, need the quiet time that I need, and contribute to the world in amazing and important ways – my introversion is not a limitation as long as it doesn't drive everything I do.

Maybe I would have complained about being made to repeat, giving me a completely different school experience; maybe even a bully-free one. I would have finished school a year earlier; gone to University earlier; met very different people; and maybe had the confidence to be myself, and follow my own feelings about the world.

Why this is all so important

Don't get me wrong, extroverts can be great and we need them in the world; I am trying to happily embrace extroverted tendencies in this project, and the current activity. But I am also learning to accept who I am and how I can contribute to the world in a meaningful way that aligns with my personality.

These messages are so important for parents and teachers to understand. I'm sure there are children at school going through the same doubts and pain I did as a child; probably more so, as we have become a more collaborative and social culture in the last 10 to 20 years. I have loaned my copy of *Quiet* to an introverted colleague at work, who is so glad to have someone else to talk to about this.

As so many things in the project are teaching me, I am not alone in many of the traits I thought made me broken and wrong. This is the power of

TED, it is the power of sharing and it is the reason I'm trying to start a movement about preconceptions and stereotypes. Maybe this post should go on the blog as well. Maybe the movement should be 'why do you think you are broken?', and we can all share the parts of us that we have actively tried to keep hidden from the world, because someone, somewhere made us feel like they weren't normal, they were wrong, or they were bad.

Is there something in your life, a personality trait or feeling, that you have always hidden from the world due to other people's opinions?

ACTIVITY 14 • 30 DAYS OF LEADERSHIP

I had always planned to do an activity on leadership and since I am currently trying to start a movement I thought this would be a good time to take it on.

The talks

There are quite a number of talks that I could have used for this activity, but the talks I have chosen are:

- *Barry Schwartz: Our loss of wisdom* – I love this talk, I've watched it about 10 times. It introduced me to the concept of moral will and moral skill, which puts a theory around something I knew was broken in our working environment.
- *David Logan: Tribal leadership* – I like this one so much I bought one of his books; *The Three Laws of Performance: Rewriting the Future of Your Organization and Your Life*. The concept of this is that there are five levels at which tribes operate, and it is the leader's job to move them to the more effective levels for performance.

I should also mention that *Susan Cain: The power of introverts* will support this activity. Mainly because it validates my chosen leadership method, or my 'natural' leadership style and the only way I'm comfortable leading.

Lastly, *Seth Godin: The tribes we lead* is also obviously a part of this.

There is a chance I might include another talk or two, there are a couple on the periphery that could be introduced, but we'll see.

The challenge

This is another one of those challenges that will be quite easy for me to outline but will be extremely difficult to execute. I don't currently manage any teams at work, I will have a project team shortly but that is unlikely to do anything much until July/August. But leadership isn't about management, it's something altogether different and I do have a leadership position in my current working environment.

From Barry's talk, I will be trying to find a way that we can empower staff to use their own initiative and decision making skills for their roles. From David's talk, and particularly David and Steve Zaffron's book, I will be focusing on working out the operating level of the tribes I am part of and then seeing whether I can use the three laws to move them forward.

The activity

There are two parts to this activity. The first is based around the 'Challenge your preconceptions' movement, and ensuring that any leadership I do around this activity aligns with Barry and David's talks. That does require me to get a tribe going, so there has to be a more practical aspect for this; which leads us to the second part. This is the main part of the activity, and it is centred around my working environment. It will involve the following tasks:

- identifying aspects of our working environment where we can better empower our staff to apply practical wisdom – moral will and skill
- working out the operating level of the tribes in my working environment, including my immediate office, the broader group, our smaller unit and the project team I'll be managing
- once I have worked this out, using the three laws I will see if there is any way I can help the tribes move to a higher level of performance.

This might be a particularly difficult activity to write about, given the nature of some of the things I might be trying to change and influence. I will be as open about these experiences as I feel I can be, especially given some work colleagues read this.

Day 212: More like standing still

Let's be brutally honest, Activity 13 is not going very well. Now let's remember that this activity is about starting a movement, so it's not necessary for the movement to be a success; although that would be very helpful.

So what's going on?

I have been trying but this does not come naturally for me. So far I have:
- included the concept in a link to the blog and *Challenge your preconceptions* post in the update email that was sent to the speakers whose talks I have used so far (where I have email contact details)
- written an article for a popular website about the concept
- reached out to an online action site to see if they would be interested including the movement on their blog
- searched the web for any related sites or posts and contacted a few of them to see if they are interested in contributing or sharing on the site.

I'm halfway through though, and I'm yet to find my first follower. How would you promote this? What other avenues would you pursue? I still have some things planned but I would love your input.

June 2012 – Difficulty level rising

Day 215: Evaluating the levels of my tribes

Yesterday was the start of Activity 14: 30 days of Leadership. As mentioned in the launch post, this may be a little difficult to write about simply because people I work with (including my boss) read this blog, but I'll do my best.

Our working environment has been very challenging in the last 18 months. That isn't saying anything that people wouldn't already know, or be able to guess when I say I work for the Tasmanian Government. We have had to find some significant budget savings, which creates a difficult environment in any business. It has caused a high degree of uncertainty including voluntary redundancies, not extending contracts, and a subsequent reduction in staff without any real change in the service levels.

This has impacted teams differently, but I can generally say it's had a very negative impact on our working environment. For me, I operate within two different tribes in this environment. There is my small team and the other part of the business that is located with us on the floor.

We are great

Our team is only three people. We're a fairly new team, and we've achieved quite a bit in the 15 months we've been established. Actually, given it has only been 15 months I think we're doing very well. We have stressful periods (high workloads and compressed timeframes) but on the whole I think we mainly stay at 'we are great' level – which is largely due to our boss.

And not so great

The other team is far from level 4, my opinion is that they fluctuate between level 2 'my life sucks' and level 3 'I'm great'.

This is the team I'll be taking a more active leadership role with, and see if I can apply some of David and Steve's teachings. The idea is to maintain them at level 3, because when they drop lower it makes an already difficult working environment intolerable.

I may very well be completely ineffectual in being able to do anything at all about this, but I would like to try.

Day 220: Lots going on but not in current activities

I'm feeling at a little bit of a loss at the moment because I don't feel there is very much for me to write about in the blog, but it doesn't feel right if I'm not writing. So I'm going to write about some of the stuff that's been happening around past activities, and give a brief update on the current ones.

Working on my How and What

In Activity 6 I managed to finally come up with a draft Why for my life:

- **Purpose** – To help people understand our world a little better and make life easier.
- **Belief** – Life should be as fair as possible and everyone should have the opportunity to reach their potential.
- **Cause** – Trying to make society more equal and help people see their own abilities/strengths/value.

I've been trying to work out whether this is accurate, and also how I might be able to achieve this; what actions I could take to make it real. Recently I came across something I think might help me move toward my Why in a very big, yet very small way.

Okay, that makes no sense when I write it down, so I will explain it. I'm considering volunteering as a Literacy Tutor. The State Library in Tasmania runs an adult literacy program that relies on volunteer literacy tutors to work with adults requesting support. I met with the Coordinator in my area this week, and I will be writing my application over the weekend.

This directly relates to my Why, moving me toward it in a big way. However, it's local is only a one-on-one activity, so it's very small at the same time. All the same I am very excited about it; I may become less excited as I have to do a Certificate IV in adult literacy, but that might be fun as well.

Continuing simplicity

As mentioned in the reflection on this activity, I always aimed to simplify things in my work. Since doing the activity though I am trying to maintain more of an awareness of the need to simplify; to make information more accessible. This has been problematic at times; a recent brief for the Minister became a very difficult design challenge, but I think we got there in the end.

I have also started reading John Maeda's book *The Laws of Simplicity (Simplicity: Design, Technology, Business, Life)*. I've only just finished Law 1, but I think there will be some very interesting points in this book that will help me continue to simplify.

And as for Activity 13

Maybe 13 is an unlucky number for me, or maybe I just always knew this would be a virtually impossible challenge for me to successfully undertake. In all seriousness, 30 days is not long enough for me to even begin to start something as significant as I have chosen to tackle with the 'Challenge your preconceptions' activity. I should have tried something more manageable and simpler. Sadly, that isn't what came to me when I thought about starting a movement, so this is what I have, and this is what I'm continuing to pursue.

It means there will be a pretty blunt and lesson laden reflection for this activity, what it also means for me is I need to start thinking about whether this is something I think is worthwhile to continue, because it will take a lot of time and energy to get traction. Maybe it needs a rethink, maybe after I've finished John's book I can come up with a way to make it more targeted, more simplistic, and a more appealing idea. All good things for me to think about coming into the final week.

ACTIVITY 15 • 30 DAYS OF REMEMBERING

The talks

This was not in my original schedule, it came about from Joshua Foer's talk at TED2012. *Joshua Foer: Feats of memory anyone can do*, is based on his experience of learning the memory techniques used by ordinary people to compete in the memory championship events around the world. The other talk is *Daniel Kahneman: The riddle of experience vs memory* in which he discusses the experiencing-self versus the remembering-self, and how they work.

The challenge

Joshua's talk is not just about how to build memory palaces and remember people's names, it is a commentary on our modern lives. Particularly, how we don't take the time to remember things anymore because we have so many devices to do that for us. As he reminds us, 'To live a memorable life, you have to be the kind of person who remembers to remember'. This feeds in very well to Daniel's talk where he explains that it is our remembering-self that makes decisions: 'We don't choose between experiences, we choose between memories of experiences'.

The challenge for me is to spend 30 days remembering to remember; to learn the ancient techniques that Joshua talks about; and to try to be more aware of taking the time to remember.

The activity

This is a fairly simple activity to explain, I will learn and practice the memory techniques that Joshua discusses, to improve my ability to remember. Particularly, I will learn the memory palace and visualisation techniques to improve my ability to remember people's names, shopping lists, and other seemingly random things.

The other underlying part of this activity is that I will take the time to remember experiences that occur in the 30 days, to see whether I feel like I am better able to recall these experiences by the end. This will involve being more attentive to things as I experience them, processing information more deeply, and focusing on remembering.

Day 226: Final day of starting a movement

I won't try to hide the fact that I am extremely glad this activity is over. As usual there will be a reflection post in the next couple of days, which I intend to make a brutally honest assessment of why I failed to start a movement.

But let's talk about more positive things

The leadership activity is going quite well. Not so much around trying to improve the tribe on my floor, which will take a more concerted effort. But my project started last week, and I'm feeling pretty happy with the working group that has been set up. I've been trying to be quite aware of talking at the level of 'we are great' and at a meeting today I felt that positivity coming through. Not that I believe the attitude is completely due to me, but we are at a good place and I think it is up to me to keep it there.

This project is kind of a big deal, actually it is a huge deal. I do get a bit daunted by the fact that it has been entrusted to me. It's not that I don't feel confident I can do it; I think we have placed enough people around me to support the processes. But there are a lot of people relying on getting this project right, and I want to deliver a great outcome for everyone who will be involved. It's important for me to remember, when I am with the working group members particularly, that I need to maintain a positive and enthusiastic attitude, even when I'm feeling daunted.

I feel I have been achieving this so far, but I just need to remind myself to keep going at that level.

Oh, and I think I have found a way to apply moral will and moral skill as part of this project. Ideas are just formulating at the moment, but I think this is a significant part of the project; I'll see how I go.

Day 228: First day of remembering
A reason to do 30 days of Remembering
Well this activity is off to a rip roaring start. I realised this afternoon that I had forgotten my eldest nephew's birthday, which is this Sunday. I know that means I did remember before it happened, but since we live interstate and it was 4.30 this afternoon, it means his present won't be there for the day.

And this is why I need to focus more on remembering. Because we have a calendar that hangs in the kitchen with important dates for our friends and families on it, but I don't remember to look at it. So I have entrusted the remembering process to a passive device I don't engage with.

Now some of you might say that if I put all of this in an electronic calendar I can get alerts through to remind me of things. Well, Derek has done this, but because I don't use the calendar he has set up I still missed it. And that is not the point of remembering anyway. The point of remembering to remember is that I become a person who remembers important dates without calendars and electronic reminders.

Learning to remember names
On the plus side for the activity, I found a Remember Names game on the web a few weeks ago. Basically they flash up dodgy pictures of people, giving them a random name; then they show a couple back to you and you have to type their name in; the number of people increases each round. I have practised this a couple of times in the last few weeks, and I am getting better at it. Although I do think that the game is a little harsh with requiring exact spelling, especially since it has some very randomly spelled names – seriously, Dorthy?!

Anyway, it is good fun and is teaching me some mnemonic tricks I need to start learning for the memory palace technique. I figure it will be about a week or so before I start trying that. I need to practice the creativity of remembering names first.

I started doing this game early to get a bit of an idea of my baseline, how good or bad I am at remembering names. The first few attempts were pretty shocking, but today I read through some material about remembering names (including the material on the game page). As a result, I managed to get 61 on my first attempt and 75 on my second, which is a marked improvement.

REFLECTION – 30 DAYS OF STARTING A MOVEMENT

Let's be honest...

This activity was less than successful, and the movement was a complete failure. I need to address these things separately because, as I said in the launch post, a successful movement was not the purpose of the activity.

What was the challenge?

This challenge was to move completely outside my comfort zone, and act more extroverted, from Susan Cain's talk. It required me to promote the movement, and try to get others to engage with it. To put myself out there; to possibly be challenged about the intent and purpose of the movement; and to completely ramp up the small things I have been doing to market and publicise this blog. Which inevitably means My Year of TED in general.

What I really needed to find was the first follower from Derek Sivers' talk. I needed to find someone who saw the value in this, preferably an extrovert, who already had an audience and could do some of this for me. That didn't eventuate, and quite frankly I don't have nearly enough of a web presence to start something this big myself. Which is lesson number one, I should have made it smaller and easier it achieve – more on that later.

So, how did I go in the leadership stakes then in relation to Seth Godin's talk? Well that would require me to have a tribe to lead now wouldn't it; I obviously failed to develop curiosity in the movement and to connect with people. I was trying to challenge the status quo though, and I think I showed a fairly good commitment to the task, although I know I could have done more. But I think that is always the case, we could always do more. In relation to building a culture and having charisma, well they are moot to the whole thing since the movement didn't get off the ground.

Let's look a little deeper at the lessons

I will start by saying that I felt I was biting off more than I could chew with this one. The activity alone was always going to be a challenge, but the movement I decided to start was a bad choice. Let's deconstruct it a bit more.

1. The movement was too large and not simple enough for people to engage with. I know this is a general problem in trying to get people to engage, and yet I didn't notice that problem when I picked the movement. That was partly due to the fact that I had spent the previous month being immersed in challenging my preconceptions, so it was no longer a complex activity in my mind. I should have made it simple; I should have made it something less all-encompassing; and I should have made it something that wasn't as challenging. I also think that in hindsight I should have made it something local.
2. Following on from point 1, I don't have enough of a voice in the world to attack a topic as huge and significant as challenging your preconceptions. If I had thousands of Twitter followers and readers of this blog then I might have been able to get some traction on this. I seriously overstretched myself, and without a first follower this was never going to happen. This one I wasn't clueless about, which was why the success of the movement was secondary to the activity itself.
3. My boss actually pointed this one out when I was talking with her about the failure of the movement – I picked something that was too confrontational for people to want to publicly engage with. So even if people were interested in the concept and thought it was a good idea, maybe even did the exercise, they weren't going to publicly talk about it. I tend to forget that I am baring my soul in this project, but normal people would tend to think twice about it – actually I always think twice or three times but I have committed to doing it anyway.
4. I didn't do enough, but I did as much as I felt I could. I'm just not the sort of person who has the confidence to say 'hey I have a brilliant idea, look at me'. This is partially because I have way too much internal judgement going on to think that I have a brilliant idea, but also because I don't enjoy being the centre of attention – seriously! Now this may seem like an extremely odd comment given the project I am doing, and the fact I'm writing a very public blog about it all. But think about it for a second, how hard have I pushed the blog? Occasionally I get conscientious and think I would like more readers, so I play around the edges of promoting it through Twitter and finding like blogs to comment in etc. I'll leave that one there.

In summation

I probably should have tried the light-hearted concept that I had for a movement, this was way too heavy and serious for a 30 day activity. The other one had the possibility of people finding it fun and engaging, but I felt it was too frivolous. So, that was a preconception I should have challenged harder, because this project is life changing enough. I should have tried something more fun and less stressful – lesson learned.

I will leave the preconception blog running, if anyone feels like contributing. I may even continue to add posts if I find other sites or content that I think are great; but I don't have the energy to keep it going. Maybe I will refine the idea and find a way to simplify it once I've finished John Maeda's book, or maybe I will just admit defeat on this one.

I learned a lot about my strengths and weaknesses, and that is the overall purpose of this project. So I shouldn't be too hard on myself, and internally I'm not beating myself up very much at all, because this was the outcome I had always expected. Maybe I set myself up to fail, or maybe my effort matched my expectations and not my goals. So much to think about.

Day 231: Status update with a moody dog

Lily is not talking to me tonight, we had her in a kennel over the weekend while we were in Melbourne. This is also partly because she is very tired, but some of it is definitely attitude. So, what does that have to do with my current activities? Nothing much really, except Derek isn't home yet and I can't even get cuddles from my dog to fight off this descending mood.

Onto the updates on the activities

I scored a whopping 193 on the Remember Names game tonight. I am getting far more creative coming up with ways to remember the names. The trick most sites give you is to make it very outlandish and comical, although that usually means they end up being not just a little insulting. That's why all the sites mention you don't let anyone know what you associate them with.

And Activity 14, well we have more project team meetings this week, so I get to practice leadership a little more. I want to focus on my language and be more aware of any unintended negativity I might be projecting. This may be impacted by own negative mood at the moment, but that is why I need to be more vigilant about it.

Day 233: It's the little things

New people I met yesterday

I attended a meeting yesterday with 11 people, only three of whom I knew. We did a quick whip around the room to introduce ourselves, and I tried hard to practice the name remembering skills I've been learning. This was a little difficult since everyone was introduced so quickly, and I had a significant talking role in the meeting, so I didn't have a lot of down time to do this slowly.

Having said that, I remembered almost everyone's names. The three new people in the room I needed to know were among the group I do remember; I can even visualise them now with the mnemonics I developed.

We are great... I think

My project team met again today. This is a very eclectic group of people, and I think we're still generally in the 'We are great' stage, well our language anyway. There was a little more negativity expressed today, but that was about the potential influencers and risks for the project. On the whole the team is still talking positively about possible outcomes of the task.

The group also readily acknowledges there might be less than ideal outcomes for this, which they are quite nonplussed about in a way. This is a problem, because while they are not extremely negative about that outcome, they are still stuck in using the language of the past. It's like they have an expectation that things won't go well because in the past they haven't. While they are accepting of this I keep trying to shift them into considering the possibility this might not be the outcome; that it might in fact turn out pretty good. It's not getting traction, and quite frankly I think they're probably right, but I'm trying to use my future-based language.

What activity would you do?

And now a question for you all. I'm at a point where I need to decide what my next activity will be. The one I had planned is probably just a little too harsh to do around my birthday (and my current mood, although that shouldn't still be here in 10 days). I have two others I'm considering but I need to do some more prep work with them, and I don't know that I have the time with my workload.

So I'm opening this to the floor – if you were doing this project what activity would you do? What TED Talk(s) would you use for that activity? I'm willing to be a guinea pig for this one, assuming it's an activity I can see something in, and it won't require too much preparation. I know that many of you who watch TED Talks would have at least one that you've thought about applying, which is it?

Day 236: Creating memory palaces

My first memory palace

I started practising the memory palace technique today. I'm starting pretty simple, memorising lists of 10 random items, but it's fun.

There are a large number of resources that explain the memory palace technique on the internet, I've read at least a dozen of them in the last couple of weeks. The technique is fairly simple. Most people suggest using a building that you walk through in the same way every time, but others have suggested you can use a journey that you are familiar with.

At the moment I've just been using our house, but the recommendation is for you to have a number of memory palaces you can use for different purposes. The concept is that you place memorable things along your journey through the house and, as Joshua Foer explains, the more creative and outlandish you make the image the more memorable it will be. Then when you need to remember you run through the journey in your mind.

Next stop is to use it to remember my shopping list for tomorrow, although I will write it out as a backup as well. I'm wondering if it's best to do this memory palace walking through the supermarket, since that would surely be a good prompt as I go through. It could cause me to break out in laughter if I use some of the crazy images I've been coming up with so far.

Remembering to remember

The more important part of this activity is simply remembering to remember. I've been trying to do this by taking small steps, like relying more on my memory rather than my Outlook calendar at work. But really, as with so many other activities I've been doing, this is all about focus.

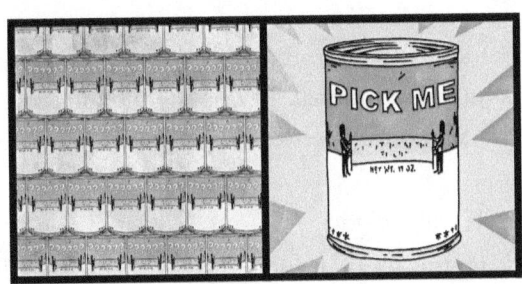

ACTIVITY 16 • 30 DAYS OF CHOICE

I had planned to do this activity a lot later in the schedule, but I've had to make some changes to my original plan. This is partly because I decided not to do a few activities, and delays in external events mean I'm not ready for a couple of others. Mainly, this month it was due to not wanting to do a particular activity for my birthday.

The talks

There are three talks that I am using for 30 days of Choice. They are *Alain de Botton: A kinder, gentler philosophy of success*, *Barry Schwartz: The paradox of choice* and *Sheena Iyengar: The art of choosing*. These are three very intriguing talks about how we make our choices; how we feel about the choices we make; and how we are swayed by very irrational aspects of our choices.

The challenge

We make so many decisions every day, and in each of those decisions we have a number of available options. Some are seemingly inconsequential, what to have for lunch or what to wear to work; others will have a more lasting impact, like choosing your phone carrier or where to go on holidays. The last group are the life changing decisions, like career and relationships.

There are a number of aspects to the challenge for these 30 days. Firstly, it is about understanding what success means to me, and aligning my choices to reach that success. This is from Alain de Botton, and will hopefully help me stop judging myself against others, envying their achievements and judging their failures.

The second part of the challenge relates to Barry Schwartz and it is about lowering my expectations and limiting my choices for the month. The aim of this is to improve my feelings of satisfaction with my choices. Related to this is being more aware of the options that are available to me, and what might be influencing my decision making, which is from Sheena Iyengar.

The activity

This should hopefully be a more tangible activity for me, since it is like remembering – a lot more internal. Maybe it's the introvert in me, but the activities that don't rely on others (or my interaction with others) seem to come more easily.

The activity itself will include:
- going back to the work around my Why and spending some time thinking about what success means for me
- being aware of any time where I am judging myself against others' achievements and failures, rather than judging myself against what I want from my life

- limiting my choices over the 30 days, wherever possible, to lessen the impact of opportunity costs (what I miss out on based on my choice)
- being aware that there is unlikely to be a perfect choice, so I can manage my escalation of expectations (related to that feeling that if there are 50 to choose from then one must be perfect for me)
- taking time to focus on all of the aspects of my decisions, and the irrelevant aspects that might be influencing my choices.

I'm looking forward to putting a magnifying glass over some of these choices in my life. If I can become clearer in my decision making, and experience less buyer's remorse that would make me very happy. If I come up with a better definition of what success looks like for me, so I can remove some of the envy and judgement from my life, I will be ecstatic.

Day 240: Last days of leadership

I've had a couple of interesting conversations at work in the last few days related to leadership. It's very hard to write about these in this forum though, due to colleagues reading the blog. It's one of the things that has made this activity so difficult, some of the things I have wanted to address are so sensitive I don't feel I can share it here. I will work very hard in the reflection post to talk about things that have happened.

For now though, the leadership around my project is continuing along nicely, I'm pretty happy with how it's going. I have a couple of days left to see whether I can have any more impact on the environment. Well only a few more days of the activity, I think that this will be one I will try to keep, but that's for the reflection post.

Memory fail

I had a complete memory failure this morning, which was a very small thing, but so small I shouldn't have forgotten it. I haven't been practising the memory palaces as much as I could, but in fairness I have been exceptionally busy at work. This might also explain why I forgot such a simple thing this morning. But I shouldn't be making excuses, I should just be doing the work.

Day 243: Eight months down, four to go

Today marks two milestones in My Year of TED. It is the last day of 30 days of Leadership and it is the final day of the eighth month. That means I am now two thirds of the way through this project, which is quite exciting. Of course it will be even more exciting at the end of next month, since that is the three-quarter mark, but every step counts.

What sort of leader am I?

I've been a bit reflective today about the end of leadership, I think the reflection post will detail my leadership style and limitations. On the whole, my initial feeling about the activity is that it went quite well. As I've said time and time again in this project, simply making something a focal point of your life makes you so much more aware of how you approach that thing. I didn't get a chance to do quite as much as I would have liked, which is why I want to maintain some focus around using future-based language (from David Logan and Steve Zaffron's book).

I am also going to try keep an eye out for any opportunities to influence and support the application of practical wisdom in my working environment. Given that I work in government this is an extremely challenging thing to achieve, but I want to improve that situation.

Remembering to remember

I'm starting to get the hang of the memory palace technique. I've been practising it a bit with completely random lists of items, and with things I actually need to remember. I've found that some days I am far better at it than other days, and I think that's a creativity thing. I know when I'm busy or stressed my creative brain has the tendency to shut down. So, because this is a visually creative activity, some days I struggle to find memorable images for what I'm trying to remember.

I am trying to be very mindful about generally remembering over this time as well, again some days this is better than others. I've had simple wins like I can now remember Derek's mobile number, something I had never bothered to do since it was in my phone, and on a card in my purse. I am also trying very hard to remember what my friends are doing, so I remember to ask them about how things have gone. This is way more successful on days I don't have a huge workload on, which isn't too often of late.

Next up 30 days of Choice

Lastly, tomorrow is the first of the month, so that means Activity 16 will start. This one should be quite interesting, I already have a rather important decision to make during the month, not life changing but important nonetheless. It will be interesting to see how I feel about the process of deciding and the choice I ultimately make – more about that next week.

July 2012 – The month I turned 40

REFLECTION – 30 DAYS OF LEADERSHIP

My leadership 'style' is one thing I've spent many hours thinking about and focusing on over the last 12 years. We spent the majority of our three months of RAAF Officer training on leadership. That was when I started to understand some of my 'failings' in leadership, and also some of my strengths. Throughout the following 12 years, and seven different positions, I've managed to improve some aspects, and accept there are some things I will never be able to do very well.

What I've learned is that I am a very participative leader, and an even more participative manager. I guess that's one of the distinctions for me; I'm not a natural manager, I don't feel comfortable telling people what to do. I prefer to explain what needs to be done, come to an agreement about everyone's role, and then let them get on with the job.

The way that I've come to view this is that I tend to lead more than I manage the teams for which I am responsible. I hate micro-managing, almost as much as I hate being micro-managed. If people need help in understanding how to do their tasks I will happily take the time to explain and teach, but on the whole I expect that people have been employed in their positions because they are capable of doing their jobs – unfortunately I do get proven wrong sometimes.

My tribal leadership experience

When I first watched David Logan's talk in late 2009 I thought about how I lead and whether I improve my tribe's experience of working, or if I make it worse. I think that, like most people, I probably do both things at different times. I thought about the team I was managing at the time, and where they sat on the scale. There was a schism in my team that placed them at three different levels, depending on how you viewed them (the sub-groups). I realised that I didn't know how to make that any better, how to pull them together as a team. I mulled it over and then, like most people, I got so busy with day-to-day activities that I forgot about how to make them a team.

When I took on my role in Housing Tasmania in 2010 I revisited David's talk, among other TED Talks, thinking this was a fresh start with a new team and I could try some different techniques. I was pretty happy with how I led that team, and feel I did improve their unity. But I will admit that I was ecstatic when I took on my current role, since I have no staff. That was when I realised the problem, it is very difficult to lead when you are so busy managing and doing.

When I no longer had to manage so much day-to-day activity, it freed my brain up to consider the issues, and how we might overcome some of them. That was when I bought David and Steve's book; I needed to understand how to move people between the five levels, not least because the situation at work is increasingly strained with all of the downsizing and cost savings.

Adapting my language

When I read through the future-based language part of the book I didn't fully get it, it just wasn't sinking in. After trying to apply it in this activity I now understand it a lot better. The problem with applying the *Three Laws of Performance* for me is that David and Steve talk about it at an organisation-wide level, and I don't have the power to play with it at that level. Instead, I was taking the basic principles and trying to apply them to the small tribes that I'm part of. I didn't improve the main issue I really wanted to address, but I gave it a go, and had a few conversations that will hopefully fester away in people's minds.

In relation to my project tribe, I tried very hard to start them at 'We are great'. We spoke a lot about the importance of this project, and having a diverse team that allows us all to learn from each other. I tried to ensure every tribe member has had a chance to have a say, that they are listened to, and acknowledged for their contribution. I have a tendency to get very task focused, so this time around I'm trying to work on the non-task aspects a lot more. I think this is going well, and I want to keep this focus for the remainder of the project. I'll keep reflecting on this as we go through and see if I can truly get the tribe to 'We are great' during the next four months.

And now onto practical wisdom

As I mentioned in the launch, I absolutely love this talk from Barry Schwartz, and given the way I explained my leadership style above that shouldn't be a surprise. It introduced me to the concept of moral will and moral skill, something that I do believe is lacking in our modern world. I have worked in government for almost 12 years now, in two States and at the Federal level, and I can tell you that it is sorely lacking in these bureaucracies – as I'm sure any public servants out there will attest.

Government is a large machine that uses taxpayers' money and provides vital services to the public. There are a large amount of rules and regulations we need to comply with, and I don't think many of us would argue these shouldn't exist. But there are also a lot of processes that make no sense; that just seem to be there for the edification of an individual or team; that get in the way of allowing us to be flexible and make our own judgements. I think that this is why Barry's talk resonates so strongly with me.

I did not make much leeway with this in the 30 days, as I suspected would be the case; but there have been some small wins along the way. These mainly related to making people reconsider putting another layer of bureaucracy into processes, trying to be a rational voice about trusting our staff and funded organisations to do the right thing as the default.

This is also something I want to keep in the back of my mind, to see if I can come across any way I might be able to get some real traction with the concept. There is one thing that I have the potential to advocate for within the organisation that falls into this category, and that is the current whispers that IT might be removing the wiki that we have. The theory is the new intranet will render it obsolete; nothing could be further from the truth. The wiki's purpose is so radically different than disseminating the 'approved' and complete information on the intranet.

The real problem people have is the lack of control, as everyone can edit it. Some people think it's not appropriate, since staff might put up inaccurate or offensive material. This is a ridiculous notion for so many reasons that I need to articulate to the people involved in the decision making. The existence and use of a wiki is a very simple, but clear example of moral will and moral skill at play for me, and I don't want to lose the functionality or the underlying value it brings.

Fairly happy overall

This reflection was always going to be a little long and rambling, you will have to excuse me for that. Leadership is so important in organisations, and I wanted to see if these talks could help me take more of a leadership role in the organisation. I've learned a few things, and have also been aware of situations where I haven't shown very good leadership; there were a couple.

On the whole though, I think this was a very worthwhile activity. I will be keeping it in mind as I continue my work project, and continue to try to find a way to improve some of the current cultural problems we are experiencing. Even if I only make the working experience better for a couple of people around me I will feel like I've achieved something.

One last thing, I promise

One last note about leadership, introversion and Susan Cain. Through Susan's book I have come to understand that a lot of my 'failings' as a leader are due to my introversion. Things I've been told I have to change and improve are simply the natural way I work as a leader. We can't all be the strong, vocal type and I think that Susan clearly explains what we would lose as a society if all leaders were like that.

What Susan's book has given me through this process is a keener understanding of the other introverts in the room, and how I need to work with them in slightly different ways to get their valuable contributions. It has also given me the courage to lead by example, to be open and honest about being an introvert and all of the insecurities that go with that. This has led to a number of conversations with people that I hope have been as valuable for them as they were for me.

Day 248: An interesting week

I'm pretty happy with how the memory exercises are going. I'm continuing to play the Remember the Name game, maintaining a standard score in the high hundreds. Wednesday night was one my lowest scores in a while; that's what pain will do to you I think (my shoulders and neck are playing up).

I'm also still practising the memory palace, not as much as I had planned to. Unfortunately I have been extremely busy with work and that has consumed far too much of my non-work time at the moment. I do hope to improve that practice in the next week though.

Defining success

I've started working on trying to define what success means for me. This is going quite well, but I'm not willing to share this here. There are some things that seem a little too personal for me to share; I'll ponder that a little more as I continue working on this part of the activity. What I will say is that I need to keep in mind that my life is very close to what I would deem as successful. There are still things I have not achieved with my life that I would like to have sorted out by now, but I am working on it.

It is quite prophetic that I'm working on this as my 40th birthday is looming. Next Sunday, as a matter of fact, I will turn 40. It doesn't feel like it, well maybe this week with some of my shoulder and neck pain, but on the whole I don't feel that old. Largely, I'm not that bothered by it, it's just another birthday. Then I have these moments where I feel like I've achieved nothing with my life so far. I don't dwell on it usually, but I think this is a fairly standard reaction to a birthday in general.

Simple choices

I haven't had to make any major choices in the last few days, but as usual a lot of seemingly minor ones. For instance, I've realised in the last few days just how many decisions I make at work a day. Most of these don't seem to be consequential, they are more related to timing and language, but there are a lot of other choices: who to include in correspondence; what course we should be taking; what messages we should be giving, etc.

I have more of these choices to make with the project I'm managing at the moment, but still there are so many daily decisions. What I've been realising with these choices is that I seldom hesitate or feel like I've made the wrong one. This is probably because the choices are usually limited and controlled, and they are part of a rational decision making process.

Now I just have to make a few more consumer decisions, which have none of the characteristics above. I did make one this week, I had to buy my sister a birthday card. Following Barry Schwartz's guidance I limited my choices by going to a small store near work that only stocks a very small range of cards. This made the selection process much easier, and I only spent about five minutes making the decision.

There are 24 days left to go in this one, so I'm sure I'll have a lot more opportunity to think about it, and put some of the theory into practice.

Day 250: Consumer choices and why we're bad at them

The Atlantic had an interesting article yesterday on how bad consumers are at making decisions – 'The 11 ways that Consumers are Hopeless at Math'. The article contends the reason we're so bad at consuming and making rational decisions is mainly due to the fact that we have no idea what things should cost. This leads to a series of interesting processes and manipulations relating to whether we feel something is a bargain or if we're being ripped off. Very intriguing with my current activity relating to choice.

Having said that, we did do some consuming today. We went into JB HiFi, which is always a dangerous thing to do. We walked out with $70 worth of DVDs and CDs that we probably don't need, and certainly didn't go in with the idea of purchasing. But that's pretty much how most shopping experiences in JB work, they're good at doing that. Although I'm extremely proud of the fact that I walked out of Officeworks without buying anything, so not all bad.

Interestingly, even though we had not planned to spend that amount of money I have no regrets about the purchases. Maybe this has something to do with having no expectations going in, so the choices were not a long decision making process weighing all of the options. Then there was the fact that there wasn't that much I wanted from the sale bins, they limited the choices for me anyway. Something to ponder a little more.

Day 251: How is my career success?

I've been trying to define what success means for me in all areas of my life. Some of this I'm not going to share on the blog, but I think with everything I've written about my career this aspect is a good area to talk about.

Follow on from my Why

I've been thinking a lot about this in the last year, I have already written about trying to define my Why, and to work out what I should be doing with my life. This is obviously one of the catalysts for this entire project, and it's a good time to try to resolve it as my 40th birthday is a week away.

So what does success in my career look like for me? The simple answer is I don't really know. Since I've never had any idea of the career I wanted, I've never had any real idea of what I wanted to achieve with my career. I have friends who have done the whole 'by the age of 30 I will be this, and by the age of 40 I will be here with my career', and I think more power to them. I've just never had that type of plan for my life, and some people may say that's my problem.

Do I feel successful?

So I decided to approach the question in another way – do I feel successful in my career? For this I would have to say yes. Having had no plan for my career, I have held senior management positions in government for over six years. I have been well respected in all my roles and have achieved some pretty amazing things. When I think of my career as a whole, I'm very proud of my achievements. I guess that makes me successful, wouldn't you say?

Since I'll be 40 next week, I've been thinking about this in a different way. While I am happy overall with my achievements, have I done enough? The problem is I shouldn't think about it in this way, because it isn't tangible.

What is enough? If I had no plan about what I wanted to achieve then how on earth can I know if I've done enough? Of course, the fact that I'm a perfectionist means I seldom feel like I've done enough, especially when I look at other people.

Cue Alain de Botton's talk – I should not compare myself to others since we are all individuals with different paths, challenges and life experiences. With that being the case, I need to remember that I am proud of myself; I am happy with what I have achieved, when I look at my situation alone.

Defining success

I still need to be able to define the things that I am happy with and what makes me feel I am successful. This is the only way I can know whether I'm making the right choices in future. More work to go, but at least I'm feeling pretty positive about where I am at the moment.

ACTIVITY 17 • 30 DAYS OF BEING WRONG

The talks

This activity is based on two TED Talks from Kathryn Schulz – *Kathryn Schulz: On being wrong* and *Kathryn Schulz: Don't regret regret*. In the first of these talks Kathryn explains how being wrong is something we learn from a young age is a bad thing, and yet it's something we should be more open to acknowledging in ourselves. The second talk is a plea to be kinder to ourselves when dealing with our regrets, and learn to live with them as they remind us that we can do better.

The challenge

There are two aspects to this challenge: being more open to the prospect of being wrong; and trying to better accept my regrets and the lessons they are there to teach me. Now, as you've been reading this you should be aware I'm a bit of a perfectionist, alright an atrocious perfectionist. So you can imagine how problematic this challenge might be for me. Having said that, I think you would have to agree that I'm also willing to be quite open about some of the mistakes I've made.

Being a perfectionist means I am not very good at accepting my mistakes, so while I might admit them I am certain to punish myself for them. Interestingly, professionally I am usually quite quick to acknowledge when I'm wrong. This wasn't always the case, but my military career and the leadership role I had, really helped instill in me the value of admitting mistakes early and working on correcting the error.

Overall, the challenge is to embrace my imperfections since that's how we learn and grow. I need to challenge my feeling of being right if people are questioning my opinion or comments, allowing me to be more open to the prospect of being wrong. Along with this I need to work on my regrets and not punishing myself for having them. Rather, identifying what I need to learn from the regret, and learning to live with it in a more manageable way.

The activity

This activity aligns well with 30 days of Choice. It's about acknowledging how fallible I am and trying to better deal with regrets in my life. The activity itself is another internally focused one; another awareness and focus activity.

So, I will focus on the possibility of being wrong and be more open to admitting my mistakes to people around me. What I would like to do is adjust the way I think of 'wrong'. Moving it out of the realm of a criticism about my intelligence or capacity, and realise that everyone gets things wrong; that those times are opportunities to grow and learn. This should also include reducing judgement when others get things wrong. We'll see how that goes.

Lastly, I will look at the regrets I'm holding onto in my life and see if I can work out how to live with them in a more beneficial way. This means you guys might get a chance to view a little more of the trainwreck that has been my life, surely that's worth hanging around for?

Day 255: A choice to help celebrate my birthday

As I'm sure I have mentioned a number of times now, my 40th birthday is very close – actually it's Sunday. It's not every day you hit an interesting milestone like this one, so I decided I would do something a little interesting to celebrate. Hence the new hair colour – I am now blonde again.

I was 26 the last time I was blonde, so it's a bit of a shock looking at myself now. I think it's more of a shock for Derek, since he's never seen me blonde before; I can't wait to see the reaction from the people at work.

But what colour to choose?

I've been planning to change my hair colour for my birthday for a few months now. I thought it would be an interesting extension from Activity 1 since it is going to make me stand out even more than usual. I only recently chose the colour.

This meant I got to practice 30 days of Choice, and this was not an easy one to make. I had been contemplating blonde because it would be the most radical change from my usual brown, but I was also tossing up red, or whether I put another colour through the blonde and so on. I decided to apply Barry Schwartz's talk and limit my choices, so blonde it would be.

But even with this choice made there are many variations of blonde, so I still had to find one I was happy with. I had wanted to be a whiter blonde, there is still a little too much gold, but after three hours and two goes at applying the colour I was a little over the whole experience.

It wasn't that easy though

I've made it sound like it was quite a simple choice, approximately eight hours over a couple of weeks of looking at haircuts online would give you some idea of how difficult it was. The bigger problem was that yesterday I went through a very common phase in my decision making process. Let's just say going from brunette to blonde is a fairly expensive process, especially for a person who usually spends very little on their hair.

So, even though I made my decision and was comfortable with it two days ago, yesterday I went through the whole decision making process again. This time it was 'is it worth the money when I don't intend on keeping the colour for very long anyway?' I won't go into how I am with spending money at times, let's simply say I have guilt issues associated with spending money 'frivolously'. So, it was only after Derek made me see it was okay to do it that I felt I'd made my choice.

This may not seem like a big deal to a lot of you, but it gave me an opportunity to think about the how and why behind my choice. It gave me a chance at insight, and demonstrated some of the ridiculous things inside my head that influence my choices. Some of them appear to be rational, others are just plain mental.

Day 257: Last day of remembering

30 days of Remembering ends today; overall I feel I've learnt some good skills to improve my memory, now I just have to keep practising them. I was

explaining how the techniques work to a couple of people yesterday, and that allowed me confirm in my own mind what I was doing and how it helps.

Of course there will be a reflection post about this later in the week, or maybe next weekend because I know how busy work will be.

The choice of hair colour

People's reactions to the dramatic change in hair colour were interesting yesterday. On the whole people seem to like it, I'm still uncertain myself. I need to sit with it for a little longer and see how it makes me feel; at the moment it's not sitting that well with me.

Tomorrow I turn 40

Tomorrow is the big day, not that it feels that way, or that I feel any different leading up to it. I don't have any issues with turning 40, probably because the whole concept of becoming a certain age has always seemed a bit surreal to me. I don't know how you are supposed to feel as you go through the ageing process, but I'm yet to hit a birthday where I think to myself 'oh wow I'm X today.' Maybe this will be the one; I'll wake up tomorrow morning feeling different about myself in some way, but I highly doubt it.

Day 261: Sometimes life gets in the way

I have to admit to not being very focused on My Year of TED activities over the last few days. I took the opportunity to have a very relaxing weekend for my birthday, to celebrate but also as the calm before the storm. Work became a lot busier this week, and it will stay that way for the next couple of months as my project gets into the implementation stage.

I had intended getting back into the swing of things in a more focused manner on Tuesday, but added to a busy workload we spent the morning supporting our boss through a very difficult day. To top it off, I have a cold; needless to say there has been a lack of focus.

The aim is to start getting back into it all tomorrow; I think I have the current tasks under control so I can shift my focus after work. So while life did get in the way for a few days I'm hoping I can get back on top of it all, and get back to choice and being wrong.

Day 262: Not entirely wrong but not quite right either

I've been trying to be more open to other people challenging my ideas as part of my project at work. This is mainly because I am not the expert in the work we're doing, and I need to rely on others' knowledge. Today I got to practise it in a very real sense.

I had come up with a method of calculating a figure we needed for the project. It was a very complex way of deriving a result, and I was pretty happy with how I'd made it work. I ran this past another person on the Working Group and they shot it down very quickly with another option for the calculation, which is much easier. My initial reaction was to defend my work, it had taken me quite a while to come up with it. Then I remembered I'm supposed to challenge my rightness, by being more open to being wrong.

So I opened myself up to listen to his idea, and realised it was a far simpler option that we should take. So, not wrong, but I didn't have the best idea.

On another note
I will be finally getting around to the reflection post for remembering in the next couple of days. Just another casualty of life getting in the way.

REFLECTION – 30 DAYS OF REMEMBERING

I used to be good at remembering people and their names. I started to lose this skill a little when I was in the Air Force, and spent a year going around the country meeting and training hundreds of people in an air tasking system. There was so much other stuff going on when we did these courses that I wouldn't remember all of the people I trained at each site, and let's face it we can all blur together a little when we're dressed the same.

The problem was, they would all remember me; well they only had one instructor whereas my usual class was around 20 people. The result was, I started to second guess myself with people's names, and once I started doing that it kept getting worse. Since I've held so many jobs that seemingly require me to learn everyone's name in the organisation; sometimes I feel like my brain just won't take any more.

How did remembering names go?
I'm generally happy with this activity. I have become more attentive focusing on people's names, and so my recall has definitely improved over the 30 days of the activity. As with all of these activities, the main thing is focus. When I focused on people saying their names, rather than focusing on what I was going to say in response, my retention naturally improved.

I have been practising some of the simple aspects mentioned by Joshua Foer and online resources. Things like repeating the name and visualising some creative hook to remember them. But the technique that works best for me is to come up with some sort of rhyme in my head, or the way that I say their name in my head. I'm not going to go into that in any more detail, I'm sure that some of these have the possibility of causing offence and that's not my intention.

Making memory palaces

I thoroughly enjoyed learning this technique, and it does work for me. Sometimes I found it hard to come up with a visual, but on the whole this technique works. I intend to keep it up, as I think it is a useful skill to have.

Remembering to remember

I was definitely more attentive to remembering things that occurred over these 30 days. Most days, when I wasn't completely flat out at work, I took a few minutes after meetings or interactions with others to just think about what happened, and make a more conscious memory of events.

This was an important time to be practising remembering because my workload has been a little insane; I've been juggling a lot of things over the last two months. But while I was more focused on remembering, I generally felt more at ease with my workload; surely that indicates a benefit for me.

So to sum up

On the whole, I've felt that this has been a worthwhile activity and I want to be more mindful of keeping it up. Not only the remembering techniques, but also the general concept of remembering. It's far too simple to be so caught up in what's going on that you don't experience these activities in a long term way; that is you don't remember them. Since I think that Daniel Kahneman's talk is completely valid, that we base decisions on our memories of our experiences and not the experiences themselves; it is important that we remember, and remember well.

This is not easy to do, since we lead such busy lives with so much stimulus these days. We are constantly bombarded with information, and I know that I often feel like I'm not consciously participating in my life; I'm just being swept along in the tide of busyness. This activity has helped me come to terms with simple things I can do to be more of a person who remembers. Yes, on the days I was extremely busy this all got pushed to one side, but that made the days I did focus on it even clearer in my memory. I get it, now I just have to remember the value of it for my life. I just need to remember to keep the focus – remember to remember.

A note on serendipity

You know how life throws you seemingly random experiences and then they turn out to be very important? Well on the second last day of remembering I had one of these. Our team from work was having lunch, and we were talking about 30 days of Remembering. We were going through a way to help my manager remember her partner's mobile number, which was breaking it down into memorable bites and noticing the patterns that exist. I must have said that number about 20 times during lunch.

On Tuesday we learned my manager's mother had passed away over the weekend. Not wanting to call her to find out about the details, and where to send flowers, my brain retrieved the number from Friday. The older I get the more randomness becomes some unexpected connectedness.

Day 265: Choices are going well, success even better

A little bit on choice

This has been an interesting activity so far, with just over a week to go. I've been very focused on limiting choices, especially when I'm presented with a lot of them. I usually do this by putting some arbitrary limitation in place, but sometimes the limitation is obvious.

For example, I've kept up the weekday vegetarian alteration to my diet. So food choices for four to five days of the week are simplified, since there is an obvious limitation of avoiding meat. Whereas, when I decided to do a little bit of op shopping last Monday I had to impose my own limitations. The limitation I imposed was that I had to think of how I could create two complete outfits out of my current wardrobe using that piece; see arbitrary.

A little more on trying not to compare

I've mentioned in a number of posts that I can be extremely judgemental. Reducing how much I do this has been part of a number of activities in My Year of TED. I think that overall I have reduced how much I do this about other people, but I'm still quite harsh on myself. That is why Alain de Botton's part of this activity is so important for me. I know in a theoretical way I shouldn't compare my life to other people's, and I have worked hard over the last few years to try to apply this, but I'm far from successful.

I have been making a concerted effort though, to try to think about my life against my definitions of success and not against other people's achievements. This is easier now I have definitions of success for each part of my life.

What I've worked out is that I'm pretty easy to please, when you get down to it. So does that mean I'm often satisfied with my life? Well not so much on a day-to-day basis, because you can always find things that aren't right, or things that annoy you. But when I take the step back and look at my life as a whole, I'm extremely happy with where I am in most areas – my relationships, finances, health, career, and life in general. Of course there is a way to go to reach 'success' in all of these areas, but I would expect nothing less, or else there would be little point to life.

A bit remiss of late...

I've mentioned the project has taken a back seat of late, but now I'm physically feeling better, and a massive step for my project starts tomorrow. So, I hope to get back to normal soon.

Day 267: Regrets... I have a few

The activity of 30 days of Being Wrong has two elements. First, being more open to the possibility of being wrong, which includes trying to be more accepting of that. Second, is trying to be more comfortable with the regrets in my life. So what are the regrets I feel I need to be more comfortable with, and why do I struggle with them?

Two failed marriages

Let's start with the big ones, since they are the ones I probably struggle with most. I was married and divorced twice by the time I was 33. Now I believe most failed relationships are a two way street in some shape or form, and I'm sure the poor choices I made in those partners had a role to play in the eventual downfall of the relationships. However, the beginning of the end of both marriages was them cheating on me – did someone say trust issues?

I never completely understood why I held onto the regrets for these experiences quite so much, especially now I'm in such a wonderful relationship. After all, as crappy as those relationships were, they got me to the place I needed to be for a relationship with Derek. They also taught me I'm a hell of a lot stronger than I ever thought possible along the way.

When Kathryn explains regret in her talk, it helped me understand it all a little better. The problem with why I can't make complete peace with these experiences is that I can remember decision points in both relationships where I should have walked away. So, because I have a very fertile imagination for torturing myself, I'm very good at replaying these decisions; wondering why I stayed; and what path my life might have taken if I hadn't.

It's all about self-respect

Please don't think I constantly torture myself with these experiences, I seldom think about my first marriage at all. I long ago came to terms with why I had to have that relationship, and just how broken I was at the time to think that he was all I deserved. That might sound arrogant and nasty, but trust me it is a pretty fair statement to say we were not well matched. But I lacked the self-respect, strength and courage to leave; being a shocking people pleaser didn't help.

The second one haunts me a little more, because I know I caused him pain; not as much as he caused me, but I hurt him a lot in the process of leaving. Also, I can remember four specific points in the first year where I thought to myself 'something isn't right here, I should leave'. So, I can easily imagine four points where I could have changed everything, and neither of us would have been seriously damaged or hurt in the process. Sadly, the reasons I didn't go were exactly the same as they were the first time around. I guess I hadn't learned the lesson and needed to learn it again.

So what do I regret and how do I live with it?

My real regret is that I've let other people make my decisions for me, that I have not had the courage to make decisions about my life. I have not had the strength to act, even when I have known situations in my life were not right for me. I have spent so much time doing what others wanted me to do, being what others wanted me to be, that I failed to understand what I wanted to do and who I wanted to be.

That's the description of the first 30 or so years of my life, particularly in my personal relationships. Sure I had moments of rebellion where I did things that broke the mould of what people expected, but they were not lasting, and were often detrimental to my overall opinion of myself afterwards. Most of that past I have come to terms with, I have found a way to accept the regrets I have around it and, as Kathryn says, those regrets remind me I can do better.

I know I'm a very different person now to the one that walked down those aisles all those years ago. I am much more confident and courageous now than I was back then, and I would not be in either of those relationships now. I think this should be enough for me; I have finally learned my lessons, and I've grown. Now I should just accept that they happened, and stop replaying them, stop thinking 'what if?' Because those experiences are part of who I am, and I'm starting to think that who I am is pretty great.

Does anyone have any advice on how to resolve this? How can I make my mind stop replaying past decisions? How I can be more accepting of my past, and a little kinder to myself for not being strong enough?

Day 271: Risk aversion is my default

It is amazing how random choice can seem to be in our lives. I love the theory of alternate universes, that there are squillions of other universes out there where other Kylies get to live the choices I didn't make. So there are universes with Kylies who have never had a failed marriage; who didn't go to university; who went to university and studied genetics (that was my other choice at one stage); who became a graphic designer; who were courageous enough to tell her lecturer she had a crush on him for four years, and so on.

I've always been risk averse

I know a lot of my choices are based on risk aversion and fear. I understand this is the most powerful, underlying factor when I make a decision. It can be very limiting, in so many ways, but I am generally not a risk taker. That may actually come as a surprise to some people who know me, because it's not like I have sat in a safe little existence my entire life – but it is true.

For example, when I chose to join the Air Force I didn't see it as a risk at all. The job I had was good, but there was no growth opportunity unless my boss left, which was years away. I didn't consider for one moment that I might not make it through training, even if I failed at Air Defence they would probably offer me something else. I was leaving a small number of friends and my brother in Melbourne, but I was okay with only a few friends, and I could usually make a couple wherever I ended up.

So I didn't see a risk; I saw an opportunity for a career that was unlike anything I had ever done. Opportunities to experience a completely different life, and the money was a lot better than I was earning doing administrative work. The choice was easy, I was going into a very structured world with few risks; it was safe.

Jump forward to 30 days of Choice, and I've noticed how risk averse I can be. I have been limiting my choices to avoid regret about my decisions, but at times those self-imposed limitations are simply to remove the risky choices. The limitations have reduced choices into my standard comfort zone. I didn't realise this at first but it became obvious as I was limiting my options around what I was eating, buying and doing. It is even more amusing when you think that a lot of the activities so far have been trying to move me out of my usual comfort zone, and in this one I have simply been building those walls back around myself.

Extending 30 days of Choice

This gives me something to ponder as I head into an extended activity. Since I've been so busy with work, my birthday and being sick, I don't feel I have given 30 days of Choice enough of a chance. I know the next week is going to be just as busy at work, but I feel I need to give this activity another fortnight, to do it justice.

I am likely to want to apply the same extension to 30 days of Being Wrong. While this one is going a little better I think it might serve me well to maintain the focus for a little longer. Being wrong is not supposed to finish for another fortnight anyway, so we'll see how I do in the next two weeks before making that decision.

I hate the perfectionism reaction to feedback

And while we're on being wrong, I've been trying to focus on it more at work in the last week. I did have an incident yesterday where I had to check my instant reaction to people commenting on my work. It's that interesting knee-jerk reaction I get when people want to make changes to my content.

I know I'm fallible, and I also know this week I've been a little brain dead at work; too much going on. So when I asked someone for feedback on content I had written, I should have been open to their comments. I was for the first two people, because they didn't have a lot they thought needed to change. The third person had quite a few comments, and my initial thought was that I knew best. But I checked that thought and instead went to my being wrong approach of, 'well maybe it could be better'. Of course, her suggestions were great and simplified some of the content I had written.

I have to learn to overcome this reaction to constructive criticism and feedback. I know my work is not perfect, I know it could always be improved with another set of eyes reading it; so why do I feel insulted when they come back with changes? Why do I feel the need for everything I do to be perfect, even when I know it isn't? Why do I feel like a basic suggestion to include something I missed or reword a sentence is a commentary on the worth of the entire document? More things to think about as this progresses I guess.

Day 272: Defining success for me

In the process of defining what success means for me I broke it down into 10 categories. These are, in no particular order:

- Relationship • Friendships • Family • Finance • Career • Learning • Hobbies • Volunteering • Mental Health • Physical Health.

These aren't necessarily comprehensive or even universal, but when I sat down to think about what success would look like for me; the things in my life I would need to have; and what I consider to be important, this is the list I came up with. I've thought about how much of this I would share with you, and then I thought 'what's the point of holding back now?' I mean, I've shared more in this project than I've shared with many close friends in my life. That's partly because this process has allowed me to realise things I hadn't identified in myself before, but nevertheless.

My success statements

So below are my statements for success in each of these areas of my life. They are of course evolving, as I think they should be, but this is how I currently view it.

- **Relationship** – I am in a happy relationship with someone who loves me and supports me in everything I do.
- **Friendships** – I have a small number of people in my life who are positive and supportive; who I can rely upon; and who can rely upon me. These are people I can be myself around without fear of judgement.
- **Family** – I have mature, supportive and non-destructive relationships with all of my family members. I am a wonderful aunt to all of my nephews and nieces.
- **Finance** – I am able to afford to live a comfortable lifestyle where I don't have to think too much about money; meaning I don't have to struggle or live hand to mouth.
- **Career** – I have a career where I am respected, valued and I am contributing to society. There is another layer to this one, I see myself as truly successful now I am doing something I love that is more creative than management.
- **Learning** – I am continuing to learn in formal and informal ways, and sharing those learnings with others.
- **Hobbies** – I have creative outlets in my life that allow me to express myself, and make beautiful objects that are appreciated by others.
- **Volunteering** – I am engaged in a volunteer role that allows me to give back to my community in a meaningful way.
- **Mental Health** – I am generally happy, a lot nicer to myself and experience few melancholic or blue moods; or depression-lite.

- **Physical Health** – I am physically healthy, and have more positive control over my weight and the minor health issues I have to manage.

Some of these I can honestly say I've achieved, and there are a couple of areas in my life I feel are very successful. Others I continue to struggle with, and some of them I acknowledge I may never attain. But it is interesting to have these definitions in place, because it does control the envy comparisons.

For instance, you will notice there is nothing in here about marriage or children. These are not things I have ever wanted in my life, and I certainly would never gauge my success by them. Other people will have them, of course, and that's great for them; but this is my list. So this means I shouldn't envy people that have these things in their lives, because I truly don't want them for myself.

There is one thing I have not included in this list, and that is the ultimate dream. It's nothing personal but I'm not willing to put that in writing and reveal it to the world – yet. I have implied it in a number of posts about this project, and I know I have all but said it, but there is still that broken little girl inside me that feels putting it out into the world would just be too much, would make me too vulnerable.

How do you define success for yourself? Do you even know what your measures are, or are you like I was before going through this process?

August 2012 – Why am I doing this?

Day 275: Do you know what today is?

Today is the beginning of the final quarter of My Year of TED. I can't believe I've completed nine months already. Of course this means in the next week or so I will do my Third Quarter reflection; I do need to get cracking with this.

I am a little disappointed that I'm starting my last quarter by extending my current activities, but at the same time I feel it is important for me to extend them.

No progress on being wrong

My work project is about data gathering from the community sector, that's probably the easiest way to explain it. The working group I'm leading was responsible for developing the collection tool, this is why I've been so busy. As a side note, I did get to practice a lot of the simplicity principles in developing the tool, a data guide and scenario, which was great.

Over the last week I've been doing information sessions to explain the data collection, and this has given me some fantastic opportunities to practice being open to being wrong. Some of the questions the sector have come up with are things we had never envisaged, and that's required me to make some quick judgement calls about how they fit into collection.

This has subsequently allowed my internal critic to have a field day, for two reasons. First is the thought that I shouldn't have missed some of the questions being asked. This has been interesting for me, since I'm doing being wrong I'm trying not to be defensive at all, so every question is legitimate (I find it hard to remember that sometimes). But for some of them I can't help feeling a little crushed when the question is something I feel I shouldn't have missed; that's when I feel wrong.

Second, usually later that night when I am trying to sleep, I realise some of the answers I've given in the information sessions are probably not the best way to deal with things. There have been two answers in particular that I'm completely kicking myself over; I think they may create a massive problem for the analysis – we'll see.

The reason my internal critic is going nuts is because I haven't been able to adjust how I think about being wrong. I'm still stuck in the mindset that it means I'm dumb, or lazy – or both. I know this isn't true for a number of reasons: I've been on an incredibly steep learning curve; other people were involved, so it isn't all down to me; I've worked my arse off doing all of this work; and I've done a pretty good job with it all. But that doesn't stop me feeling like I've failed because I didn't factor in every possible permutation.

I do need to work on this, but I'm at a loss. I have tried to reduce the impact of my inner critic for a long time to little avail. I'll keep trying since it is the only way I'm likely to catch up on some sleep; I don't know if I will ever get better at this.

QUARTERLY REFLECTION 3 – THREE MONTHS LEFT

The completion of the third quarter snuck up on me in many ways. The last two months have been crazy busy at work, so My Year of TED project has taken a bit of a back seat. That's been a little challenging, since most of the activities for this period have been very involved; hence the reason I'm currently adding a fortnight to the end of choice and being wrong.

30 days of Preconceptions

I realised how quickly I categorise people, and how wrong those categorisations are if the surface is scratched.

I enjoyed this activity in many ways. It stretched me beyond my comfort zone to write some of the posts I did during this time, particularly the asylum seeker post. It surprised me how much I do categorise and, as a result, judge people I come across. This shouldn't have surprised me, I know I can be very judgemental, but I was quite shocked about it.

I did challenge myself to go beyond that initial judgement though, to consider the other stories in people's lives; to adjust the way I thought about them, and interact with them accordingly. I also started the *I am not just a…* blog, which became important for 30 days of Starting a Movement.

I have tried to be more mindful of this after completing the activity. It's not something I am vigilant about, but a number of times I have caught myself in interactions with others taking a mental step back, and trying to think about what else is going on.

This was an important activity to do, and I believe everyone should take time to realise just how quickly they label and judge the people they meet every day. It's a real eye-opener, which is why I tried making it a movement.

Thank you Chimamanda, Bill and Derek for three wonderful talks that made me think about how I view and interact with other people. These are invaluable lessons I think we all get too busy to remember in our daily lives – I'm going to try hard not to forget.

30 days of Letters

Writing letters allowed me to connect with some special people in my life, and let them know how important they are to me.

There is a power to the printed word that becomes more influential when you hand write it. This was an extremely challenging activity, since I was saying things in the letters I had never said before. I don't know why it made me feel so incredibly vulnerable to do this. Maybe it's because the written word can be interpreted in so many different ways; but I think it was mainly due to the fact that, like many people, I'm bad at saying the important things.

I enjoyed the creativity of this activity. It was wonderful to get some of these feelings out and I think that all of the letters were well received, I haven't heard from one recipient. I still have to write my parents' letters, I will do that before the project ends. There are a couple of other letters I should consider writing; I'll think about that before I finish.

One last thing I will say, a couple of the people sent me back a letter, and in this very electronic age there is nothing quite like getting a handwritten letter in the post. There is something so special about knowing someone took the time and effort to hand write the words for you; try it and you'll find out what I mean.

Thank you so much Lakshmi for a wonderful talk that has helped me say things I was never brave enough to before.

30 days of Starting a Movement

This was a great reminder that I need to keep my limitations in mind when I come up with ideas to tackle.

This activity was a classic example of biting off more than I could chew, and I think I knew this going in. I've said this many times, I'm an introvert, so promoting a movement and trying to get some traction was always going to be an extreme challenge. I'm not going to go into the whole post-mortem about this activity again; feel free to read the reflection post if you want to know why this one was a failure.

But I learned a lot from the failures in this activity. If my current activities are teaching me anything it's that we can often learn more from getting things wrong than being right. Since the initial reflection post I've had a little more time to sit with this activity, and the things that went wrong with it. What I've come to realise is that as a leader I am a great follower, and no that is not counter-intuitive.

This activity put me further outside my comfort zone than probably any other one to date, and I did that knowing I was going to fail. But I wanted to see what I could do when I put my mind to it, and I am proud of the fact that I pushed the whole 30 days; that I didn't give up on it.

Thank you Derek, Seth and Susan for talks that helped support me through a very challenging activity. They helped me understand what I was striving for, and what I failed to achieve.

30 days of Leadership

I now understand my leadership style better, developed an understanding of future-based language, and learned how valuable it can be.

There was always going to be an activity based around leadership; this is something I've spent a lot of time thinking about over the last decade. I've always had a concern that I wasn't a very good leader, but what I've realised is that in many ways I was confusing leadership and management. The main limitations I thought I had were more management than leadership related.

What I've realised through this activity is that I'm quite happy with my leadership abilities, although I could always improve on them. Saying that, I did improve a little by finally understanding what David Logan and Steve Zaffron mean by future-based language.

More than anything though, I think the most important thing to come out of this activity was an acceptance of my introverted leadership style. Susan Cain's talk and book have been such a revelation for me. Not only do I understand that my style is not 'broken' as I felt previously, but I'm also clearer about how I can support other introverts as well.

Thank you Barry, David and Susan for the inspiration. I know I tried very hard to incorporate them, and do them the justice they all deserve.

How do I feel at the nine month mark?

In a word, tired! Due to the way I've been doing the quarterly reflections I have not spoken about the activities for July in this post, but I am including them in this reflection on my feelings at the nine month mark. I think that human beings are only capable of coping with so much in their lives, and I've had a few days in the last month where I've felt I'm reaching that point.

The activities I have been taking on are not easy to do. They are challenging aspects of my personality that are fundamental to the way I view myself. Moreover, every time I challenge part of this I have to acknowledge the weaknesses I know exist in my personality but I choose, as I'm sure most of you do, not to think about most of the time.

It means I've had some very confronting moments over the last nine months. Some have made me very teary; some have made me anxious; and others have made me angry. I don't know where I will end up on the emotional scale at the end of this project though. At this stage I guess I'm quite proud of myself, given the things I have achieved and the growth I have experienced so far; but I also carry some disappointment.

I guess I'm feeling a little stripped bare and vulnerable, but at the same time I feel more courageous and centred. In all honesty, I'm glad I only have three months left of this project. I don't know how much more I can challenge the intrinsic parts of my nature, especially since I know a couple of the activities that are still to come.

A question for you, the reader

As I'm being very reflective on the last nine months while writing this I have some questions for you guys. Has there been an activity that you have enjoyed more than the others? Is there anything I haven't covered that you think I should have? Are you getting anything out of this blog at all?

Day 281: Avoiding poor purchases

It constantly surprises me how poor some of the choices I make can be. There are so many random things that get in the way when we make decisions, even when we know the rational choice. This shouldn't be surprising though, organisations have spent billions of dollars to work out how to manipulate us into buying things we don't need, and choosing their products over others. But I for one, am continually dumbfounded by how ridiculously my decisions can be manipulated.

We all have items we buy and don't use

Take the simple things like buying clothes for instance. I know I'm not the only person who, over the years, has purchased items that I've never worn. It's a fascinating process that I've spoken with other people about as well. Sometimes they are items of clothing that I want to be able to wear, even though I know they don't suit my body shape or colouring, so I buy them anyway. Other times it's simply that I have spent so long looking for something I pick an item that is better than the other options, even though it's not right.

I bring this up because over the last week I have walked away empty handed a number of times when I've been shopping. I have managed to control the instinct to buy a number of items that would not have been right for me, this includes: mascara that was on sale when I was bored waiting for a prescription to be filled, that I didn't need; a lovely top that was completely the wrong colour for my skin; and, trying on four pairs of black pants for work, none of which were quite right.

Focusing on choices has made me realise just how poor some of the decision making behind my product purchases can be. Don't get me wrong, I have still bought things during this activity, things I'm happy with. I guess I'm just a little more aware of the random things that influence my choices, and lead to poor outcomes. I'm not saying I will never end up with a bad dress or uncomfortable shoes again; I'm just saying that at the moment I'm hyper aware of it, which is saving me money, and buyer's remorse.

Day 283: Acknowledging the elephant

I've been struggling with something for a few days on my work project. It was a thought that came to me last week as a minor passing caution I guess. It popped up and I dismissed it, because it was a thought that I'd gotten something quite wrong in the analysis; I had missed something important.

It came back on Monday as a fleeting thought, but I was so busy it was easier to ignore it again. On Tuesday I had to stop and realise that I was putting this thought off because it would mean I had to admit I was wrong, and I would have a lot of work ahead of me to fix it. So I asked the question that had been playing on my mind, hoping I had not been wrong – unfortunately I was.

I don't know why, even when I am focused on being wrong, I kept putting this thought out of my mind. Surely it would have been easier for me to acknowledge this concern and ask the question early, then get it resolved. I think it had a lot to do with having put so much effort into doing the survey that I didn't want to acknowledge I had missed something so obvious. The most disappointing thing was I'd gotten halfway there, my brain just hadn't reached the final logical conclusion.

We all have elephants in the room we ignore for one reason or another. There's a considerable amount of work ahead of me to resolve ignoring this elephant. Maybe that's a good thing as it will remind me I'm fallible (oh so fallible), and I need to acknowledge nagging thoughts earlier; regardless of whether they are there to tell me I'm wrong or not. Undoubtedly I will learn this lesson again and again, these sort of lessons are like that.

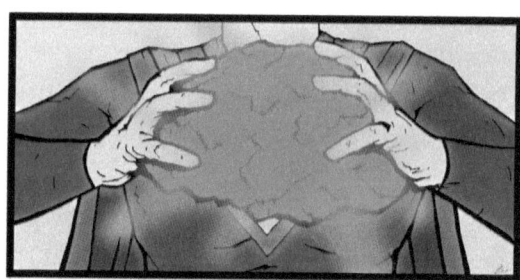

ACTIVITY 18 • 30 DAYS OF VULNERABILITY

We're rapidly approaching the end of My Year of TED, with only four more activities to go. With that in mind, I decided it was time to kick it up a notch and take on the big one. You all had to know that a dedicated vulnerability activity was on its way; time for me to fully embrace the concept.

The talks

This activity is based on three talks, the first two being Brené Brown's amazing talks on shame, vulnerability and courage – *Brené Brown: The power of vulnerability* and *Brené Brown: Listening to shame*. Brené's talks inspired me so much I bought her book *The Gifts of Imperfection: Let Go of Who You Think*

You're Supposed to Be and Embrace Who You Are to get into it a little deeper and prepare myself for the project as a whole. The third talk is *Eve Ensler: Happiness in body and soul*, which is a very inspirational talk about owning your truth and giving away what you want the most.

The challenge

I've mentioned a number of times that this entire project is an exercise in vulnerability. That means I should probably have saved this to be the final activity of My Year of TED, but it aligns so well with 30 days of Being Wrong that it's better placed now.

I've tried to be painfully honest in this blog; as well as more open and vulnerable in the interactions with people in my life. There have been times where this has become too much for me, and I've felt my natural impulse to withdraw and protect myself kick in. Sometimes I push through this, other times I let that impulse take over to censor posts or isolate myself from others for short periods.

So, part of the challenge for me in this activity is to focus on, in Brené's words, 'excruciating vulnerability'. This not only means being courageous and embracing connectivity, but also being more compassionate to myself and others. This last thing is something I have improved upon, but mainly towards other people; I'm still way too harsh on myself.

The second part of the challenge is about telling and owning my truth. I feel I've done a lot of that in this blog; there are things I've said here that I've never told anyone outside a select couple of truth-holders in my life. Added to this, through some of these activities I have been more honest with the other people around me about things I could never share in this space. But there is more that I can do in this aspect of my life, and part of that is fully understanding my truth.

There is another part to Eve's talk – giving away what you want most in the world as a way of healing yourself. I've thought quite a lot about what this would be and I have some ideas, but I'm not sure how this will play out.

The activity

There are so many facets to this, so many ways I can embrace vulnerability in the next 30 days. The main things I think I need to focus on are:
- continuing to push my courage by being more authentic, rather than being what people want or expect me to be
- actively practising self-compassion; trying to kick my perfectionist trait

- trying to reconnect with a couple of people from my past who I have fallen out of touch with for a long time now, and in the process sharing things they probably never knew
- I also want to try to understand what my truth is on a deeper level, so I can ensure I'm telling and owning it.

The last part of this is to try to work out what I would want most in the world, and whether there is some way of giving that away. I doubt I will resolve that in the 30 days, but you never know.

A final note: I believe I am prepared for this activity, given everything I have done in the project so far. But that does not mean I am under any misconceptions about how difficult it will be.

Day 288: Last day of choice

Today is the last day of my extended activity on choice, and I've had some interesting revelations in the last few days. Some of this I already had a general awareness of, but it seems to have come together when I was thinking about regrets and being wrong.

This starts with the fact that I think we have far too much choice, and I don't like it. It's one of the reasons I wanted to do an activity on choice, because I have often struggled with making choices, and being happy with the choices I've made. I wanted to see if I could find a way to be more comfortable with my choices by understanding them a little better.

It has certainly made me more aware of decisions, but more than that, I've realised how much of my life I've spent avoiding choices. I'll expand on this in the reflection, I need a few days to understand it more clearly myself.

Update on volunteering

In relation to my definitions of success there has been something I have been meaning to mention. I raised it in the post outlining my definitions of success; it relates to the volunteering aspect of my life.

Next week I start my training course to become an adult literacy tutor. To be entirely honest, yes even before vulnerability starts, I'm just a bit terrified with the concept; both of studying again, and then actually being a literacy tutor. It's not that I don't think I can do it, it's just that taking this on is a pretty significant step for me – and yes there is also a bit of the perfectionist fear creeping in.

This is a bit of a rambling post, welcome inside my brain people. I'll try to get it under a little more control as I start vulnerability tomorrow. Work is occupying so much time and energy at the moment that I need to make space for writing, and reflecting on the activities I am undertaking. Oh, and yes I do realise I should probably be meditating to help clear my mind from the work stuff, but that's just added pressure I don't need at the moment.

Day 290: No self-compassion for me today

Today was a fantastic learning opportunity, putting a positive spin on pretty a crappy day. I'm paying the penalty for making a wrong assumption two years ago, and not following it up to make sure. A simple phone call or email a year ago would have saved me a few hundred dollars, and a lot of grief.

Since I was already in a bad mood today, well let's just say that self-compassion is not something I'm succeeding at just now. In truth it was a very simple mistake that I had assumed there were fail safes in place to guard against. I would love to have a dollar for every time one of my assumptions was incorrect, it means I would be able to pay off the bill I received today.

Anyway, this was just a very brief post to get that off my chest, admit that the mistake was mine and that I was wrong to not follow it up. I'm not ready to be lenient on myself about it yet, that will take a little longer.

REFLECTION – 30 (OR 45) DAYS OF CHOICE

The outcomes of this activity were very surprising for me, especially when I was doing it in conjunction with 30 days of Being Wrong. There were two facets to this activity – understanding my definitions of success; and being more conscious about the random aspects of the choices I make.

Starting with success

The thing about Alain de Botton's talk that strongly resonated with me when I first watched it, was the aspect of envying others by making comparisons that are not realistic, yet we feel they are. I've mentioned a number of times during this project that I've never had a real plan or vision for my life; this talk pointed out that I need to understand what success looks like for me for a whole different reason.

I had been primed for this through a number of other activities in the project so far, but mainly from 30 days of Drive. This meant coming up with success statements for all aspects of my life was not as difficult as I thought it would be. I'm not saying they are complete at this point in time, but they are a good indication of what I think a successful life looks like, for me.

I've already used these statements twice, when I was judging myself against other people's achievements. Not only did they remind me that what these people had achieved is not even in my definition of success, but one of the achievements would have required the person to make commitments and sacrifices that I am, quite frankly, not willing to make. It's a nice leveller, and something I will definitely try to keep in mind in future.

Onto actual choices

I was successful in limiting my choices and being generally more aware of my thoughts and feelings when making choices during this time. This definitely had an impact. I was more considered in my choices and didn't just buy something for the sake of it when none of the options were quite right. I've never put such a concerted effort into making choices as I have over the last 45 days, and there were still a few outcomes I wasn't very happy with, but at least I know I considered all possibilities when making them.

Some of the bigger choices included:
- what colour to dye my hair – I'm finally happy with blonde, even though it didn't quite come out as I pictured it
- where to go for a holiday next month – based on the two most important elements; price, and being able to take Lily with us
- a few visual decisions on the house we're building – largely colours around the windows, which I'm happy with
- a few pretty major choices about how we'd approach my work project and how the work would be done – mainly census questions and structure, which I'm happy with, even with the error I found.

And the surprising aspects?

The semi-surprising thing is that I don't like the amount of choice we have in our lives. Who needs to be able to choose from over a dozen varieties of shampoo or toothpaste? And what are the differences between them anyway? I know I live in a capitalist society, and I'm supposed to revel in the large variety of choices that are available to me in all aspects of my life; sometimes a benevolent dictatorship, or even a utopian socialist community would be so much easier.

Don't get me wrong, if all of these choices were taken away tomorrow I would bitch and protest with the best of them, but sometimes the sheer amount of choice we have in our lives is so overwhelming that I just want someone to tell me what to pick. This is not just for consumer products, I can definitely see the appeal of having your career or life partner chosen for you – not that I would trust my parents to do it, but given some of my decisions they couldn't have done much worse.

The greater surprise for me is the realisation that for the majority of my life I've allowed choices and decisions to be made for me. By this I mean I haven't been a very active participant in the direction and choices in my life. I've just moved along with the choices that became available to me, I haven't made things happen for myself. I have also missed out on opportunities because I avoided making choices when there was a need to.

But it is so much more than this; I've been so scared of actively making choices and creating opportunities because what if I get it wrong? It's easier to take the options that present themselves particularly if they aren't different or risky, because there are so many things I could do or be in this life, and there are so many ways I could fail. Funnily enough, it is when I've been at these crossroads in my life that I've made the worst choices imaginable. But in each situation, they were the simple choices that didn't require risks; where I could look back and think 'well it wasn't what I planned on, life just got in the way' when they failed.

Take my first marriage for instance, and this is another moment where I'm sharing more than I had ever planned on in this forum. I met my first husband at a point in my life where I was at a complete loss where I was going and what I was going to do. I had just completed my honours year at university, and had decided that I wouldn't stay on to do a Diploma of Education to become a teacher; something I had thought I would do for the three years prior to this. I had become so busy doing my thesis that I had effectively distanced myself from the few friends I had in my life, and it had been well over eight months since anyone had shown any romantic interest in me. Added to this, I now realise that my mental health was extremely problematic for the last couple of years I was at university, and this was an exceptionally low point in that time.

So, rather than sitting down and making a plan for my future, and what I would do now that I had finished study; or taking a risk and telling the person I had a crush on for four years how I felt about them; or putting myself out there to try to re-engage with the friends who meant so much to me – I made no active decision about my future at all. Instead, life threw this trainwreck of a relationship at me, and I felt it was easier to just take it and go along with the flow; yes, I had a very messed up concept of 'easy'. That way I didn't have to take any risks; I didn't have to make any plans that might fail; I didn't have to put myself in situations where I might be rejected and hurt; and I had one anchor point in a complete time of flux.

I hope that this is making some sense, it's become quite clear in my head but I don't know that I'm explaining it that well.

This hasn't always been the case in my life, I have had moments of clarity about what I wanted and where I wanted to be. When my first marriage broke up I came up with a list of three things I had always wanted to do: skydive; go to Florence, Italy; and join the Air Force. Within 12 months of coming up with that list I had done all three of these, and the sense of achievement around this was huge. But then I hit another bout of feeling completely ungrounded, and not knowing how things would turn out; that's when husband number two came into my life.

Anyway, all of this is to say that, over the last eight or nine years I have been a much more active participant in the choices about my life, and I feel much happier about it as a result. But thinking back about all of these things I realise that at times I do still abdicate responsibility for the decisions in my life. It's usually not the big things any more, but that tendency still remains.

In summation

This activity has been incredibly important in helping me understand quite a few things about myself. I highly recommend everyone do the success statements exercise. It is amazing how powerful writing this down can be in calming the envy you might have of others. There are still people that I feel bad comparing myself against because they have what I want, and I think the comparison is fairly valid. But it has become more targeted, and I hope to maintain that aspect.

As for choice, I think I need to maintain an awareness around my choices so I don't fall back into crappy consumer choices. I also think this activity has shown me I need to be more active in making choices, especially the difficult ones, and taking risks in those choices. I will try to maintain this awareness in my life, especially when the next big life decision comes up; since I didn't have any during this 45 days.

What about you? Are you an active participant in the big decisions in your life or do you tend to go with flow and see how it turns out?

> Subscribe to my newsletter and get the free workbook based on these exercises. It's called *Living an Aligned Life*, visit kyliedunn.com.

Day 295: Regretting what didn't happen

In the reflection above, I mentioned I've had periods in my life where I've actively abdicated the responsibility to choose, and have instead just gone with the flow. The outcome of these periods resulted in my biggest regrets.

My two failed marriages fall into this category, or more importantly one of my marriages, and how I dealt with the end of the other. But, since I've been focusing on this in the last couple of months, the biggest regrets I have are for the things I didn't do; opportunities I missed; things I let slip away. I think this is because when you take an action, even if it turns out to be wrong, you generally learn something from the experience. So even though I feel like I wasted time in those relationships, I learned things about myself and what I wanted from my life in the process.

It is the times I've missed opportunities to do and say things; when I was too scared to take action; and especially the times I have been too scared to do the right thing, I struggle with most. Because with these events my imagination can run riot, and trust me it does. I don't mean all of the time, but when I'm feeling stressed or in a more fragile state of mind, these things take on a life of their own. As a result, I spend far too much of my brain space imagining the outcome, if only I had been a stronger or more courageous person at that time.

Like many of the characteristics I've spoken about here, I'm absolutely certain I'm not alone in any of this. So I figure that while I'm trying to also come up with a better way of thinking about being wrong, I also need to come up with a way of shutting down these thoughts running through my mind. I thought I would ask any of you reading this how you deal with these sort of regrets? How do you accept the things you didn't do?

'Vulnerability hangover'

This is a phrase that Brené uses in one of her talks, and I think I experienced a little of this last week. My stress levels with work are pretty high at the moment, and I had another minor meltdown about the fact that our house is not progressing as quickly as I had hoped or we had planned; okay pretty major one. Add to this the My Year of TED project, and this blog; suddenly last week was not surprising.

Sometimes I forget how difficult this project has been for me, and continues to be. I've been tackling ingrained personality traits along the way. The stuff I've shared with people close to me, and with you here has made me feel increasingly exposed and vulnerable. Having said that, let's just leave it at me having a very bad time; I don't think I have it in me to explain what occurred at this point of time.

Day 299: Self-criticism induced insomnia

I am writing this post at 5.20am because my brain simply won't let me get back to sleep; after 90 minutes of tossing and turning I've given up. 'And why is your brain keeping you up?' I hear you ask, well this is some of my lack of self-compassion at its best, and I thought I was doing so well.

This is the insanity of how the human brain functions, and I don't just mean mine; I'm pretty sure this sort of thing is universal for people capable of empathy and other such emotions. The reason I cannot get back to sleep is I'm beating myself up about not calling my brother for his birthday. You know the amazingly talented brother who does my activity artwork, well his birthday was a couple of days ago, and I still haven't called him to wish him a happy birthday – I'm not entirely sure why.

I did text him to say happy birthday, and I consciously didn't call during the day because I know how busy he gets and didn't want to interrupt his flow – wow, that sounds defensive! But I simply cannot fathom why I didn't call him that night or yesterday even! This is very unlike me, and my brain is punishing me for it. I not only have the voice telling me I'm a bad person, but it is amplified by the fact that I cannot explain why I haven't called. I even made a comment on his birthday cake photo on Instagram last night, and still wasn't prompted to call – WTF is that about!

This may not seem like a big deal to some of you, but it's unlike me not to contact people for their birthday, and especially my little brother. I don't forgive myself these sort of things easily; while I'm sure Matt is fine with it, I don't feel he should be.

There are a lot of interesting family dynamics around these events, depending which family member is having the birthday. If I had my way we'd just call them all off and move on with our lives, because they can be such emotional minefields. We have had some interesting history around birthdays in our family, and there is a lot of guilt and negative emotion associated with them. But that doesn't explain this oversight, or maybe it does? From memory I think I have done something like this before with Matt's birthday… it's too early in the morning to be going there.

So now I just have to wait until a suitable hour to call and explain that I have no idea why I didn't call. While I wait, my brain will tell me how horrible

I am, it will remind me of all of the nice things Matt has done for me over the years, and all of the other ways I have let him down. I'm trying very hard to kick myself out of this spiral, because I know that in the scheme of life this is not that big a deal; sadly I don't get to pick the things my brain gets hung up on. Those choices were created a long time ago, and had much less to do with me than people around me — otherwise known as parents — imposing their expectations and guilt onto me.

I will probably read this back later and decide that I should never write blog posts this early in the morning, or when I'm this emotional. But I'm embracing vulnerability and trying to silence the shame monster on this one. Added to that, this is kicking that perfectionist image of myself in the head, which I do like. Unfortunately, it's not as successful at moving my brain to a place of self-compassion; 'yeah, good luck with that' I hear that little voice in my head utter. I will end this rambling post here by saying Happy Birthday Matt, and I'll call you later this morning.

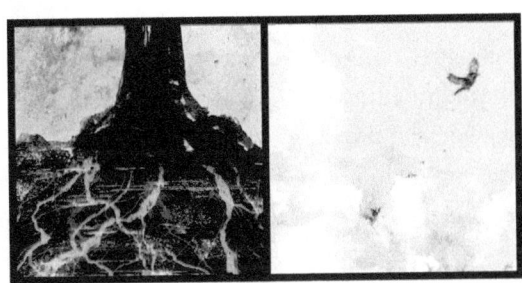

ACTIVITY 19 • 30 DAYS OF TIME

The talks

This activity is based on *Philip Zimbardo: The psychology of time*, which is short talk that's always resonated with me as such an interesting concept. The idea that we have a time perspective which alters the way we function in the world, was intriguing for me. *Joachim de Posada: Don't eat the marshmallow!* talk also influences this activity. He discusses the idea that children who are able to resist the temptation to eat the marshmallow so they can get two when the adult returns, have better impulse control that seems to benefit their entire lives.

The challenge

The main part of this challenge is for me to better understand my time perspective and try to improve it to the 'ideal' time perspective outlined by Philip. The ideal perspective versus my current perspective is:

- Past Negative   1.95   Me: 3.90
- Past Positive   4.6   Me: 2.33
- Present Fatalism   1.5   Me: 1.44
- Present Hedonism   3.9   Me: 3.07
- Future   4.0   Me: 4.23

The thing is, as I'm sure you are acutely aware by now, my Past Negative is far too high, and probably influences my life too much. Interestingly enough, and I will expand on this in my next reflection, I actually think my negative opinions of my past have been exacerbated by the recent activities I've been doing.

Regardless of this fact, as my Zimbardo Time Perspective Inventory results indicate, I need to fix my perspective on the past. I need to stop focusing on the gnarled roots of my past so I can achieve a more positive focus on the vast possibilities of my future.

The activity

I'm using the exercises in Philip Zimbardo's book *The Time Paradox* as its basis. These include answering questions about who I was, who I am, and who will I be. I should mention here I will not be practising vulnerability by including these answers on the blog; a reflection of the process, and what I learn from it will be included. Quite frankly, even though I'm doing vulnerability, there is only so much I can share with you all, and I've probably overstepped the mark on the things you actually want to know.

The activity also includes daily gratitudes, yes back on that one; it's only for two weeks this time. I will also be trying meditation again, or some activity that will bring me back to the moment.

I'm still finishing Philip's book, which I hope to complete before the activity starts on 1 September. I will post up the additional parts of the activity as I find out how he recommends shifting my time perspective.

Day 301: Another milestone down

Wow, I've done 300 days of TED! I feel like that's pretty damn impressive. In some ways it certainly feels a lot longer than that, but not always.

I only have a few days left of Being Wrong and I will be so glad when this activity is over. It's been a great area to focus on, and I have realised a few things about how I deal with the possibility that I may be wrong, but it is not a productive mindset to be in. Particularly the part of the activity that has me focusing on dealing with regrets, that's just too depressing.

Owning my story

I've been spending a bit of time thinking about the Eve Ensler part of 30 days of Vulnerability. This has added to the negative feelings around regrets and being wrong, but I'm not going to talk about that at the moment.

The thing that I have been focusing on is what I might want to give to the world. While I did not expect to resolve that during this activity, I think I have come up with a couple of things that appeal to me. I am entirely certain these ideas have little to do with this activity, and much more to do with My Year of TED as a whole, which is partially why I scheduled vulnerability for so late in the project.

I'm still conceptualising this, but I can say that what I'm thinking I want to give the world is the ability to learn about yourself; mainly the sort of things I've been learning about myself throughout this process. I don't know exactly what that means, or how to achieve it, but it's the beginning of the idea that I'm assuming will become my focus after My Year of TED ends.

This of course aligns to one of my three words for 2012 – Share. I'm open to suggestions on what you might want me to share, or what you think might be good to expand on? As I said, I'm in the conceptualisation phase at the moment, so feel free to offer your input.

Day 304: Last day of being wrong (if only)

As I mentioned in my last post, I'm very glad this activity is over and there will be some interesting comments in the reflection. In hindsight, I don't think I should have extended this activity, although I did learn quite a bit.

To make the final day more interesting I had a bit of a humbling experience today. I've mentioned the work project I've been doing and the census tool we developed, then the issues I've had analysing all of the information. It's been a very interesting journey over the last month about overlooking things, or just not quite appreciating the importance of approaching things in a certain way. That meant I have spent this week completely redoing the collection spreadsheet to capture the relevant pieces of information, or rather to better capture the relevant information.

Today, one of the members of the working group, the one from Finance, pointed out the calculations I did in the census data collection tool were flawed. It turns out that there are far smarter ways of doing what I was trying to do in Excel, and Shane knows how to write those formulas. So today he rewrote all of my calculations and we spent time updating the 180 responses; well he did more than me, and we aren't finished yet, but you get the idea.

I hope this is the last time I'm proven fallible on this project. I don't know that I can handle doing any of this collection again – and we're not even finished with the analysis.

And in other news…

We just finished watching the second series of *Go Back to Where You Came From*, the great SBS documentary that takes people from both sides of the asylum seeker debate and puts them through the 'boat people' experience. It was great, although I think it lacked something in not having any 'average' people involved this time – they were all celebrities/politicians. Watching it reminded me of my 'Asylum Seeker Debate' post, of which I'm quite proud.

I'm also two weeks into my adult literacy tutor training. This will be an interesting course, and has a very eclectic collection of people participating. I'm trying to be open minded with this, not judging people based on my preconceptions, but some people are very challenging. I think that it will be good to practice some compassion with my class mates though, because compassion and empathy will be a requirement for the literacy tutor role.

September 2012 – Turning a corner

Day 306: The fear in connecting with people from my past

Today was the start of 30 days of Time, which will hopefully help me shift my time perspective, at least a bit. I was hoping to have finished Philip Zimbardo's book, *The Time Paradox*, before starting the activity. This week has been crazy so I'm only two-thirds through. It's quite fascinating so far, can't wait to get through the remaining hundred pages.

Vulnerability and connection

The connection I want to do during Vulnerability is to try reconnect with people from my past. I have contact details to get in touch with two of them; I hope to do so next week. I thought it might be a good thing for me to explain why I feel it's important for me to do this.

I don't have many friends in my life from school and university. Actually I probably only have three people in my life from that time who I stay in contact with at all. This has not been an active choice I've made over the years, it's just that I've been pretty bad at the friendship thing. By that I mean, and I've said this many times before, I haven't been good at letting people know how important they are to me. More importantly, I have not been willing to put myself in vulnerable positions to keep people in my life. I've usually waited for friends to make and keep this contact.

Now that is an incredible generalisation, I have had some friendships in my adult life where I've felt very comfortable, and worked hard to maintain them. But for many of my friendships, especially those when I wasn't entirely sure the other person wanted the friendship, the description above is more accurate. That may sound a little strange to some of you, for others I'm sure you know what I am talking about, since I know I'm not alone in this. It is a self-esteem/self-confidence thing, partly driven by actual life experience, unfortunately. The easiest explanation is there were people who I considered friends, but I'm not sure whether they valued my friendship or tolerated it.

That is a very brutal way of explaining it, but like I said – self-esteem issues combined with some not so great experiences with people I truly thought were my friends. Anyway, all of this is to say that there are a couple of people who I do think truly were friends but I was afraid to make the step of putting myself out there to try to keep the friendship. So now I'm going to put myself in the ultimate vulnerable position, to contact these people over 20 years since I've seen them to find out if they were my friends and if they want, in some small way, to rekindle that friendship.

It's taken a long time for me to muster the courage to do this, I'm sure it will go better than that nasty little voice in the back of my head tells me.

Day 309: Authenticity challenges in the workplace

Being authentic is not an easy thing to do, otherwise we'd all do it. I've been trying to be more authentic since the beginning of this project, which is why I've said this project is largely about vulnerability. However, now I'm focused on stepping up that authenticity, I've realised just how often I'm not.

This is usually done so I won't upset or offend other people, but sometimes it's because I do not want to deal with the confrontation that may arise from being authentic. This is why I'm focusing the courage aspect of vulnerability towards authenticity, because I'm not courageous enough.

A light-hearted but mind-numbing example

I've had a pretty rough couple of months at work, and that's made me a little more blunt than usual. So while I'm trying not to upset people I'm not feeling the need to stroke their egos or get involved in inane conversations with them. By 'them' I'm referring to a couple of staff in the office that have the capacity to drive me completely insane. The authentic me wants to shake them and tell them how annoying they can be, and how they should not equate their inane tasks with the other people in the office who are truly busy. The compassionate part of me understands they are functioning at full capacity, so they do honestly believe they are as busy as everyone else. The outcome is that I simply don't engage when they talk about how busy they are, I come back with some sort of statement like 'aren't we all' or, of late, simply avoid conversations with them altogether.

Sidenote: one of these people actually equated her three week cold with knowing how people with a terminal illness feel 'being so run down and not being able to do the things you want'. I kid you not! She has said this to three people, one person mentioned it to me, two other conversations I overheard in the office. Now, given it is still quite recent that we lost Derek's dad to cancer, well she should be extremely glad that I'm in disengaging mode.

This is probably not a major thing in most people's worlds, but I am a people pleaser, so listening to other people and validating their whining seems to be a built in reflex. It's a reflex I feel bad about indulging, particularly when I do not believe what the other person is saying. Now, if they're people who are close to me I do often have the courage to call them on their shit, or calmly explain to them there is another point of view they may want to consider. But how do you deal with the people you want to beat to death with the phone when they start talking in their babyish, condescending tone of voice?

I don't believe it is authentic of me to be nasty to other people, but I don't want the authentic me to be a people pleaser either. I'm fairly comfortable with how I've been dealing with it in the last few weeks, but I cannot continue to just disengage with people; our office is way too small to keep that up. I need a way where I don't have to confront these people, but where I'm not seen as supporting their behaviour or opinions either.

Or maybe I just need my project to be finished, and take some leave so I can get back on a more even keel. Then they may not annoy me so much that I fantasise about harming them in the office. I'm sorry this has been a little rambling, but that is my brain at the moment – unfocused and random. If only I had more time in the day.

Day 312: Back onto daily gratitudes

One of Philip Zimbardo's activities is the Who Was I? test. This involves a list of 'I was:' repeated 20 times; you have to fill in the gaps. I'm not going to share my responses to this test with you, because while I'm practising vulnerability I'm still not ready to share some things with you. Maybe I feel this way because it's a particularly negative representation of me as a person, and explains the Past-negative focus in my time perspective.

Anyway, the next part of the process is to complete the 'Reconstructing a Positive Past' worksheet. I'm still tossing up whether I share this with you or not. I have already spoken about some of these during 30 days of Being Wrong, I promise to have that reflection done soon; but I need to sit with the list for a little while I think.

The next part of the process is to complete a daily gratitude list for two weeks, and then do the Who Was I? test again and compare the answers. So, for the next two weeks I'll be doing daily gratitudes again, which I'm sort of looking forward to for a couple of reasons. One of them is it gives me a focus for writing in the blog, because my brain is seriously scattered at the moment. This is why there has been a lack of posts in the last couple of weeks, and why the reflection on being wrong is taking so long to write.

I'm not entirely sure what this is about, but I'm going to blame general fatigue. My work project has taken it out of me; I've even missed my last two days off. It's amazing how much I have gotten used to working only nine days a fortnight, and to lose that for a month has added to the stress levels quite considerably.

Another compassion fail

One last thing before I go as well, for those of you who might be keeping score with this sort of thing, my post the other night was a serious compassion fail. Yes, the person I work with should learn to have a greater deal of empathy for the people around her and what they are going through in their lives. Yes, she needs to realise that her job is actually a lot less stressful than many of ours. And yes, she needs to learn to shut it occasionally, and put her whining efforts into doing said job.

But I also need to realise that her ability to cope is very low, and I don't know everything else that is going on in her life. That I should not judge her and how easy I perceive her job to be. It is wrong of me to do that, and the fact that those thoughts and feelings became so consuming that I vented here about it is very disappointing for me. I don't expect this project to turn me into a paragon of virtue and compassion, but I do need to not let her crappy behaviour impact on the things I should be less judgemental and more compassionate about.

So the criticism on her insensitive and ridiculous comments about terminal illness remain, but I should not let my anger about that turn into such a judgemental and mean assessment of her in total.

REFLECTION – 30 (OR 45) DAYS OF BEING WRONG

I've mentioned in a number of posts during this activity that this was very uncomfortable and difficult. On the whole, I feel I did it justice, but it was a hard won success in many ways.

So let's start by breaking this activity down into its two parts: being wrong and regret. I'll start with being wrong, because focusing on regret was probably the more damaging part of the activity.

Being wrong

Going into this activity I was fairly happy that, at least professionally, I was capable of admitting mistakes and rectifying them. While I'm a perfectionist and hate being wrong, I know I'm often wrong. I think that, like many of you, I am often 'wrong' when I make a decision without having all of the facts to hand. This makes it a lot easier to admit being wrong, because it's more a case of revising a decision now you are better informed.

This was often the case during the activity, when I was wrong at work it was due to overlooking a fact, or in the worst case ignoring a nagging thought in the back of my mind. I think this has been the breakthrough to me trying to re-conceptualise what it means to be wrong. Maybe being wrong is not a commentary on my intelligence or ability, rather it's the result of me making a decision without considering all of the information appropriately.

I can't claim that insight as my own, thinking back on Kathryn's book *Being Wrong: Adventures in the Margin of Error*, this aligns to a lot of her discussion about being wrong. It's funny that I didn't consciously remember that from the book when I started the activity, but as I've been reflecting on it these things have come through.

So now I just have to remember that wrong is not bad, wrong is how we learn and grow – something I think we all know at some level. For the future, I will try to keep this in mind and take a minute to think about what facts/information I was missing, misunderstood or overlooked that might have led me to be wrong. I'm not naive enough to think I can achieve this and suddenly it will be all right to be wrong, but I will try to do this for a while and see if I can remove some of the sting that comes with wrongness.

And as for regrets

Do not do an activity that examines choice and success when you are doing an activity looking at being wrong and regrets. It is not good for your mental health or self-image – just saying.

I've written a bit about discovering my inability to actually make choices at times in my life. I'm not going to go into it too much in this reflection, but I will reiterate the majority regrets in my life centre around my lack of decision making. This not only goes for the things I did do, but also the opportunities I didn't make or take.

What will I take from this?

What I learned in this activity is a reiteration of what I've learned in pretty much every activity to date – when you are focusing on something it shifts the way you think and act. So when I was focusing on regrets and being wrong, my thoughts and actions became very negative. I should have known this would be the case, or I should have at least worked out earlier the impact it was having and not taken on the additional 15 days.

So I guess I will take two things from this. The first is the new appreciation of what wrong means, to hopefully be a little kinder and less judgemental to myself and others. The second feeds into my current activity on time, which is to try to shift my focus away from negative thoughts of the past, and the regrets I have.

One last thing

This is the only activity I've done that I would not recommend anyone else take on, especially if you are prone to depression and self-confidence issues. It is a very hard road to travel being so focused on all of your faults and failings. The only thing I'm glad of is the complete serendipity of scheduling Vulnerability and Time, alongside and after this activity.

Day 314: What a difference happy thoughts make

I did start daily gratitudes yesterday, but didn't post them up because of the reflection post. It may seem like a weird thing but I don't like to do more than one post a day if I can avoid it, and I don't like to include anything in the reflection post except the reflection. So today you get two daily gratitude lists for the price of one.

Gratitudes for Saturday
1. I managed to get the reflection post done on being wrong, so I can stop thinking about that whole thing for a little bit.
2. We found door handles and locks for the new house at an absolute bargain price – pretty much the front door lock/handle in a pack with six other internal sets and door stops for only $50 more than the front door lock/handle on its own!
3. The universe seems to be trying to find a way to be nice to us at the moment – I can't elaborate on that one yet as I don't want to jinx things or add pressure.

Gratitudes for Sunday
1. A lovely sleep in, which we both desperately needed.
2. Glorious sunshine to allow us to get some more work done on the house – quite lovely even with the very gusty winds.
3. Our crazy dog who always has the ability to make me smile.

Was it just the weather

It is quite interesting that in the last week I have been feeling a bit brighter. This may be due to breaking the back of my project and coming up with a positive result. Or maybe it's because we've been moving forward quite quickly on the house build. Or maybe it is simply a brighter outlook because I'm not focusing on negative things and I'm actively trying to be nicer to myself. Or it could just be that we have had a burst of spring weather, (not counting rain and snow down to 400 metres) and the apples are in bloom.

Who knows what it is, all I know is my mindset has greatly improved and I'm enjoying the change. I'm also hoping that the daily gratitudes will lift that a little more, especially given this will be a stressful week at work.

Day 315: A short note on self-compassion

I've been working hard on the self-compassion thing, as mentioned in previous posts this is a failing of mine – yeah that's great self-compassion. Anyway, I've had some great opportunities to practice self-compassion of late. The major issue I have is that perfectionist gene. The not-so-little voice that can always find the negative in everything I do: my appearance; how I interact with other people; how I perform my job, or do any other task; any sort of random decision I might make; or anything I do/think/feel really.

30 days of Being Wrong was a huge start to more self-compassion, but there is still a long way to go with this. For instance, the amount of times I have internally called myself an idiot and chastised myself for all of the mistakes in my work project is a little crazy. I've had a few wins though, times where I have been able to convince myself there is no way I could have been prepared for the issue that came up.

And it turns out that after going through all of the negativity and mentally kicking myself, it turns out that by going back and forth to resolve the issues that came up, I am so much more familiar with the data and comfortable with the decisions that have been made. If I had gotten it completely right the first time, I would have needed to spend a couple of weeks going back and forth through the data to get to this level of comfort.

Onto today's gratitudes
1. Finally working out how to graphically represent data for my report.
2. How closely connected we actually are to everyone else – this led to some interesting news.
3. The beginning of school holidays; huge reduction in commute traffic.

Day 316: Only gratitudes today

My brain is a little trashed from looking at spreadsheets and trying to explain how the equal remuneration order gets applied today, so I'm only going to write up my gratitudes. They are:
1. Derek's opportunity continuing to sound quite positive.
2. Finding out that one of the external inputs into my project is finally progressing, and I may get to be involved in the discussion.
3. Sharing an interesting conversation with someone at work about Deadwood, always nice to have someone with shared interests.

Day 317: Grateful I finally got to go home

Wednesday was a pretty busy day in my world. I'm writing the options paper for my work project at the moment, so that's consuming a lot of my brain power. Today I realised that I had failed to include some of the funding in the modelling, so I had to redo all of the figures – argh!

I have gone back to getting into the simplicity principles again though. What I am trying to explain in the paper is a very complex process and set of data, especially for people who aren't as immersed in it as I have to be; I still realise new things about it that I failed to recognise earlier. So I've had to come up with a way of graphically representing the information to simplify it for my audience.

The problem is that the information has three different audiences at the moment; there will be another two once we have everything signed off and approved. That adds more complexity. But I think we might have finally come up with something which will satisfy, now I just have to get the last pieces pulled together.

Daily gratitudes

Which brings me to the things that I am grateful for today, and yes I am writing this on Thursday because last night was my Adult Literacy Tutor course and I got home late and too tired to focus.
1. A lovely boss who is very concerned I might be pushing too hard on my work project, and is appreciative of everything I've done so far.
2. The usual table we sit at for the course was full.
3. Jo decided to do the volunteer literacy tutor thing as well, it's so nice to be doing the course with her and getting to know her better.

ACTIVITY 20 • 30 DAYS OF COMPASSION

The talks

Time for another one of the big ones, an activity dedicated to compassion. This one could probably have a hundred TED Talks associated with it, but I've selected a couple that have really resonated with me for the activity.

The first is of course *Karen Armstrong: Let's revive the Golden Rule*, which I also used during Activity 2: 30 days of Thanks, Praise and Mindfulness. The second is *Chade-Meng Tan: Everyday compassion at Google* which I found to be an interesting talk about how they train their leaders to be more compassionate, and encourage staff to be involved in compassionate activities. The final talk that will inform this activity is *Daniel Goleman: Why aren't we more compassionate?*, which is a great discussion about various aspects of compassion in our society, and how we might improve it.

The challenge

This is a pretty simple challenge, to spend 30 days being more compassionate. It's something I've been trying to be better at since Activity 2, but I know I have a long way to go.

I'm just finishing an activity focused on self-compassion, to try to improve the way I judge myself internally. I think this is a great opportunity to turn that focus outwards and spend 30 days on compassion for others.

After Activity 2 showed me I'm less compassionate than I would like to be, I bought Karen Armstrong's book *Twelve Steps to a Compassionate Life* and have been endeavouring to read it so I can learn how to improve this aspect of my personality. After eight months I still haven't finished it. This is partly because it took so long to get through the first part of the book, about the Golden Rule in religion. Even though I'm an atheist I don't have a problem learning about religions, I have spent a lot of time learning about them to come to my atheist decision. But this was a very hard read and I will admit it put me off the book. I will attempt to finish it in the next week though, so I have greater guidance to this activity.

The activity

There is one specific aspect of Chade-Meng's talk that I intend trying. When I interact with people during these 30 days I want to do it with the thought in my head 'I want you to be happy', to see if that improves my focus on compassion.

Apart from that, I have no explicit guidelines for this activity; simply a desire to become more compassionate in my daily interactions. This is a very subjective measure, even more than the other activities. After all, only I know how compassionate I am, and whether that's more or not.

The other thing I would like to do in this activity is see if I can find a way to improve the compassion of people around me. This concept is still formulating in my mind, and I think it's something I need to engage with the people at work about. The idea is to come up with something that makes us practice compassion as a group. This does strike me as an odd statement given that I work in Human Services, which is supposedly all about compassion; we're quite poor at extending that into our office environment.

Day 319: The end of vulnerability

How I wish the title of this post was true for my entire life, but it's just the end of 30 days of Vulnerability. The activity actually ended yesterday, but with the launch post for 30 days of Compassion, which starts tomorrow, I decided to leave it until today to talk about it.

This one seemed to fly by, partly because the last month has flown by for me I think. I feel like I did get something out of it, but I will write more about that in the reflection post in the next few days. Brené Brown's new book *Daring Greatly: How the Courage to Be Vulnerable Transforms the Way We Live, Love, Parent, and Lead* came out the other day as well. It sounds like it will be an interesting addition to the content of her TED Talks, and her previous book *The Gifts of Imperfection*.

Daily gratitudes

I'm feeling a bit out of whack with gratitudes, since I didn't do them yesterday. So I will try to catch up today.

For yesterday my gratitudes were:
1. Having a chance to sleep in a little bit.
2. A handful of new Twitter followers, which is always nice.
3. Successfully making a new recipe for dinner.

Today they are:

1. Finalising my position paper for the project, and preparing for the next step in the process.
2. Being able to leave work a little early and get a few hours helping Derek with wrapping the latest wall.
3. It's Friday – obviously today has not been very eventful.

Day 320: Overcoming what you are 'given'

I've been reading more of Karen Armstrong's book, I'm up to step five of the 12. So far I've done 'Learn about compassion'; 'Look at your own world'; 'Compassion for yourself'; and 'Empathy'. Next is 'Mindfulness'.

I wish I'd read this quote from the 'Compassion for yourself' step earlier:

> 'So much of life is a "given": we do not choose our parents, the genes we inherited, or the upbringing and education we received.' (p.70)

The discussion is about how there are so many things out of our control in our make-up that we might need to overcome to achieve compassion (internal and external).

This morning when I was reading this it was one of those little epiphany moments that you get in life. It's not like this was an entirely new concept for me, but the way it was written and the context it was in gave me an 'of course' realisation. I've had a lot of these when listening to TED Talks, and reading the books of some of the speakers over the last year; this was one I thought was definitely worthwhile sharing. I read it as this – *So much of your life is given to you, but it is up to you to adapt or overcome that stuff so you can become the person you want to be.*

I will explain a little more about why the wording of this might have struck me so deeply. As children, when we visited one of relatives' houses they had a saying, which my cousins would always take great joy in reiterating: 'You get what you're given'. This was the statement if you complained about food or drink, but it meant a lot more than that. It was the mantra of that family, that you could not complain or question my uncle in any capacity whatsoever because 'you get what you're given'.

I didn't enjoy going to visit those relatives very much, and to say the children have turned out very broken individuals is a gross understatement. But that saying affected me, and stayed with me in a very subconscious way. This morning I read that quote in Karen's book and that saying just came back at me with a vengeance. Reading her words was a very freeing experience from those words. While I may have gotten what I was given, it's up to me to change that to what I want and need.

Today I am grateful for

More daily gratitudes, did I say I was looking forward to doing this for a couple of weeks again?

1. Lovely sunny weather which made working on the house today a lot more pleasant.
2. Derek having a photography excursion so we didn't have to work on the house all day.
3. New episode of Doctor Who tonight.

Day 321: Trying to become more Past-positive

Today I am grateful:

1. All of my aches and pains from yesterday's building work were gone this morning.
2. Finding brown paper lunch bags at the supermarket, now I can start doing microwave popcorn for snacks.
3. A few hours completely for myself today; some complete down time where I didn't log on to the computer or worry about anyone else.

More activities to try to shift time

There are a number of other activities that Philip Zimbardo mentions in his book to try to shift time focus. None of these will have any impact in the remaining fortnight I have for the activity; shifting time perceptions is a long term process. But I'm trying to see if there are a few of these activities I can start now and continue to incorporate into my life once the 30 days are over.

What I need to do is significantly reduce my Past-negative, while increasing my Past-positive. As for my present and future perspectives, my Present-hedonistic is probably about right, could be a little higher, but my Future should be just a little lower.

As well as doing the worksheets I mentioned in an earlier post the other activities I'm trying to adapt into my daily life are:

- Setting goals for after the end of My Year of TED.
- Do the Who Am I? and Who Will I Be? worksheets.
- Try a new restaurant.
- Incorporate relaxation/meditation into my day – yes, I have attempted this a couple of times, sometimes successfully sometimes not.

- Get back to nature a little more – hopefully I will do a lot of this when I take time off work next week.
- Place happy pictures of my past in my home – this may be a challenge but I do want to recreate a more positive history for myself.
- Trying to make sure that my parents' visit down here at the end of October is positive and enjoyable.

Day 322: Chocolate was my saviour today

I'm feeling exhausted after a draining day today, so this is going to be short and sweet. Today I am grateful for:
1. A very short line in the bank.
2. A huge effort from Derek to get some windows and doors into the house today – still a long way to go.
3. Chocolate – it was the only way I got through this afternoon.

Day 323: Looking forward to a week off work

I'm feeling remiss for not having done my reflection post on Vulnerability yet, and since tomorrow night I have my literacy tutor course after work, it's not going to happen tomorrow either. It's a little bit indicative of the last two months of My Year of TED. I feel like I'm dragging my feet with things; that I don't have the passion and drive for the activities that I had earlier.

I think this has a lot to do with how much work is taking out of me at the moment, because I'm still feeling very inspired by the activities I've been doing. Hopefully, having next week off work will help rejuvenate me for the final month of the project.

Another set of daily gratitudes:
1. Lily only has a mild case of kennel cough – trying to see a silver lining.
2. I didn't have too many interruptions today so I made good progress on my benchmarking.
3. More progress on windows and doors, the house is looking great.

Day 324: Simple gratitudes today

A very quick post tonight, since I've not long gotten home and will be heading off to bed shortly. Today's daily gratitudes are:
1. Lovely compliment from a friend on recent blog posts – a nice boost.
2. My interfering paid off for someone who deserved it.
3. Leftover morning tea from one of the meetings in the office – yes that's all it takes to make my gratitude list some days.

Day 325: May have benchmarking sorted

Today I am completely stoked that:
1. I may have come up with a way to benchmark the results of my work project – this has been a long and arduous process that is not necessarily perfect right now but it's pretty close.
2. Having a slightly slower start to the day, I find an extra 20 minutes makes such a difference on Thursday after such a busy Wednesday.
3. A lovely lunch with good friends.

Compassion fails and wins this week

I've had a few compassion fails at work in the last few days. This is mainly because I seriously need some time off, but that's still not appropriate. Having said this the compassion fails have been mainly internal, usually just judgemental thoughts, but I've made a few comments to close friends.

I've had a couple of compassion wins though. A couple of incidents where I felt annoyed by something, but took a second to think about the person/situation so I could be more empathetic and understanding of the potential issues that might be influencing them. I hope that having a week off work will make it easier for me to start from a place of empathy.

REFLECTION – 30 DAYS OF VULNERABILITY

This was always going to be an interesting activity, since I have said many times that a large part of this whole project is about vulnerability. So to step up that focus for 30 days was always going to be a challenge.

There were four specific things I wanted to include in this activity, so it is probably best if I address each of these separately. The first three are based on Brené Brown's amazing talks on shame, vulnerability and courage – *The power of vulnerability* and *Listening to shame*.

Courage and authenticity

I've needed to dig deep into my courage reserves for so much of this project, but in this activity I wanted to push that a little further. I'm not entirely sure I managed to do that, but I'm also not entirely sure I had much opportunity to be more authentic. I have had a couple of minor incidents where I was a little more vocal than I would usually be. None of these have been life changing, but they have required me to risk confrontation by speaking up.

One such incident was during the literacy tutor course I am currently doing. There is one guy on the course who does not stop talking when the teacher is trying to explain stuff to us. A couple of weeks ago when we were packing up for the evening he made the comment that the he didn't think the teacher liked him because she kept glaring at him throughout class. I just looked at him and stated very simply 'that's because you talk all the time', then just went back to packing up. He seemed to dismiss the comment, and certainly didn't call me on it. There was a chance though, that he would call me out on it, and I would be involved in a conversation I would not have been comfortable with.

This may seem like nothing at all to many of you, or maybe you are like me and you understand that this sort of flippant remark does not come easily. Anyway, as little as it may seem I did give myself a mental pat on the back for the comment and standing by it; you know not laughing it off as a joke.

Self-compassion

I had some fairly major self-compassion fails during this activity. I did get better at being more compassionate to myself as the activity progressed though. I think the initial failings were because of the very negative mindset I was in after completing choice and being wrong. A major trigger to improving that situation was the emotional and vulnerable conversation that I had with my brother on Day 299.

My perfectionism trait has taken a beating over the last 11 months, but I managed to lay the boot in a few more times during this activity. It's not easy to kick the habits of a lifetime, but being a little more self-compassionate when I'm pointing out my failings is helping. This will take a lot longer though, and in all reality I may never get there.

Connecting, or reconnecting

This is an incredibly simple one to reflect on. It took me three weeks to get up the courage to make a phone call and send an email, and I am yet to hear anything back from either person.

I'm sort of okay with that though, because as nice as it would be to hear from them again, I didn't expect that to happen. It's been too long; I let those friendships die and I have no right to expect to be able to revive them just because I would like to. There is of course still a chance I will hear back, but I'm not holding my breath.

Understanding my truth

The last aspect of this activity was from *Eve Ensler: Happiness in body and soul*, about owning my truth. I did develop a much deeper understanding about some of this; the conversation with my brother, mentioned earlier, provided some great insight. This is still evolving, and I'm not sure how much of my truth I'm willing to share in this forum. I will say that, combined with a lot of other activities and realisations along the way in this project, I have realised the thing I have always wanted in the world is encouragement and support. I have this in my adult life, I have found people who give this to me readily; but I feel like I missed out on so much because I didn't have this for so many years, and for the incredibly important formative years.

Yet again, I know I'm not alone in this one. I know there are a lot of people who feel exactly the same way about their childhoods and probably their adult lives as well. There are a whole lot of things I have started realising about the impact this has had on my life, and I know that at the end of this project I will have a lot more to say about this aspect of it. For now, I'm scared out of my mind about what this realisation has given me, but I'm very excited at the same time.

And so...

Overall I think this one was pretty successful. I'm glad I decided to do a dedicated activity on vulnerability. As hard as it has been, there is so much I have gained from it, and so much more to do with it. Thank you Brené and Eve for your amazing talks and all they have given me.

Day 327: Grateful for the break

Yesterday's gratitudes were:
1. That it was my last day before a week off work.
2. Lovely support and compliments from my manager – thank you.
3. I made a few people happy today, which was nice.

Today was a lovely, relaxing day, and for that I am probably grateful enough to cover three gratitudes. But I will do them anyway:
1. A lovely, relaxing day.
2. A couple of great finds at op shops.
3. Derek being patient enough to let me go through the op shops.

Day 328: Starting to relax into my break

There's not a lot to say about today, except that we had a very relaxing day driving around the countryside. The weather could have been a little better, but otherwise it was a lovely day with Derek and I having a chance to chat about a lot of things. He has helped me work out what my last activity will be; more on that later in the week.

Daily gratitudes for today are:
1. The rain held off for most of the time we were out of the car.
2. A cheap, secondhand copy of *Watership Down*.
3. Lily being a wonderful puppy, and mostly well behaved.

Tomorrow I hope to complete some of the present/future exercises mentioned in the Day 321 post, so I may have more to say about time. I found the trick to compassion as well, have very little human interaction!

Day 329: How do you think of yourself?
I wish I'd done this 11 months ago

I mentioned yesterday I'd be doing the present and future worksheets from Philip Zimbardo's book today. Basically, the present worksheet is answering *Who I am* and the future is *Who I will be*. These of course complement the past *Who I was*, which was a very painful list for me to complete. I wish I had done this before My Year of TED, it would be an interesting comparison.

On the whole, I see my past self as being weak, easily manipulated, unhappy and very alone in the world – gee, I wonder why I'm Past-negative? I see myself now as being much stronger, happier and generally a good person; still not as confident and successful as I would like to be though. If I am able to become the future-self I have described in the worksheet I would be extremely happy. While the list is not that dissimilar to the present list, the couple of words that differ are incredibly important.

I am trying to re-frame my childhood and latch onto some happy memories. I don't want it to sound like I had a completely miserable childhood, I didn't. But there are a lot of painful experiences there that have spent a long time becoming the dominant memories.

I think I know why that is the case – remembering the person I was and what I have overcome to get to where I am, is something that makes me feel good about myself. What I have to do is realise that where I am is enough, I don't have to keep comparing that to where I was. That might have helped me get here, and driven me to make a better life for myself, but I need to find a way to change this message.

And you know what's next

Today I am grateful for:
1. Beautiful and stunning scenery when touring around today.
2. A couple of great op shop finds.
3. More slow time to spend with Derek and Lily.

Day 330: Last day of gratitudes for a while

I've decided that today will be the last day of gratitudes. While 30 days of Time does not end for a few more days, I had only planned on doing the gratitudes for a fortnight, and I have already gone over that time. So tonight is the last one for a while.

My gratitudes for today are much the same as yesterday:
1. A beautiful day with stunning scenery.
2. Crazy birds teasing Lily, it's like they got together and planned it.
3. Starting a fantastic book that my brother gave me, *Robopocalypse* – very promising story and storytelling.

Day 333: A lovely week with nature

It would be nice if everyone else in the world was practising compassion as well. I had to stand in the rain in a carpark today because the guy in the car beside us had started to back out on an angle that meant I couldn't get into our car – but he then stopped and did up his seat belt, looked right at me and chatted to the other person in the car for a bit before deciding to finally pull out of the spot so I could get in. Did I mention it was raining?

I've realised in the last couple of weeks that while I do have the occasional compassion fail, overall I'm pretty aware of how I might be impacting other people around me and I'm generally quite considerate of other people. I'm by no means perfect, and I want to improve this, but I don't believe I am ever that man in the car today; I am grateful for at least that level of compassion.

Nature helping my time perspective

Derek, Lily and I have spent the last week in the North East of Tasmania. The natural beauty of this part of the world is exceptional, and the fact that we are close to the only people around has made it even more enjoyable. Getting back to nature, and spending time in the moment, experiencing the beauty of the situation, is part of moving my time perspective from past to present. I feel like it has been working, but I feel like I need to shift a little more into the grand planning stage to get the future focus balance.

ACTIVITY 21 • 30 DAYS OF BALANCE

The talk
This activity is based on *Nigel Marsh: How to make work-life balance work*, which is an interesting talk, and one where you get to hear the rare Australian accent on TED. One of the key parts of Nigel's talk is that if you don't design the life you want then someone else will design it for you.

We need to attend to the physical, intellectual, emotional and spiritual sides of our lives; not just one or a couple. It's about small changes that can radically transform our life, and make it more balanced.

The challenge
While this activity will focus on using aspects of Nigel's talk, it is of course a culmination of the last 11 months of TED activities. It requires me to look at everything I've learned about myself; what I want from my life; the parts of activities I want to keep; and what else I might need to think about.

The real challenge will be to pull together all of the things I've learned about myself, and what I want from my life throughout this year. This will require a further reflection on all of the lessons and knowledge I've acquired. More importantly it will require me to try to pull them together into some sort of integrated outline for my life.

The activity
The main concept for this activity is to come up with a model 'perfect day' for myself. That is designing a perfect work day for myself, outlining all of the components that will and will not be included.

I'm hoping this activity will allow me to tie together a lot of the learnings from the last 11 months so I can move forward with a practical road map. It won't include everything of course, but I think it will be a fantastic way to end the project.

Day 335: Last day of time

Today is the last day of Activity 19, and boy has this one flown; I must have been having fun. Maybe it's because we had a week away during the activity, but I don't feel like I was doing this activity for 30 days.

As always, I'll to the reflection post in the next few days about my feelings on the activity. My initial reaction, it was just what I needed after the three activities before it. I know that anything I feel I've achieved at the moment is only fleeting, but it helped shift me out of a bad place.

Compassion progress

30 days of Compassion is continuing along nicely. I'm all but finished Karen Armstrong's book, so the theory behind all of this. Of course, putting that all into practice is the difficult part, but we'll see how I go returning to work after a very relaxing week away. I'm hoping that by recharging my batteries I am calmer and more able to cope with some of my work colleagues – and I might be easier to deal with as well.

Final activity

Tomorrow I begin the last activity in My Year of TED, 30 days of Balance. This is a big day since it is the last month of what has become a huge part of my life. I truly hope I have the time and energy to pull this all together in the end. I am trying to practice some self-compassion by not putting too much pressure on myself.

October will be a very busy month for me. I will be meeting my first adult literacy student next week; I still have a lot of work to do to complete my study for adult literacy tutoring; I have to finalise the recommendations and implementation of my long-running work project; and my parents are coming to visit at the end of the month. So I do need to maintain a very realistic approach to how much more I can cram in, but I will try my best to make this one count.

October 2012 – The final push

Day 337: Struggling a bit at the moment

I may not know what my perfect day looks like, but I certainly know some of the things that won't be in it. It will not involve an early start that requires commuting with some gifted drivers; it will not involve listening to tedious conversations at work; it will not involve remaining in the office during my lunch break; and most of all it will not involve extremely repetitive tasks that don't feel like I am getting anywhere with.

Yes, I am struggling being back at work.

Thinking more compassionately

This morning I was quite annoyed when I stopped to get fuel, just a simple thing of someone pulling into the pumps the wrong way so I had to use the pump on the wrong side of my car.

Then I stopped and watched the woman putting fuel in her car. She was harried and obviously running late for something. It was the perfect chance to be compassionate, because I realised I had no idea what was going on in her morning. So I took a breath and relaxed a little, stopped scowling and gave her a little smile when she came back to her car from paying.

This whole incident probably had no impact on her day, whether I was annoyed or not. For me, thinking more compassionately about her reduced my stress levels, which made my day a little better.

REFLECTION – 30 DAYS OF TIME

This was a rejuvenating activity to do after Choice and Being Wrong. A nice complement to Vulnerability; I generally feel good about it.

The important part of this activity was to try to shift my time perspective, or at least start. There is no way this is a short term project, but I think it was a good start to making long term changes. The main problem is I am too Past-negative in my time focus. Apparently, according to Philip Zimbardo's talk and book, the perfect time perspective is much higher in Past-positive and Present-hedonistic, and lower in Future than I was.

The worksheets

Completing the worksheets from Philip's book was a very enlightening experience for me, particularly the *Who I was, Who I am* and *Who I will be*. What I realised from these lists was that my entire past conceptualisation of myself is pretty much based entirely on the negative experiences from my childhood, and early adult life. As I mentioned in one of my previous posts:

> On the whole, I see my past self as being weak, easily manipulated, unhappy and very alone in the world – gee, I wonder why I'm Past-negative?

Interestingly though, when I completed the *Who I am* list I realised I'm a lot stronger than I often give myself credit for. This has come out in a few activities throughout the project, but I think I realised it more with this list.

I realised that, although I still have a long way to go to become the person I want to be, I'm a lot closer than I thought. There were only a few words that were completely different from the *Who I am* and *Who I will be* lists, which was very positive for me to discover.

Process of re-framing

After these realisations, and reading more of Philip's book, I've been in a process of trying to re-frame how I think about my past, and how I think of myself now. This should be no surprise, since this entire project has been a personal development process to try to change myself and the way I view myself in the world, but this was a more focused activity.

What the revelations helped me understand is, I've held onto all of the bad things in my life, and the fact that I have not only survived them but have done quite well for myself. Framing myself like this has been one of the ways that I've felt proud of myself and my achievements. The problem is, when I started thinking of things in this way I realised that I shouldn't have to hold onto past misery and disappointment to feel good about myself and my life. I don't need to keep hold of how far I've come to be proud of where I am and what I'm achieving.

The re-framing will take a lot longer to sink in, so when I'm not focused on making these changes I don't slip back into my old mindset. It will be a long process where I need to spend time shifting my past focus to being more positive and finding a way to realise that I am enough, right now, without a comparison to the past.

A happy childhood

I've been trying to remember the happier memories of my childhood; there are many of them, especially before I was 12 years old. I've also been going through old photos to assist this process; I've shared a couple on the blog.

I'll leave the more embarrassing ones from my teens to your imagination, let's just say that 80s' fashion and hairstyles were not kind to most of us.

More to do

There are still a few activities from Philip's book that I want to do, there just wasn't enough time to do it in the 30 days. As I said, this will be a long process; if I can keep my current mindset, I think I'll be generally happier with my place in the world.

This was also an important activity to have completed before I start to sort out Balance. I only wish I'd done all of the worksheets before I started My Year of TED, because I'm certain the present and future answers would have been quite different over 11 months ago.

Thank you Philip for all of your TED Talks, but particularly for introducing me to the concept of time perspectives and the impact they can have. I am certain this will change my life in a very positive way.

Day 343: May not seem like compassion, but...

I've been more forthcoming in talking about things I would previously have avoided of late. A good example was a conversation I had with my mother last week. I will preface this by saying my maternal grandmother is a piece of work. I have referred to her as evil Nana for the last 20 years or so; she is a very bitter and nasty woman who seems to take great pleasure in trying to belittle any positive achievements by anyone in my family, but I digress.

When I was younger my mother used to say that this distance between us was her fault, since she stopped talking to my grandmother for about eight years when I was two. I've always said it isn't Mum's fault her mother is a bitter old cow who cannot be happy for others – stick with me people this is about compassion I promise.

Anyway, Mum was telling me how upset she is with Nan and Alan, my uncle who lives with Nan and looks after her. They failed to call my Mum to tell her that Nan had a minor stroke and was in hospital for a week. This will also tell you a little more about my Mum's personality, but that isn't what we're focused on right now. Mum informed me she'd cut the conversation short with Nan, and hasn't spoken to her for over a week. She stated that she'd finally had it, this was the last straw, and she would only speak to them again when they called her.

Something just clicked in my mind when she said that, I think it had something to do with all of the deaths of parents that have happened with people I know, including my father-in-law of course. So I said to Mum that I completely supported her decision, after everything Nan had done to her over the years. BUT was this the right time to finally make this decision. Nan just had a stroke, and if she had a more serious one, would my mother be happy with this being the last conversation they ever had?

This is a big thing for me because I have never taken Nan's side in a discussion before; I usually just switch off when Mum talks about her. But this was more about my mother than my grandmother. Mum still thought it was too much and she was over it, but I hope this conversation, there was a lot more to it, has made her rethink her decision. Or she'll be certain she could accept the outcome if the worst were to happen.

What will be the outcome of balance?

I am working on this activity, but there has been a lot of internal pondering in the initial stages. I should have some stuff to start writing soon.

I was walking past a construction site this afternoon where they've recently demolished the old building that was there. I thought this was a great analogy for what I'm doing at the moment. I'm going through the planning and design phase at the moment, but there is a big part of the balance activity that would require me to demolish sections of my current life, so I can construct my new balanced life. That's a scary thought. I don't think it would be a complete demolition, but there is part of me that feels like this is what I'm doing at the moment.

Day 348: Baby photos and Wii tennis

This week has been a massive failure in balance, work has been consuming far too much of my time and energy. I haven't had a chance to think much about either of my TED activities, which is why I haven't been posting. I'm hoping I can rectify that this week, although there is still a lot I have to do on my work project.

Having fun with Mental Health Week

One of the things I did do this week was try to improve the morale and mental health of the people I work with. I've mentioned a few times, mainly during 30 days of Leadership, the culture in our workplace has deteriorated quite a bit with all of the recent changes. So, since this week was Mental Health Week, I decided that maybe we should do something fun to try to lighten the mood and get us all interacting a little better.

We ended up doing two activities. The first was the Baby Photo Competition, where people brought in a baby photo and caption, and then we all had to guess who was who. I was a little concerned that people would think this was a dumb idea and wouldn't get involved, I couldn't have been more wrong. We only had seven people from our broader team who didn't submit a photo, and many of these had wanted to but didn't have one, or forgot to bring it; there wasn't a lot of lead time on the activity. The second activity was a Wii Tennis Tournament. We had a dozen competitors, as well as a few spectators, and everyone had a great time.

It is amazing how two very simple activities completely changed the feel of the office for the week. People were generally more chatty, they all mixed a little more, and had some great laughs. I think it was a fantastic way to end 30 days of Compassion. I say that because I had an extremely busy and stressful week, but it was a great opportunity for me to put my work colleagues' wellbeing first, which I think helped me get through a shit week. I feel it was a bit of a leadership achievement as well, which also felt fantastic.

Day 350: Big day tomorrow, I meet my first student

Yesterday was my last day of compassion, and by that I of course mean the 30 days of Compassion activity, not a general statement about any massive changes I might have made for interacting with other people. Since I am no longer spending Wednesday nights learning how to be an adult literacy tutor, I'm hoping to have the reflection on this done before the end of the week.

And while we're talking about literacy tutoring, I meet my first student tomorrow afternoon. This is extremely exciting, and just a little scary. I hope this works out; I think it will be a fantastic way for me to contribute to society, and get some balance in my life.

Which segues neatly into talking about 30 days of Balance. I haven't spent as much time on this as I'd planned, because my work/life balance is so incredibly out of whack at the moment. It's made me realise that I need to plan my perfect week, because I don't want to just plan my perfect working day. This will allow me to factor in a lot more detail and get a feeling for my balanced life.

Day 353: Using my lessons for tutoring

As mentioned in my last post, I had my first tutoring session on Tuesday. I'm trying to practice self-compassion and my new conceptualisation of being wrong while reflecting on how this session went, because it wasn't that great. All jokes aside, I'm not being too harsh on myself because I don't know how many other people would have been able to explain the gerund and infinitive grammar rules off the top of their head.

So the last few days I've been spending quite a bit of time polishing up my English grammar skills. You see, when I went through school we didn't learn a lot of grammar terminology or explanations of the rules. We learnt what all of the common parts of language were, but I don't remember learning phrasal verbs and all of the conditional clauses in a formal way. So I've had a bit to refresh, to make sure I get the rules right.

This tutoring role will actually require me to use a number of things from activities so far. I will have to focus on simplicity to develop activities and materials for our tutoring sessions; compassion to make sure I have the right attitude in teaching and accommodating my student; listening, particularly active listening and channel listening if I can't get the tutoring room; and I'm sure there are other bits and pieces that I'm just not thinking of yet.

Importantly, doing this tutoring is a big part of the current activity on balance, so I'm glad I'll get a few sessions in to get an idea about it before the activity is over.

REFLECTION – 30 DAYS OF COMPASSION

When I look back at what I had hoped to achieve in this activity I didn't hit the mark very well. I don't think I failed the activity, but there were a few things I wanted to try that I didn't find a way to do.

The main problem with practising compassion during the 30 days was that work was extremely stressful, and I've found that an ability to maintain a compassionate focus on other people is significantly reduced when you are in a 'My life sucks' mode – yeah it could be seen as a leadership fail as well. Anyway, what I mean to say is I was far too self-focused for a large portion of this 30 day activity, but not all of it.

Thinking positive thoughts

I did find that maintaining a positive thought about the person I was dealing with, like Chade-Meng's 'I want you to be happy' thought (it wasn't always that exact thought), was particularly powerful if there was someone being very challenging. It really can shift your focus onto them and their needs, rather than how they might be interrupting you and your needs.

Pretty big compassion win

One of the things I had wanted to try to do was improve the compassion of people in my office. I didn't have an opportunity to focus on that explicitly but, as I explained in a previous post, I did organise a couple of very successful activities in the office to try to bring them all together a little more. It's been a week since we did these activities, and I can say that the overall changes were not long lasting, but this isn't the sort of thing that changes overnight. It was the beginning of a process that's lightened the mood a bit, and for at least a week it helped people in the office engage with each other.

On the whole, I am happy with some of the things I achieved during the activity. This is an area I will have to maintain focus on for a long time before it becomes an integrated part of my personality. The important thing is I want it to be a larger part of my personality, and I'm willing to spend more time getting there. I know I'll stumble and fail a lot in my compassion (for others and myself), but this is one area I've been trying to improve since Activity 2 of this project; I am not about to stop now.

Day 358: One week to go, can you believe it!

So tomorrow is one week until I finish My Year of TED. That is incredibly surreal for me, I can't imagine the project being over. I mentioned to work colleagues yesterday there was just over a week left and they also couldn't believe it had been a year already.

I've been thinking about what I will do when the project ends and have come up with a few things I will continue to write about on the blog. There were a number of activities I had planned for, but other things didn't line up with them. So some of these I will write about, and some of them I will do when the time is right.

Then of course the final activities need a little time before I can do a proper reflection on them, so it's not like everything will stop at the end of October. But it is still very exciting that My Year of TED finishes in a week.

I'm in a slightly rambling frame of mind so I do apologise for that, and should probably end this post here.

Day 364: Visiting parents and only two more days!!!

I've been a little absent from the blog for the last few days due to a parental visit. My parents came down for a short visit. It's only a few days since our current house is quite small, and having anybody stay for longer than that drives us a little insane.

Anyway, it was nice to see them, but it also brought up some unresolved issues. I've mentioned a few things about my childhood and my parents, and I don't feel the need to rehash it all at this point in time – needless to say that like many people, at times I have an interesting relationship with my parents.

I bring this up because they don't know about My Year of TED, or this blog. I thought about telling them at one point during the visit, but then I thought better of it. Being introspective and wanting to understand yourself and others is not big on my parents' agenda, and they already don't understand a lot about the decisions I've made in my life. For those reasons, I thought it was better left unsaid for the time being.

Seriously out of balance

I'm very glad the extremely time sensitive component of my work project is nearly at an end, because it's taken a lot of time from me. I feel very off-kilter with it all, which is unfortunate during 30 days of Balance. On the plus side it's made me realise a few things about my perfect day/week that may not have come to light as clearly in a normal work period.

I'm planning to write this up for the reflection, but a couple of the things that need to be factored into my perfect day/week are:

- time for myself where I can just be
- enough down time so I can sleep without weird circular work dreams
- a few days a week where I have the time and energy to cook, and I mean really cook not just simply prepare dinner
- time to not feel rushed about my literacy tutoring, either preparing for it or actually doing it
- a general return to the slowing down principles, specifically taking lunch breaks and not multi-tasking at work.

As a complete aside to all of this, I find it incredibly amusing that the standard spellcheck in Google Chrome when I am typing my posts does not recognise the word blog. Seems like a bit of a limitation for a blogging tool don't you think?

Day 366: The last day of my project

Wow! This is the last day of My Year of TED, and I get to enjoy the final day activity-free. Yesterday was the last day of 30 days of Balance, a reflection on this one will occur later in the week. Technically I could have called yesterday the final day, but I started this thing on 1 November, so a whole year would be 31 October, and here we are.

A few of the people at work who have known about this all along, had a little congratulatory morning tea for me yesterday, which was lovely of them. They are all proud of me for getting through the year, and for all of the work involved in trying to apply these activities to my life. I'm pretty proud of me too, although I don't know I did enough – but that could just be my perfectionist side kicking in.

So I guess this means the year of experimentation is over. I've spent a fair amount of my non-existent spare time over the last month thinking about what the end of this project means and where to go from here. There have been quite a few things that have come up throughout the year, some sparks of ideas for me to pursue. I'm going to spend a little bit of time working on some of these, mainly offline to get some of the thoughts clearer in my mind.

I have become so used to writing this blog and sharing all of this self-discovery with you, so I'm going to continue to write it. It will just become a lot broader in some ways, and potentially more focused in others. Of course, there is still so much to reflect on over the last three months, and the project as a whole.

But today is a day of celebration, and a little bit of sadness in a way. I would just like to take this opportunity to thank all of you who have been following along and all of the speakers for their amazing talks. I was asked yesterday which bit I enjoyed the most, and quite frankly I couldn't easily answer that.

End of 2012 – Starting to sum it up

REFLECTION – 30 DAYS OF BALANCE

I've been bemoaning the complete lack of balance in my life during this activity, and the issue has not been resolved yet. I know this will improve, as my work project continues to roll along; it's just very frustrating and has been dragging on too long at this point in time. But this is the reflection post, so I need to talk about what I'd hoped to achieve and how it all went.

The real aim of this activity was to consider the lessons from the project and design my perfect day. Since it's about work/life balance then this was about designing a perfect work day. With work being a little crazy and overwhelming, I was primed to identify the things I needed to improve to achieve a perfect day.

Learnings from other activities

As you would know by now, during 30 days of Slowing Down I made the decision that I needed to reduce my hours at work. This was a goal in moving to Tasmania; that neither of us would have to work a full-time office job, so we would have more hours for the things we want to do. But, I felt I couldn't reduce my hours because Derek doesn't get paid to build our house. But I successfully managed, with Derek's wonderful support, to drop one day a fortnight. This is important because I don't want to work for someone else full-time. There are too many other things I want to be able to do; write, design, and create things that are not related to my job for starters.

From 30 days of Drive and 30 days of Choice, I went through processes to attempt to better understand my purpose, and how I define success for myself. This helped me understand some of the things I need to include in my perfect day, or my perfect week. So, from these activities; other things that I have learned about myself; from starting my volunteer literacy tutoring; and from things that I know I need to get into my life…

…an outline of my perfect day and other things to improve my balance

Creative Pursuits
In the perfect world I would find a way to earn enough money from creative pursuits to remove the need for an office job at all. But that's a pipedream for now. So the schedule would have at least one non-weekend day for me to pursue the things I have as creative outlets.

TIME WITH FRIENDS AND FAMILY
The other important aspect of this is time to connect with others. This is time set aside to socialise, but also keep in touch with people not living near us. This is not to be contained to weekends.

DEFINING 'WORK'
There is an assumption in this 'perfect' day that I will still be travelling to Hobart for work. This is not my ideal situation, well not 5 days a week. My aim is to reduce office hours to 3 days a week (eventually) with the possibility of a fourth day working at home. This may require a change in the role or career to achieve.

Time for Volunteering
This schedule assumes time for me to continue the literacy tutoring I have recently started. This would take about 90 minutes a week in tutoring and the same in preparation.

Meditation; like exercise, there is a need to include more of this in my daily schedule. I'm yet to really work out how/when this will work for me.

ELEMENTS OF MY PERFECT DAY*
6.30 - Wake Up (I'm a morning person)
- Exercise, not in the current schedule but I would like to change that
7.30 - Breakfast, Shower and Prepare for Day
8.30 - Head to Work, this needs to be properly defined
12.30 - Relaxing Lunch Break, time away from my 'desk' to be with friends or simply centre myself
1.30 - Back to work
5.00 - Finish work and head home
6.00 - Discussing the days with Derek and preparing dinner - includes pats and play time with Lily
7.00 (or so) - Eat dinner and clean up
- Watch TV and wind down
- Creative pursuits, reading and writing
10.30 - Bedtime

* This is my realistic/achievable perfect day, within some current constraints but moving towards where I would like to be.

Ok, so this is not my "perfect" day, but it is the perfect day for the foreseeable future. I had put thought into what I would want my ultimate perfect work day to look like, but I couldn't articulate it. Maybe this is a lack of vision, maybe it is just indicative of how stressed I currently am, and how that is impacting my creativity. Either way, I felt this was the best option at this point, to plan for the next stage; the one that I can start moving towards now but can't achieve until after we are in the new house.

So how was the activity?

I'm comfortable that this was the point I wanted to reach, but I didn't get to spend as much time or energy on it as I had hoped. As the final activity for My Year of TED project I don't think I could have planned it any better. I will try to think about this a little more during the next couple of months and in the quarterly reflection on the last couple of activities; we'll see whether I come up with anything else.

Have you ever thought about your perfect day and what it would entail? It's an interesting activity, and you may be surprised with what you include. Like most of the activities I have done this year, I would highly recommend taking the time to imagine it; you never know what you might discover.

Finding my voice

Earlier this year I applied to be part of the talent search for TED2013; well you never know your luck, and I have been doing a vulnerability project. Anyway, I thought it might be time to share the brief synopsis of the talk – there is no way you are getting the YouTube video, seriously no chance.

The topic I chose was Finding my voice, since that's been a core part of the project. The script for my one-minute application was as follows:

> There are so many people in your life who try to influence who you are, and how you think of yourself. Your parents, your teachers, relatives, friends, enemies, colleagues, bosses and partners all clamour to influence your identity, and sometimes control your voice.
>
> You spend your life hearing that you should say this; or you shouldn't do that. Worse, people telling you what you are and what you aren't. And the thing is we are different people with different voices depending on our environment, which leads to more confusion about your real voice.
>
> Until you find yourself, at the age of 39, wondering who you really are, what your authentic voice is, and what you can possibly contribute to the world.
>
> That's sort of what drove me to My Year of TED project, the stark realisation that I didn't know who the authentic me was and that somewhere inside me there was a voice that really wanted to contribute in a meaningful way to the world.

I'm still working on how to contribute to the world in a meaningful way, but I think I've come a long way in finding my authentic self. Most importantly, I feel like I understand my voice a lot more now, and I'm comfortable using it.

This will of course come up in a lot more detail in the reflection for the overall project, this is just a teaser for now.

And while we're talking about reflections...

The more observant reader may have noticed that there should have been a fourth quarter reflection by now.

I will try to get this done by the end of the weekend, but ongoing work stress is not conducive to being quiet and reflective.

Almost a fourth quarter reflection

Okay, so I was thinking about writing the fourth quarter reflection this weekend, and then I realised if I wait until the end of the month I can include all of the completed activities in it, and I wouldn't end up leaving the last two out. That's my excuse and I'm sticking to it.

That led me to start thinking about the reflections a little more, and it struck me that this time last year I was well into 30 days of Fashion, and a couple of days into 30 days of Thanks, Praise and Mindfulness. It's quite surreal to me that it has been over a year since I started the project, and since I started changing my relationship with clothes and accessories.

On my final day of the project I mentioned to a couple of people at work that I'd finally finished. One of the women, who has known about it from the start (I didn't tell everyone), said that I was looking a lot more stylish these days. She then got extremely embarrassed and started back-pedalling, concerned that she had offended me by the suggestion that I wasn't stylish before. I just laughed and accepted the compliment, because it is a valid point that I do take more care with my appearance these days.

This is one of the simpler changes that has occurred in my life from My Year of TED, but it is the one that is noticeable to everyone; it appears a lot of people do notice. I can honestly say I've received more compliments about my clothing and accessories in the last 12 months than I would have in the last five years, at least. Probably the most interesting aspect of this is that I still have days where I wake up and struggle with the concept of wearing more colours, and some very different styles of clothing than I did just over a year ago.

But 30 days of Fashion, and Jessi Arrington's talk, have taught me that I should push through these feelings. Clothes can be fun; they can change your mood, and the way that you think of yourself. Added to this, when you buy them secondhand you can achieve all of this at a very reasonable price.

This has been an extremely important point in the process, if I was trying to be more playful and adventurous with clothing while paying full price for it, well the whole exercise would not have been as successful. As a result of using op shops I have had more items come into and leave my wardrobe in the last 12 months than in any year previous. So not only have I benefited from this, but the local charities have also been doing well from the activity.

Are you conservative in your clothing choices? Do you treat clothes as something you wear to get through the day, or do you treat them as fashion that can change the way you and others think about you? I used to treat my clothes as a way to blend into the background, but it isn't scary to stand out.

Explaining how I want to be praised is not easy

A large part of Activity 2 was trying to become better at asking for praise; this meant asking for praise when I wanted it and explaining how I would like to be praised. This was not a successful component of the activity, but I did have a few wins in this area.

Since the activity finished I've tried to be more forthcoming with people around me about praise. I still have a way to go with this, and my current project is a good example.

What I've been doing most is watching others and seeing how they like to be praised and acknowledged. I've always known that people like to be thanked and praised in different ways, but I don't think I've ever understood this for myself. The last few months have taught me a little more about how praise and acknowledgement works for me. This pretty much boils down to two facts:

1. I don't enjoy gushy praise, it makes me uncomfortable being the centre of attention.
2. I do need to be acknowledged for my achievements, especially when they are significant and/or exceptional.

An example of something that worked well

A good example of this was my time in the Air Force. I was involved in a project that required me to go completely above and beyond my years in the RAAF, and my rank. I was expected to learn things no one else knew, and teach them to people who had a lot more experience and seniority than I did. As a side note, it's taken quite a few years to be able to succinctly say 'I did a great job'; if I was saying this to you in person I'd be blushing now.

When I was given my Chief of Air Force commendation I finally felt acknowledged for the work I had done, and all of the effort and passion I put into my role. It took far too many years to happen; it only occurred because I finally had a boss who had the people skills to acknowledge that praise is important, and wasn't just looking out for his own success.

But I was very glad they presented it to me in a very small morning tea, with pretty much just my directorate. Other presentations of this sort had occurred in base briefing sessions or at larger morning teas. I would have been mortified to have to get up on stage to accept the award, but I was incredibly happy with the acknowledgement of my efforts.

Personally, I think that not liking people to publicly talk about my achievements has a lot to do with the fact that I don't like to talk about them. I will talk about them if the conversation leads to things, because they are mine and I'm proud of them. But I can't do that whole 'have I told you how amazing I am' thing that some people can, and I certainly can't do it in large groups. I think this is a bit of an Australian thing, definitely a female thing.

Now the hard part

All of this is to say, that now I've realised I need to talk to my boss about it, because her way of praising doesn't work for me, which is my issue. I have a lead in, she did ask me months ago how I would like to be acknowledged for the work project that has been consuming me for the last five months. I just have to find a way of articulating all of this so it makes sense, and gives her an actual idea of what that praise might look like; that is the bit I'm still a little uncertain of in this case.

Do you know how you like to be praised and acknowledged? Are you a big fanfare, or a less public person? How about the people around you, do you know how they like to be praised? Have you ever thought about it?

QUARTERLY REFLECTION 4 – ALL THAT REMAINS

Because of the way the quarterly reflections have been timed, I have seven activities to include in this final quarterly reflection. This is partly the reason why I decided to wait a month to do the fourth quarter reflection, otherwise I would have had to do a fifth one with the last two activities. Anyway, enough of the preamble, let's get on with the show.

30 days of Remembering

I've realised that it is not just about having techniques to be able to remember, but about being a person who actively remembers to remember.

This was a great practical activity, which are always a little easier to do than the introspective, intangible ones. I learned a few memory techniques that I have promptly forgotten to consolidate. Okay, that may be a little harsh, but I have been so busy and scattered in the last couple of months that I haven't been taking the time to remember.

This is particularly disappointing for me because I felt there was a lot of value in this activity, and in keeping some of these things in my life. The ability to easily recall someone's name, and feeling like I was on top of everything going on in my life, were two things I found incredibly valuable in this activity; as well as characteristics I would like to keep in my life.

So, I need to make time to refocus on this; to remember and get back some of confidence that this activity gave me.

30 days of Choice

> I finally understand that I need to stop allowing circumstance to make choices for me, and I have a clear set of definitions about what success means for me to help.

This was a very powerful activity, which also meant that it was very difficult. Due to a busy work schedule, this activity and the next one were both extended out to 45 days. In hindsight, this was not a very positive thing to do, as these two activities did bring about a very negative mindset.

But enough of that. There were three very important lessons I took from this activity, which have stuck with me. The first was defining what success means for me in 11 key areas of my life. While I had a general understanding of these things, the power of articulating them into defined statements has been very positive.

The second point was improving my consumer decision making, which I think I have kept on top of. I haven't had any buyer's remorse in the last couple of months, and the holiday destination for September was a great success. I'm still trying to limit my choices, and it's proving to be of benefit.

Lastly, the part that impacted my mental health; the realisation that I have not been an active participant in a lot of important decisions in my life. I haven't had any major decisions to practice on yet, but it is something that has continued to play on my mind.

30 days of Being Wrong

> It is extremely important to rephrase the way I think of wrongness, but focusing on being wrong and regret is not very healthy.

As I said in the reflection for this activity, I wouldn't recommend that anyone spend 45 days focusing on being wrong and their regrets, especially when you're also acknowledging the poor 'non-choices' in your life. I'm not saying that people should not listen to Kathryn Schulz's talks or read her book, just don't focus on it quite so intensely.

I have been a lot kinder to myself about the things I get wrong since this activity, it did help me rephrase my mindset. Of course, I still kick myself when I make mistakes that could have been avoided, but I am gentler when I get something wrong that was the best decision with the information I had at the time. And by trying to focus on the lessons I can learn from each wrong decision or action, at least there is a positive outcome.

This reflection should also include a note on regret, since one of Kathryn's talks focuses on this issue. I have worked very hard on overcoming some of the regrets I have held onto, and understanding why they continue to plague me. That doesn't mean that I am free from them, but understanding why I hold the regret means I have started to think of them differently, and maybe one day I will be free from some of them.

30 days of Vulnerability

I now understand that I am more courageous than I had ever hoped, and that practising self-compassion helps me be more compassionate to others.

There had to be a 30 days of Vulnerability, this project would not be complete without it. This was one of those activities that theoretically most of us understand the principles of, but putting them into practice is a different story.

I'm trying to continue being more courageous and speaking up about things, it's challenging but it's incredibly important for me to do. Just like it is so important for me to be nicer to myself, which I'm also doing quite well.

The last part of this activity was understanding my truth, and what I need to give the world. I've been continuing to work on how I might progress this concept, and this weekend might provide me with some further direction. I've volunteered to help out at TEDxYouthHuntingfield being held near Hobart on Sunday. I have a feeling I might meet some people through this event that can help shape this idea even further.

30 days of Time

This activity changed my life, and I was not expecting it. Understanding my time perspective and how to shift it has been so powerful.

This was such a positive activity after Choice and Being Wrong; it helped pull me out of the Past-negative focus from those activities. I generally have quite a strong Past-negative time perspective, and understanding how this permeates through various aspects of my life makes me want to shift that even more.

The activities from Philip's books are so incredibly simple, but so powerful in pointing out the things that have to change. I still continue to try to re-frame my past, to focus more on the positive aspects than the negative ones. I have a long way to go before I'll feel that I am more positive than negative, but I have started down the track and just starting has had a positive impact.

30 days of Compassion

After trying my compassion wings out again, I still need to do more, but I am continuing to grow in this area.

It's true of me, and everyone I know, that we could all be more compassionate. Karen Armstrong refers to this as The Golden Rule, and I agree that if this was the basis we all had to our lives, the world would be a much better place. But for me, I found a problem with Karen basing this on all of the religions, and not just dealing with it as a purely human trait. For me, you do not require religiosity to be compassionate; if anything, I think religious dogma can get in the way of compassion.

Getting off my soap box, Chade-Meng's very simple idea of maintaining the thought 'I want you to be happy' when dealing with others is great.

Having said all of this, I have a long way to go before I think I can call myself a truly compassionate person. I continue to work on it, and believe I will work on this my entire life.

30 days of Balance

A chance to work out how I can entwine some of the amazing lessons from My Year of TED into my life. I have a basic outline, that I need to find a way to achieve.

This activity allowed me to outline my perfect day, well my perfect day within some of the confines of my life that are not likely to change any time soon. Combined with my success definitions, value definitions and other aspects defined in 30 days of Drive, I now have a great idea of who I am and what I want from my life.

I still have a long way to go to bring this balance into my life, but having it defined is a million miles from where I was before I started this project.

A brief summing up

These last lot of activities were incredibly challenging and taught me a lot about myself. They have occurred during an exceptionally busy and stressful time with my job, which probably made things more difficult than they had to be. I feel I've definitely grown through these activities, and they will form a large part of my complete reflection; coming later in the month.

Thank you to all of the speakers who were part of this growth and these experiences; more on that later in the month as well.

So what comes next?

There will be a complete reflection coming that ties all of the activities together, and this will be followed with a much longer and detailed explanation about the whole thing. This is because I am going to try to pull all of this together and write a book – come on you had to know this was coming. Writing a book about this is my goal, but I'm finding it so hard to get motivated on this task. That is partly because I'm worn out, and partly because I'm petrified to write this up. Does that sound insane to you after reading all of this? Because it sounds insane to be after spending over 12 months writing on this blog.

There is a distinct difference though, between putting effort into this blog and not expecting to have a lot of readers, and taking the time to pull this into a book that I would have an expectation people would read. There is a massive fear of failure that is creeping in at this point; a fear that I can't write it; and that it's not worth writing. I'll leave that there and move on though, because I do intend to do this, it's just getting over the confidence issue.

Leftovers from the original schedule

In planning for My Year of TED I watched approximately 300 talks in the couple of months leading up to November 2011. There were talks I knew I would be including and other talks I knew wouldn't be a fit, but I had 23 activities to plan for, so there were a lot of talks to watch and re-watch.

This process introduced me to a lot of talks I hadn't seen before, and reminded me about some I had forgotten. It also introduced me to a number of talks I didn't make it all the way through, because the topic wasn't right or the presenter didn't appeal to me for some reason.

Anyway, from all of this viewing I came up with 24 activities, but some of them were a bit iffy – I wasn't sure if I could make them into a tangible 30 day activity. During the course of the project I dropped some of these activities due to changes in the schedule, and a couple of others were dropped because I had planned for them to align with things in my life that were delayed – I should probably explain that.

Activities that have been delayed

There are two 30 day activities, and a project, that were put off because they were scheduled to coincide with us moving into our new house, unfortunately that didn't happen during the year. If you remember, Derek and I are building a strawbale house in southern Tasmania. This is an owner-builder adventure, and if any of you watch Grand Designs you should know that they never go to plan.

We've had a number of delays in the process, some are attributable to trying to get tradesmen on-site, some relate to the weather, some relate to unrealistic assumptions about how long things will take, and then there was the very sad delay around Derek's dad's illness and subsequent passing.

The three activities that will happen at a later stage are:

- 30 days of bees, which involves planting a meadow on our land and finding out more about beekeeping down here, possibly letting someone keep some hives on our land. Given all of the diggers and trucks we still had coming to the house I decided that we wouldn't attempt to start a meadow until much closer to the moving in date.
- 30 days of less, which is about cleansing more crap from our lives as we move into the new house, and also trying not to buy anything new that we don't need. For this activity we've been trying to reduce waste while building, partly to reduce costs and partly to be environmentally conscious with the building. But that's Derek's job, so not an activity I could take on for myself. That means I will wait until we are moving into the house to really consider *less*.
- There was also a project based on fresh air, which involves getting the right combination of plants into the house to help generate fresh air and remove some of the toxins that are off-gassed from building products. Again, that will wait until we are almost ready to move in

There were a couple of other ideas I couldn't see developing into a 30 day activity, or developing into one I was capable of doing. Maybe I'll find a way to tackle them later, but I think that it's likely they will just cease to be ideas for me.

Continuing with the concept

Over the last month I've been thinking a lot about whether I continue to conduct 30 day activities in my life. I must admit that I do miss the structure and the focus of attempting to change something in my life. I'm not ready to make any decisions yet, but given the activities I would still like to do I think there will be some structure created to continue these changes.

The Extras

I had considered ending the book with 2012 drawing to a close, but it didn't feel right to end it without the Wizard of Oz, and some of the experiences that happened after. What follows is a collection of some blog posts from 2013 and 2014. I have chosen these because I think they help you understand what the project has meant to my life since it finished in 2012. They aren't all of the blog posts from this period, but they round out the story, and bring you up to date a little more.

Following the yellow brick road – January 2013

This is a post I've been thinking about for a long time, but I just haven't quite gotten around to writing. I think that's mainly because the idea is so central to how I felt about My Year of TED from about five months in, and I wanted to get this post right. But if all I ever do is write it in my head then it will never happen, and I can always improve on it later, so here goes.

At about the five month mark in My Year of TED I had this realisation that my life was something like the Wonderful Wizard of Oz from this project. I started developing the analogy and realised I was like the four main characters. The activities I was doing and the main themes that were underpinning them followed what the main characters wanted.

The characters and me

As the Scarecrow I wanted a brain. I wanted wisdom, a greater understanding of my life, and the world around me. Part of writing the blog, and trying to absorb all of the knowledge of the TED Talks was theoretical; it was about improving my mind.

As the Tin Man I wanted a heart. I wanted to be more compassionate to myself and others. This included connecting on a deeper level with the people around me, as well as the purely compassion-based activities themselves.

As the Lion I wanted courage. I wanted to be braver, so I was more willing to stand up for my authentic self, and the things that were important to me. There were so many activities that required me to be more courageous, and of course writing the blog[5] was the ultimate in making myself completely vulnerable, which is a very courageous thing to do.

What about Dorothy? Well, in the Wonderful Wizard of Oz Dorothy is a small girl who takes on some very difficult challenges in the hope of being able to return home. In this analogy, I see Dorothy representing authenticity, she is discovering who she is, including the strengths and abilities she possesses, so she can return home. For me, this was trying to rediscover the things I truly want from my life; after a lifetime of allowing other people to influence and sometimes even make those decisions for me.

Which brings us to the witches and the wizard, where do they fit into the journey. The way I see it, the tornado dumped me into Oz when I started My Year of TED, crushing the first evil witch of self-doubt in the process (okay she's not actually dead, but very much diminished). The other wicked witch represents all of the other negative self-talk and weak behaviours that I've been attempting to destroy in the process.

The characters and other people

Glinda was my internal champion, but she also represents the people in my life who helped guide me through this journey. They are the amazing TED speakers whose talks I used in the project; and the people around me who helped me through this very challenging year.

And the Wizard, I think that role would have to go to TED's Chris Anderson for making TED what it is today, and making it something that helped me find my own way home – I know the Wizard was a flawed character, I'm ignoring that.

Lastly, and this is certainly not in order of importance, I think all of this makes Derek my Toto. He has been by my side the whole time; suffering at the hands of my misguided decisions, and helping keep me sane throughout.

---

[5] Let's not even go into how much courage it's taken to turn this into a book.

Like I said in the beginning of the post, this became a very important analogy for me during My Year of TED. It helped me focus on what I was trying to achieve from the project, and it was fun to think of myself as the characters at certain times, especially during the tough activities. It also gave me an internal soundtrack for some of the activities, centred on the gloriously profound lyrics of *Somewhere Over the Rainbow* – of course I dared to do so much more than dream.

An explanation about lack of posts – March 2013

You all know I've been trying very hard to be totally open and honest with you; it's been a big part of the project and the changes I've been implementing. This is one of those quite personal posts where I do feel concerned about sharing some details, but at the same time it's incredibly important for me to talk about so take a deep breath…

Since I've previously written about my depression this is probably not going to come as any great surprise to you, but it did come as a surprise to me. For the last couple of months I haven't been feeling very well. I assumed this related to a general fatigue after the stress of the last year, I didn't go any further than that. In mid-January I went to see the doctor about it, because I was over feeling like complete crap.

My symptoms were extreme fatigue, disrupted sleep, a complete lack of focus (explains the writer's block), frustration and snappiness, headaches, apathy and being on the verge of tears all the time. The doctor's immediate response was 'I think that you have clinical depression', which pushed the 'verge of tears' into real ones. I cried in relief, but I also cried because I couldn't believe I hadn't thought of depression for the symptoms. I should have identified it earlier, but I guess being in the situation and all that.

What now?

The upside (well sort of) is that I'm now being treated for it. I hate taking medication, but it was a case of feeling so bad that I could not imagine how I would get out of that state by myself, psych or no psych. Hopefully it is just short term, but something I've realised about myself throughout the project is I've probably had depression since I was a teenager, with a number of quite significant episodes in my 20s that were never diagnosed. Yes, and even though I worked this out during Choice and Being Wrong I still didn't click that this was the problem.

I know what brought this on. I had a very full on 2012 and I wasn't taking enough care of myself. It is completely stress related, just think about last year: Derek's dad passed away; I was doing My Year of TED, and going through some very challenging activities about who I am and who I want to be; I did that ridiculous project at work, including the Commonwealth negotiations (enough to depress anyone); I found out my ex-husband passed away; I took on the adult literacy course and started tutoring; a lot of my friends and family had some pretty crappy stuff going on their lives (illness, separations, work dramas, deaths etc); and, of course, we are still building our house, which is all the more stressful being owner-builders.

What next?
So I'm on the road to recovery, and feeling a little better every day. I have some lovely friends who I know are very concerned about me at the moment. I've tried to reassure them that I believe the worst is over, and I'm finding ways to make sure I look after myself and reduce my stress. They don't seem convinced, but I know how I feel and I know there are so many wonderful things just around the corner; and Derek and Lily of course.

I also know that depression has been part of my life for a very long time, and will continue to be there long after I have gotten back to my usual self this time. I just need to make sure that I don't wear myself down so much in future, and certainly not take on so many stressful activities at once. I should have remembered the benefits I discovered from 30 days of Slowing Down and kept more of that mindset in my life, I will have to work hard to do that in the next couple of months.

This has been hard to write, it's taken over a week of drafting and editing, which is why I've been so quiet on the blog. I felt it was important for me to talk about this for many reasons, the main two are that I've been practising vulnerability for over a year and I shouldn't stop now; but more importantly, to just say that it's okay to have mental health issues, so many of us do. I don't intend to make the blog about my depression. If anyone has any questions or wants to know anything I'm more than happy to answer, but I don't intend on bringing you all down by doing a running commentary on my state of mind and how the progress is going.

Instead, I need to focus on getting better so I can get back to writing and load myself up with more stress on the book – I am kidding, well sort of. I feel like I've turned a corner on this and am getting on top of it, and like I said there are so many exciting things coming up. Just today we put the last windows in our house, finally getting us to lock-up and a huge step closer to being in by the middle of the year. For now I think I need to just post this up and put it out in the world, so over to you guys.

Reinvigorating past lessons

I've been tapping into some of the activities from this time last year to help me restructure some things in my life at the moment and generally remove some stress. This time last year I had just completed Simplicity, had completed Slowing Down before that, and started More Happiness. It's these three activities that I've been trying to focus on at the moment.

Slowing Down is of course one of the activities I felt would be very beneficial in reducing stress in my life. When I did this activity last year I felt energised by being focused on reducing multi-tasking and remembering to take time for myself – even the not so successful attempts at meditation had a beneficial impact. So, I've spent a lot of time in the last two months trying to bring some of the slowness back into my day-to-day life, and dragging other people along with me. And before you ask, no I haven't tried meditation again yet; soon though.

Taking time for ourselves at work

One of the things I've been trying to do is get my work colleagues and friends more engaged in taking some time out at work and connecting. There are a few of us that are a bit crafty, so I bought us all little felt animals to make. Some of us have also been making paper animals as well – just taking that five minutes to focus on making something cute with your hands makes a real difference at work, and is also a very simple way to break up your day.

The other thing we've done is started a jigsaw puzzle in the recently designated 'lunch' area. I love jigsaw puzzles, and apparently a lot of people I work with do too. I thought it would be something we could do to take a break from the keyboard, even just spending a few minutes getting respite from the stress of current tasks. It's been working well for me so far, except I always want to stay longer.

A lot of these activities and connections have been a large part of my daily gratitudes; yes I have started them again but I decided not to include them on the blog this time. Instead I have developed a new notepad page to capture them, which I made into a beautiful hand bound book for a lovely friend of mine as well. Maybe this will be a follow up to the Do-Pad.

I should mention though that the most fun has been had with *The Walking Dead's Dead Yourself* app, which I've been using to turn most of my work colleagues/friends into zombies. We've all been having a great laugh about how disgusting some of the photos have come out.

And talking about happiness

On a positive note, I have a lot to be happy about of late, which has been very helpful. The house is moving along at a rapid pace, it's amazing how quick the internal stuff happens after finally getting to lock-up. The bank has allowed us to borrow the money we require to finish the house, which was a huge weight off my shoulders. We had a couple of significant wins in my work project; it seems like all of the hard work and stress was worth it for the community sector, which is fantastic. But all of this pales in comparison to what will happen next week. I've been very cagey about this because I haven't wanted to jinx it by talking about it too much before it happens, but I will post crap out of it in a couple of days – it's very exciting, trust me.

I guess the big thing is that while the lessons from these activities had been dropped while I was too busy at the end of last year, I managed to pick them back up quite easily and find new ways to apply them to my life. Had I not discovered the value of these things it might have been harder to find a way to start bouncing back. Thank you again to all of the speakers who contributed to these activities, and therefore to my recovery process now.

How about you, how do you reduce stress in your life? We all have different tactics, what works for you? Do you meditate, exercise, read, write? Or maybe some less healthy activity helps you keep the stress at bay? Suggestions are always accepted with enthusiasm.

Best day ever

Okay, maybe the heading is a little hyperbolic, but it's definitely right up there at this point in my life.

So what makes today so special? Well technically it was yesterday that was special, but since we are 15 hours ahead of New York, I was asleep at the time it actually occurred. All of that is to say, I'm celebrating it today (my time), and will be celebrating for quite a while.

Anyway, that gets you no closer to knowing what has happened, so to cut to the chase – today I had an article about My Year of TED published on **the TED Blog** (you need to picture me almost exploding with joy when I say that, which says a lot at this point in time).

I was approached just over a month ago with a completely surreal email asking if I would be interested in writing a piece for the TED Blog. After careful consideration, nearly a whole half second, I jumped at the offer!

This is one of those exceptionally exciting things I was talking about when discussing my depression. It's just not possible to feel completely hopeless about life when you know something like this is on the horizon. I'm so glad the drugs have kicked in for me to get more enjoyment out of this though.

It's one of those surreal and mind-blowing experiences I had hoped for but never expected to happen. I am so grateful for the opportunity to have something I've written published for such a wide audience. For today, I'll just be buzzing with what has happened, and anticipating what might occur. At the very least it has given me a boost to get stuck into writing the book.

Massive realisation about frustration with work – April 2013

I intend on approaching this post with the same level of honesty and openness as the rest of the blog. This is a little difficult because my boss occasionally reads the blog, but this is an incredibly important thing for me to write about. So I will caveat this by saying I don't hate my job, and that has been contributing to the frustration about all of these feelings – so if you are my boss, don't take this personally.

I've been struggling a bit with work over the last couple of months. Initially I thought it was to do with depression, and while I think that is part of it, it's not the main issue. See, everything else is going so well, especially with all of the excitement over the TED Blog post and a couple of opportunities that have come out of that. My workplace still has a few issues though, and I have just been feeling very disconnected from my job.

Realisation number one

Last Friday I had an important revelation that helped explain a little bit, and sowed the seeds for the big realisation. My entire working history I have based my identity and value mainly on the job I had at the time. This means that my work has always been important to me, as it has been the most significant part of who I was, which sounds quite sad when I write it out.

This has now changed, because of My Year of TED.

My work is still important to me, especially the need I have to do a good job, and to be respected and valued for my contribution. There is a shift though, towards the importance of this blog and taking advantage of the opportunities that have arisen from the experience. For me, this is now the most important part of my life – the part that defines me.

This shift has been so slow I didn't realise it had occurred, although I probably should have been prepared for it in hindsight. I've even added Blogger as a role on my LinkedIn profile, which was a big shift for me.

Realisation number two – the big one

Yesterday morning I had a major epiphany about all of this. I'm sure some of you have already worked this out, but it's taken me a while to get there. As I said, I've been feeling disconnected from my work. I am more easily frustrated with things I would usually just shrug off. Most disappointing for me is I haven't been going the extra mile, which is usually part of the job.

So, I have worked out that I don't identify myself by my job, and I feel frustrated being there at the moment – and I couldn't work out why.

Then it struck me. I spent a year trying to understand my authentic self; what I want from my life; and what I want to contribute to the world – and I'm not doing it! Of course I'm going to feel frustrated by this, especially when other opportunities are coming up that I don't have enough time for.

This leaves me in the position of trying to figure out how to make this situation work for me. I still get satisfaction from my job, I still have the ability to contribute to something greater – I just need to work out how to progress the other things in my life so that I don't feel as frustrated.

I'm happy to take any advice on how to achieve this. I think realising it has been a massive first step, now to make some peace with it all.

An exciting April of courage – May 2013

The traffic on the blog has maintained a steady level since it levelled out after the TED Blog post. It's been wonderful to see so many more people on the blog and get more feedback on posts. It feels like I'm not upholding my end of the bargain though, since I haven't been posting very much.

What's been going on

I've been a bit busy with a number of things going on in my life. So I thought I should probably update you on those, so you know I'm not slacking off entirely:

- **Our strawbale house** – quite a few weekends and public holidays in the last month have been spent trying to get all of the internal render ready for the painters to come in just over a week. We've actually become quite skilled at the rendering, considering we were completely new to the process when we started the house.

- **Writing the book** – this has come in fits and spurts, but I feel that I've started to get a good structure in place for telling the story. There is another part of this process that has taken a little time as well, and that is writing a book proposal. It probably isn't detailed enough, but one of the exciting events from the TED article was that I was contacted by a literary agent about getting them a book proposal. Oddly enough, I was so incredibly excited about this and stressed about getting a couple of chapters written that I didn't actually confirm I would get them a proposal as soon as possible! Yeah the week after the TED article was exciting but I wasn't very focused.[6]
- **Disruptive event** – the other exciting invitation that resulted from the TED article; I was asked to be involved in a leadership event as part of the *Festival of Voices* in Hobart in July. The program for this event will be online shortly (don't worry I'll publicise it), and it will involve me talking about My Year of TED, among other things. I'll provide more details about this as it comes closer, but if you're in Hobart or will be coming for the Festival, then please come along.

All of this, along with doing my job, will give you some indication of why I haven't been posting very much. But that's not important now, what is important is how I've gone about these activities – this last month I feel that some of the lessons from MYoT (I'm tired of writing it in full) have come to fruition. This also means that the depression has definitely lifted, and not just because of the medication.

Authenticity, vulnerability and extroversion

In the last month I've done a large number of things that would generally make me feel uncomfortable and anxious. Things I would normally run a mile from or that I would have suffered a great deal of self-doubt about. These include talking with people about sponsoring the Disruptive event; sending a book proposal to a literary agent; meeting with people I didn't know and being very frank about my opinions; and putting myself onto a conference program where I will be talking very openly about myself.

Now maybe it's because I've been riding high since the TED article, but I'm usually great at turning positive things into anxiety-ridden episodes of waiting for the other shoe to drop. So the fact that I've remained generally positive, and stepped up to increased exposure is a little shocking for me.

---

[6] This refers to the 'other book' of course. I wasn't even close to having a good structure in place, and the book proposal didn't go anywhere (of course). But I'm still trying with that.

As I've mentioned a number of times, one of the main things I learned about myself was that I'm more courageous than I thought. That is now the internal story I have about myself, and why would a courageous person be concerned about the list of things above?

I've had the courage to believe I am interesting enough for people to want to hear my story, and make myself vulnerable to the possibility that I'm not.

I've displayed my extroverted side to casually have conversations that would normally make me feel anxious and tongue-tied. I'm not saying I didn't breathe deeply before ringing the people involved, but when I started the conversation I wasn't self-conscious.

More than anything though, I feel like I've made a massive step in embracing the authentic Kylie, the one who used to be the quiet voice in my head that the other voices would criticise and shout down. I feel like I've been more authentic in my thoughts, feelings and actions in the last month than I can ever remember being – and it scares me out of my mind!!! It's invigorating, and I hope it continues to grow, but when the world is quiet and it's just me and my thoughts, it's a tad overwhelming.

Having said all of this, if I don't hear back from the literary agent shortly my head will explode – not in a good way. You can't change the habits of a lifetime completely in a year.

How about you? Have you been your authentic self of late? Have you stepped outside your comfort zone and trusted yourself more than usual for anything? I'd love to hear your stories of courage.

Values alignment and leadership training

Last weekend I had the great opportunity of being involved in the *Festival of Voices* leadership program, which is being done with the University of Tasmania. I still have the final assignment to finish, but there have been a few other things consuming my thoughts at the moment – more on that at a later stage though.

The weekend was wonderful, Paul Kooperman did a fantastic job pulling it all together. We had a number of sessions about different aspects of leadership, with three to four speakers in each session. These were interspersed with group activities about leadership, and possible events that we could introduce to the *Festival of Voices*.

How much is there to learn?

I did hesitate about doing the program, mainly because I've done a lot of leadership training (formal and informal, I do include TED Talks in this) and I wondered what else I could get out of the weekend. On the whole there wasn't a lot of new material, but it was a great refresher on things I need to remember. More importantly, it was the anecdotes and storytelling from this sort of event that had the greatest impact.

New people

The other important aspect was the dreaded 'n' word – yes networking. I met some lovely people, a few which I will try to maintain contact with. I was also a little proud of myself because I didn't just sit back and consume, as I generally do in these sort of events. I did voice my opinions, and more than that, I stood up in front of everyone at the end to do a plug for Disruptive – the *Festival of Ideas* event that I am part of – all without blushing I should add.

Vocal challenge

One of the most unique parts of the weekend was the choir activity. I haven't been in a choir since I was 12 years old, and doing it again was great fun. Since the program is part of the *Festival of Voices* they did this as the ice breaker, the best one I've ever done in for a workshop. We formed a choir, learned a song and performed it. The sense of achievement, combined with the sense of shared experience set a great mood for the weekend.

The problem with clearly knowing your values

There was one theme that struck a chord with me: values alignment. A couple of speakers talked about ensuring you employ staff whose values align with the organisation, which we know is important. This made me think about the overwhelming feeling that's growing within me for a few months now. Since I understand my values clearly now, it has becoming obvious to me that the culture of the organisation I work in does not share my values. I won't go into any more detail here, but this is what's been causing me angst.

This TED experience has given me a lot of insight into myself, and it has changed my life in many ways. Maybe what I failed to realise was how much more I would need to change, because once you know something about yourself it can't be forgotten or ignored. We'll see what happens from here.

How about you? Do your values align with your organisation? Or more importantly do theirs align with yours? I'd love to know whether other people have this disconnect and are able to work through it.

Some pretty big news

There are changes afoot, and I feel very confident they will be for the better. I resigned from the public service yesterday, which was a huge decision. There were a few things that aligned for me to make this step, which make this seem inevitable.

The first thing was that I've come up with a concrete idea for how I might satisfy my Why, and it's not what I was expecting. I'm not ready to share it all yet, but it's exciting. This was important because it means I know my current job is not helping me progress towards this goal.

The second thing was the Leadership of Voices program I did the other weekend. This inspired me about the arts community, and raised some very complicated feelings about my current working environment and my values.

The third thing was Derek started a job last week. We're very close to finishing the house and an opportunity came up he couldn't refuse. This gave me the freedom to resign from my job, with nothing else to go to.

I'm not concerned about it though, which is amazing since I am normally very risk averse. I've gotten to the place where I have confidence I will find the right thing for me, and that I am making the right decision. At the very least it should give me some time to set up the house and get some writing done (that has stalled of late).

As I mentioned in my last post, this project has changed my life in many ways, but I think there are still a lot more changes to come. That is a bit scary, but also very exciting.

Serendipity, change and kindred spirits – July 2013

As I mentioned the other week, I have resigned from the public service. I am still here for another week, but making the decision to pursue my dreams, and focus on making sure I'm okay, has created some significant changes over the last couple of weeks.

I feel a great sense of relief, which makes me even more confident that I am doing the right thing. I also have a great deal of nervous energy, which I have found a little challenging to direct at times, but I think I have that sussed now.

One of the most interesting things is the amount of responses from my work colleagues that are 'I'm so jealous that you are following your dreams' or 'It's so inspiring that you have the courage to do this'. There's this little part of the conversations that I've had with people that makes me feel like I have to succeed for them, that I'm carrying all of their dreams along with my own into this next step.

> It made me wonder about how many people never get the ability to follow their dreams, or sit in jobs that they hate just to pay the bills, because they don't feel they can change it. I understand that I am in a bit of a unique position, we could have survived for a while without me having a job. However, I would not be able to progress my business idea without getting some part time work to build up some capital. So I have been very fortunate in finding a job that I think will support the development process.

This was a blog post I started writing the other week, but didn't get around to finishing. It was going to be about change and how many people have considered these big changes like leaving a job or moving interstate as extremely courageous, but they aren't the ones I'm scared of. It was also going to be about how people should be more willing to take on the risk of change, because it can be such a wonderful thing to pursue your dreams.

This is where the serendipity comes in

Then I got my regular email from Scott Berkun outlining some of his blog posts, and the title of this one struck me 'Changing your life is not a (mid-life) crisis'. I don't know whether life throws these things in your way when you are thinking of a certain topic, or by thinking of it you are just more in tune with seeing the topic you're focused on – either way I love it when this happens.

So I read the post, which has some very valid points from my experience, and left a comment (because as a blogger I know how nice feedback can be). This is where it gets a little weird. Scott tweeted about My Year of TED and the blog and a couple of his followers retweeted as well.

One of these was a woman called Saya Hillman, and I noticed in her blurb that she was a TEDx speaker. I looked up her talk from TEDxBloomington called *How to define a life of yes!* Everything in that talk resonated with me. So much of it was things I learned and things I want to achieve from My Year of TED – it was like finding a kindred spirit. I've been looking through what Mac & Cheese Productions (her company) do, and I love the ideas – in some ways she is living the life I want to have. In other ways there is a difference to how she is doing things, but I can see many similarities in how I picture my business venture and the energy she has in hers.

Have you made any changes in your life that people think are a 'mid-life' crisis? Or are you like me and lucky enough to be surrounded by supportive people who can see the benefits in change?

The good, the bad, the ugly... and the brave – August 2013

So, I've been on anti-depression meds since January this year. I mention this because a few weeks ago I decided it was time to see if I could start tapering off the meds; I started this on my birthday. The last couple of weeks were going to fun anyway, but then there was so much more going on.

The good
- We moved into our gorgeous house (a culmination of about six years, three and a half planning and two and a half building) – which is proving to be better than we imagined, even at only 80% completion.
- Disruptive went very well, and I've had wonderful feedback about the event – some delusional ones have even complimented my talk.
- I've made a wonderful new network of amazing and supportive people, to add to the one I already had.
- An outcome of Disruptive has been the opportunity to speak to a group of teenagers about my experience, and particularly about values and being true to themselves. This falls into one of the areas I'm incredibly passionate about, so I'm psyched about the opportunity.
- I've had some interesting tasks with my new job, and I am loving working from home.
- I have started writing the book again, and overcome one of the big problems with the structure.

The bad – well the not so good
- We had to move, and there is still more to go. The amount of crap we have is amazing, but we have been culling fairly well in line with 30 days of less (yep, started a 30 day activity to coincide with the move).
- Disruptive was draining and took a good couple of days to get over.
- I've been so busy with locals I've been neglecting my online network.
- Working from home can get a little lonely at times, especially when I'm on a rollercoaster.
- I'm constantly distracted with competing priorities (work, unpacking, writing, cleaning etc).

And now comes the ugly...

The week after Disruptive I was desperately trying to get back on top of my day job; there was a lot to do. I'd been on half doses of my medication for a week and I was getting a little forgetful in taking them. By the end of the week I was starting to feel a little off; by the middle of last week I was downright melancholy, and feeling very scattered.

But that does not excuse my mindset on Thursday night. It's like someone let that nasty, insecure voice inside my head off its leash, and it was baying for blood. I went full negative, judgemental mode – somewhere I haven't been in a while (since going on the meds), and it wasn't pretty.

Worst of all, I happened to be socialising (unusual for me) with people from Disruptive. Now I will preface this by saying all of this remained internal, but it does not make it any better, and it made me physically ill. I was listening to this lovely woman talk about the opportunities she has had from Disruptive, and how she feels like she is finally reaching her dreams. And my brain just went a little nuts… I'm just going to leave it at that, none of you need to know what goes in my head – trust me.

On the way home I berated myself about the thoughts I had about this person (which sort of bled out to judging other people in the room). I didn't get what it was all about. Then I analysed the jealousy, the fear, the insecurity – they were all there because this woman and I share the same sort of dream.

I woke up the next morning feeling ill – my gut brain was very unhappy with me, thank you for helping me understand that Sally-Anne. I took a little time to think through it all and I realised that: the jealousy was because she was further into it than me; the fear was that she was taking all the opportunities and there would be none left for me; and the insecurity was that I'm not good enough to do this anyway.

With a calmer brain I realised she is further along because she's been doing this longer and has worked her arse off, taking the risks; there are thousands of opportunities, I just need to make some for me; and I'm enough to take this on and do it – and because of people like her, I don't have to do this alone, I can use the wonderful network I now have.

And the brave?

I wrote all of this into an email for the person I had been internally nasty to. I let her know what had happened and I was truly sorry for my reaction because she deserved my support and encouragement. And she graciously sent a lovely response back, forgiving and thanking me.

Letting her know was completely unnecessary, but I felt like I had to do it, that she deserved an apology from me. Maybe we spent too much time talking about being vulnerable at Disruptive, but I just felt it was the only way I could be authentic about this situation. The outcome was that I felt like I had been true to myself about the situation, and I think we have developed an even stronger connection.

Permission to change: or why the construct was such a good idea – December 2013

I've been thinking a lot lately about some of the mechanics of My Year of TED, and some of the subconscious parts of the whole exercise. It's interesting when I reflect back now on what I thought the project was all about, as opposed to what I've learned it was actually about. One of the big things I've been thinking about is what the construct of a year-long, totally immersed project was for, and these are some of the things that I now believe that structure gave me:

- **Immersion** – When I explained what each of the concept talks gave the project I mentioned that AJ Jacobs' talk gave me 'the whole concept that I can experiment on my life, and the idea that changing my behaviour can change my mind.' I was intrigued by the concept of spending a year immersed in a topic, and seeing if it could truly change my life. I loved AJ's book, *My Year of Living Biblically*, and think it's a great example of that. It was definitely the inspiration of a year-long immersion, but that was something I already knew going in.
- **Writing** – This was a massive part of the process, giving me a topic to write about, and to hopefully be able to write a book about. I say that a bit sheepishly because with everything else going on I have stalled on the book. I will still write it, even if I have to self-publish it, because it's important, and a big part of the project. I just need to slow down a lot of other things in my life.
- **To remember** – I remember more about that one year of my life than possibly any other year. Having a project like this meant everything was broken into time period milestones, and that has allowed me to remember a lot more clearly than I would otherwise – even without referring back to the blog for prompts. There is a little part of me that misses that structure, and misses that established memory process.
- **A plan** – quite simply it gave me a plan to follow and, if you haven't worked it out, I like structure. The construct of the project was the most structured a year of my life has ever been, and it catered to that organised part of my brain. It meant there was a lot of day-to-day activity and decision making I didn't have to worry about, as strange as that may seem, because there was this whole aspect of my life that was known. I'm not sure how much sense that explanation makes, but I'm sure there is at least one person out there going 'yeah I know what you mean'.

- **Accountability** – I explained this one very early on, before the project had even started. Creating the construct of a massive change project that I shared with people in my life, and committed to writing about on a blog, made me accountable for following through. I know that there are times I would have seriously given up on particular activities, if not the entire project, if I hadn't had to do that publicly.
- **Permission** – more and more I've come to realise how much of the construct was about giving me permission to change. After all, I could have made any of these changes in my life, or focused on any of these activities, without having this massive construct around me to do that. But I never did, because like many people I'm usually not quick to shake my life up. Let's look at the facts:
  - I went through with two weddings I knew weren't right, just because there was nothing obviously wrong with them at the time – I've often felt I don't have the right to change something just because I'm not happy with it, there has to be a 'justifiable' reason.
  - I have stayed in a couple of jobs that have driven me to complete distraction, because change is scary and I didn't know what else I could do – I will say though that when it is finally enough I tend to make very radical changes on that front, they just take a while.

The permission aspect has been the idea I've been exploring the most of late, because a lot of other people talk about this sort of thing as well so it keeps coming up. It's the notion that 'if it ain't broke' then leave it the hell alone – but why do we believe that is the best way to go? Why do we feel we don't have the right, the freedom, or the permission to make random changes in our life that might make us happier; even when we aren't necessarily unhappy? Just think about how much capacity you, or the people in your life, have to endure – to put up with crappy, or not satisfying lives, just because change is scary, or the unknown is scary?

One of the more interesting things I've realised recently is that I was apologising for My Year of TED while I was doing it. I let people refer to it as my mid-life crisis, which is total bullshit by the way; sometimes I even referred to it that way myself. I think they used that explanation because it's just not normal for someone to do what I was doing, especially not as publicly as I was doing it. So, since they couldn't explain it away with 'women's issues' it became a mid-life crisis.

I also think it freaked people out so much because I had given myself permission, and I was willing to make these changes in my life that I felt had to be made – and that's challenging to people who are just putting up with things, and not making changes for themselves. If someone else around you is doing it then it removes one of your excuses about why you aren't making changes.

Apart from mid-life crisis, the other comments were: *but you don't have children so you can do that sort of thing; you must have a lot of spare time on your hands,* implying they don't so that's why they're stuck; or even flattering comments like *it takes a lot of courage/focus/guts to do something like that,* trying to convince themselves it was extraordinary – which I don't believe it was by the way.

I'm not sure what the purpose of this is, except to share my thoughts about what a construct like My Year of TED can give you around change. It wouldn't work for everyone, but for me it was a structured and supportive way of going through with the activities I wanted (or needed) to do.

How about you, is there something you want that you are not giving yourself permission to do? Are you enduring a situation or part of yourself that you should be changing? Be brave, I give you permission…

There were a few blog posts that discussed the fact I was selected to speak at TEDxHobart in mid-January 2014. This is a subsequent post from that event.

The ups and downs of my TEDx Talk: Part 1 – January 2014

Okay, so you know I spoke at TEDxHobart on the weekend – and if you don't well where have you been?! I'm going to talk about the experience here, and for any of you who have done public speaking, I'm sure some of this will be very familiar. For those of you smart enough to decide that sitting in the audience is a great way to spend the day, this may reaffirm your decision.

Applying to speak

As with many TEDx events, there was a call for speakers. A chance for us to stick up our hands and say 'yes, I have an idea worth spreading, pick me'. As an introvert, who still has far too many 'I'm not good enough', 'who would want to listen to me' demons, this was a difficult thing to do. But the chance to give a TEDx talk was one I couldn't pass up – and being in Hobart meant it would be quite small and 'safe'. *Then came the waiting…*

Getting the email

When I got the email saying I'd been selected my head almost exploded. I was so excited, for about three hours, and then the reality of what it meant kicked in. I managed to push the reality demon away for a little bit though, so I did enjoy being accepted for about a week before the doubt kicked in.

What the hell am I going to say?

Most people only get one chance on a TED/TEDx stage, and since the exceptions are people like Brené Brown, Derek Sivers, Barry Schwartz, Malcolm Gladwell and Hans 'king of statistics' Rosling – well let's move on.

So what to do with my one shot? Of course I would talk about My Year of TED, that was the point, but what would I focus on? I toyed around with the permission and accountability aspects of the construct, but then I decided I needed to talk about the Wizard of Oz analogy. In the end I think it was the best approach – and I got to have some funky shoes for the day!

I've never rehearsed so much... for anything!

Then there are the limitations you have to work within, which I think are great in so many ways, but make the whole experience that little bit scarier. No notes! Don't go over 18 minutes! Oh, and remember that this will be recorded and placed on YouTube with a TEDx tag on it – no pressure!

I think I was going through the talk in my sleep. I woke up a few times part way through the talk so I can only imagine what my brain was doing. I kept making changes up until the last few days – which I don't recommend when you have to memorise your content. Fortunately they were minor changes to improve the flow, so not too bad. But there were two parts I kept messing up; two rather important parts, so I was pretty freaked out.

Dress rehearsal

It's one of the tips they give on public speaking and calming your nerves, see if you can rehearse at the venue beforehand – and I give that piece of advice a big thumbs up. We had a dress rehearsal the day before, we'd had other smaller rehearsals in the build up that were great, but not at the venue. I was incredibly happy with how well I remembered things, and how well I recovered when I stumbled a little bit. All that self-compassion practice paid off, and I left the rehearsal feeling happy, confident and calm(ish).

And then Saturday came

I was still calm when I woke up on Saturday, I even slept in to a reasonable time; not 4 or 5am like the previous couple of mornings. Getting everything together was fine, and then we headed off for the day. Since I was calm, let's say I started the day at 0 out of 10 on the stress meter; it was probably still a 3 but it felt calm. The 10 minute walk to the venue generated so much nervous energy I felt like I needed to run there, but that was still okay.

Registration was fine. I saw someone I knew and we talked for a little bit, which was distracting so great; although the nervous energy was building.

We went in for the first session, walking in the room kicked the stress up a little, not too bad though – after all I was scheduled to talk last, so I had hours before I had to hit the stage.

Then Robin, the first speaker, came out – the spotlights went on and the lights dimmed, and my head exploded because we didn't have this lighting in rehearsal and all I could think was 'I won't be able to see people'. This is a bad thing for a person who likes positive reinforcement when they present. Yes I could see the benefits as well, but not at that point. Since Robin's talk was so interesting I got back on track quickly, but the seed was planted.

Morning tea

I survived pretty well through the first session, after the spotlight shock. Morning tea was good, I chatted with a few people and I started climbing to about a 3 on the stress meter. There were more people there that I knew, this is Hobart after all; and it felt like a pretty nice crowd which was reassuring.

Session two

This was a little up and down – I loved the talks in this session, well I enjoyed all of the talks but a couple of these were really fascinating. So my brain was a bit distracted from the fact that the day was pushing on, and my time on stage was approaching. But during the final talk of the session my stress level jumped to about 6 for some reason, even with lovely people reassuring me; and then it was lunchtime.

I grabbed food but after I ate a couple of sandwich quarters I felt queasy, so I stopped eating. We spoke with some more people, and if you were there that day I'm sorry if I was disjointed because only a small part of my brain was functioning in the moment. I tried to distract myself, to no avail.

During lunch I went into the room to do a last minute check of my slides, and see what it was like with the spotlights. I was a little more relaxed when I walked out but then I saw everyone and my stress level started climbing again. Then my body decided it did need food, too much nervous energy.

Session three

Speakers sat down the front in their session so they could easily prepare to present – which meant I wasn't near Derek for support. I remember only snippets from this part of the day, I listened to the talks but my brain didn't take a lot in. There was a TED Talk played before mine, so I had a lot of time to get the microphones attached, and wait to present.

If I was an 8 on the stress meter when we came into the room for session three, standing on the side waiting for that talk to end would have put me at 12, and yes I know the scale is 10. I just kept running through two things, my opening line and the bit I kept forgetting.

Standing on the dot

When I stood on the dot I was suddenly quite calm, probably just dropped down to 10 in reality. This was the moment of truth and my inner champion must have sedated my inner critic, the only thought I had was 'I know this, I can do this'.

I don't really remember giving the talk; I remember being able to see a couple of people at the front of the room. I forgot to think about making sure I was standing properly, and not blinking too much. About halfway through, when I was talking about some particularly personal things, my hands started to shake, but that was okay. And then it was over – no stumbling, no forgetting, and with 30 seconds to spare.

The initial aftermath

People were very complimentary, but it was the end of the day and a lot of people left straight away. I was buzzing on adrenaline by this stage, and when we left I felt great about the talk and proud of what I'd done.

About 90 minutes later I saw the still photos that were taken during the talk and I wanted to die – I know I'm overweight, I mentioned the other day that I need to do something to connect more with my body and increase my fitness, but the photos are... well let's just say I dropped back to reality pretty quickly. What if the video looks that bad? Why did I wear that outfit? My internal critic was awake and primed.

I spent Saturday night alternating between 'it went well and I'm really happy' and 'I just want it all to have never happened'.

The next day

Yesterday was even worse, because I woke at 4am with a massive headache and vulnerability regrets. Why did I make the talk so personal? I can't believe I told them that? That's going to be on YouTube you idiot? And other such comments kept me awake for about an hour.

I tried to distract myself with retail therapy, well we did need some rugs and there was a rug sale so it wasn't mindless retail therapy. I just wanted to curl up in a ball, but I did try to be productive; and I tried to spend some time with positive self-talk to improve the situation.

And now... I'm a bit numb if you really want to know. I think part of that is because I wanted to do this talk so much, and now it's over. Another part of it is anticipating what the video will look like; but really, I think it's because I don't know what to do next. I'll admit that I am feeling very lost at the moment and I just don't know what to do.

So I will do my job, because I'm paid to do that; I will make some more jewellery, because I have a market in two weeks; I will write this blog post, because this is what I do. And while I'm doing those things I will stress about the fact that I want to do more speaking about the project, but I don't know how; that I want to finish the book, but I'm stuck with it at the moment; and that I don't know what to do with everything else I've learned – I don't know what to offer people, and I'm not certain of the next step in that.

But I will remember that I did it. I faced up to the challenge and gave my TEDx talk, and I'm proud of how it went. I was brave, I just need to continue to be brave.

You will be happy to know I don't intend on writing about this again, until it goes online and then I hope you will indulge me for a Part 2.

The ups and downs of my TEDx Talk: Part 2

Nothing is as scary as you think it is going to be – if you're anything like me, your fertile and critical imagination is always going to be worse than how things turn out in the real world. I forget this fact far too often, and the experience around talking at TEDxHobart is another reminder of this truth.

A few days after the talk I published a post about the experience. I mentioned that I would be writing another post after the video went onto YouTube, so here it is.

A surprising Monday morning tweet

I found out that the talk was on YouTube in a very random way – through this tweet from James Marino.

> jamesmainonyc
> @dinkylune Great talk, Kylie. I feature a TED Talk on my blog everyday – yours will be going up in a few hours.

My sleepy brain was initially 'oh that's nice he liked my talk' – it took a couple of seconds for the synapses to connect to, 'What!? Featuring my talk on the blog?' A quick YouTube search later confirmed that the talk had indeed gone live – nervous excitement was the first emotion to hit me.

You know how there are the things you know about yourself? Well I knew I wanted to blast this news out to the universe, but I also knew that if I didn't do it quickly I would end up going into vulnerability mode and hesitating. So the next half hour was spent tweeting, facebooking (is that even a word), putting up a quick blog post and emailing a lot of people.

And then, sure enough...
The feeling of excitement started to shift about 45 minutes later. Oh, I was still excited about it, I'm still excited about it now – but the other emotions started coming thick and fast. The same dread that came after giving the talk, combined with the fear of it suddenly being out there for anyone to find.

I rode that wave of emotions far better this time than in the days after giving the talk, but it was a slightly terrifying day. Of course it was helped by all of my wonderful friends who watched it, giving me enthusiastic feedback – and getting up the nerve to watch it myself was very beneficial as well.

Then of course there was the never-ending generosity of TED speakers whose talks I used in the project. The feedback from some of them was extremely lovely, and I can't believe so many of them watched it.

Wouldn't change a thing
I mentioned previously that I didn't know if I would watch the talk; for anyone who has never watched themselves do something like this, it's an odd feeling. We all know our voice sounds different inside our heads than it does outside our heads – listening to your recorded voice is a strange thing. But listening to your external voice, married up with the image of you, and talking about something extremely personal; well that's incredibly surreal.

I'm very glad I watched it because I'm happy with how it came out, although I did cringe at the nervous giggle that I thought I had under better control these days.

Overall, it's an experience I'm so glad I was able to have, and one I will always remember. I hope to share my story with other people through more public speaking, but sharing it on a TEDx stage and with that community has been something incredibly special for me. It sort of feels like it's all come full circle in a way, and that's a great feeling.

The Final Chapter – For now

I've thought a lot about how I would close this book. There is part of me that wanted to just leave it at the last blog post; then I thought I needed to give you some sort of conclusion to all this – not that there is one.

I continue to learn more and more about myself, largely based on the lessons from My Year of TED. Other TED Talks have contributed to that along the way of course: *Larry Smith: Why you will fail to have a great career*, *Dame Stephanie Shirley: Why do ambitious women have flat heads?*, *Monica Lewinsky: The price of shame*, and *Morgana Bailey: The danger of hiding who you are*, to name a few.

I'm even doing a new 30 day activity to coincide with finalising and promoting this book – 30 days of Asking based on the wonderful TED Talk, *Amanda Palmer: The Art of Asking*. I thought it would be a great way of focusing on being brave and asking people for help with this book launch, and a couple of days in I'm already right.

In July 2014, I was very fortunate to have a small group of TED speakers give me some of their precious time for interviews about their talks, their purpose and my project. These were all speakers whose talks I used during the year, and those conversations helped solidify some of my lessons. I'm converting some of their wisdom into articles for *Huffington Post*, other parts will be used in the book – what I've been referring to as the other book.

Collecting the blog into this book has been a fascinating process, and more difficult than I imagined. Reliving My Year of TED in such a short timeframe to edit the posts into this format was an intense process that sometimes made me teary; sometimes made me cringe; but always made me proud – the fact I can even write the last part of that statement shocks me. It's a very raw process to relive such a life-changing experience in this way, but it also makes me realise that the other book is shockingly personal; although it didn't start out that way.

See, there were things about my past that I didn't explain in the blog. I chose not to go into detail about many experiences that contributed to the broken person I was. Initially, I had kept that mindset in the other book and then I realised what the writer's block was all about. I was approaching that book from an intellectual viewpoint, which cannot work if I'm trying to make real connections between the wisdom of TED Talks and my own experience – makes a lot of sense.

As for the discussion about a literary agent and book proposal, I'm still working on that but it hasn't turned out as I was hoping. I remain ever hopeful, but self-publishing that one as well is always a real option – watch this space.

As for everything else...

I cannot begin to explain here just how different my life is now from when I started this crazy journey four years ago. Is everything perfect now? Nope, life doesn't work that way. But it is better, in real and tangible ways. I'm still working on the how and what to achieve my Why, but it's closer than I'd ever imagined.

Early in the book you might remember I called this project a 'potentially ill-conceived experiment with my sanity' – nothing could be further from the truth. With the perspective of hindsight I now realise that My Year of TED had less to do with my depression than the other things in my life at the time. I believe I would have ended up depressed regardless of My Year of TED, but I would not have recovered as well without the experience and positive changes it brought into my life.

Interestingly, one of the most significant outcomes from My Year of TED is that my comfort zone has shifted to the point that I don't fully recognise my life anymore. Sometimes I refer to this as 'fear being my constant companion', because intellectually I know that previously I would have been scared out of my mind by the things I do now – like self-publishing this book for example. That's only partially true though, because emotionally the fear is not constant, it ebbs and flows. In all reality, I think a lot of the fear is probably just excitement about what I'm doing, but excitement is not something I've historically done well – I'm not going to expand on that here.

Taking a step back to the very beginning of this project, AJ Jacobs' influence about the idea that *changing your behaviour can change your mind.* After this experience, I would have to completely agree with that idea – I find it increasingly difficult to even remember the mindset that allowed me to be as broken as I was before. Growth is interesting in that way, especially when it involves characteristics that you previously felt defined you as a person.

For me, I now define myself as a strong, courageous, capable woman – I own my life now, and I live by the ethos of do, share, inspire that came about through My Year of TED. *Forza* and *corragia* is no longer my mantra, because that was a wish, or a plea – now it is something far more positive than that:

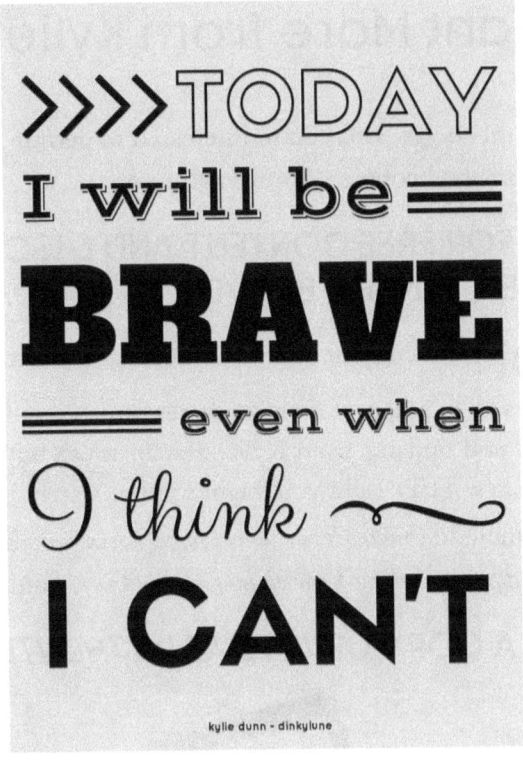

Today I will be BRAVE – even when I think I can't

You can be brave too, you just have to believe it – as Adie, my aerial circus instructor,[7] always says, 'I believe in you!'

---

[7] Yes, I do aerial circus now (think trapeze) – but that's for the next book.

Want More from Kylie?

If you enjoyed this book, and you're interested in getting more content from Kylie, there are a couple of options for you.

SIGN UP FOR FREE CONTENT AND DISCOVER A WISER, KINDER, BRAVER YOU TODAY!

Join Kylie's mailing list at www.kyliedunn.com/toolkit.

You'll get access to a range of free resources and printables, as well as regular prompts and updates from Kylie. Stay in touch with the ongoing discoveries, and new TED Talks you might want to watch.

Free resources include *Finding Your Way Home*, *Living an Aligned Life*, *Less Stress – More Happiness*, *Selling Yourself into a New Career* and more.

BUY A COPY OF *LIVING WITH INTENT*

This ebook and printable workbook will guide you through Kylie's process from 30 days of Drive. If you still don't know what drives you, or what your why is in this world, this resource will help you discover those things for yourself. Visit www.kyliedunn.com/lwi for more.

Acknowledgements

This project relied on passive and active support of a number of people – those in my life and those I only know through their wonderful TED Talks.

Firstly, I need to thank Derek for being his lovely, supportive self during this project. I know I wasn't the easiest person to live with at times during My Year of TED – I'm not an easy person to live with outside of the project at times as well. But my gratefulness for Derek's love and support goes much further than that. I doubt I would have had the courage and drive to do this project if it wasn't for Derek.

My wonderful brother Matthew Dunn, who contributed to the project through the amazing activity art pieces. It was very special to have him collaborate with me on part of this project, but his encouragement was more important to the process. Matt commented near the end of the project that this was the cheapest therapy he'd ever seen – he's probably right. He's also been a fantastic sounding board for ideas and concepts over the project, and throughout my life.

My friends and family, those who knew about the project and provided support and encouragement throughout; and those who found out later and have continued to encourage me. You all played a part in helping me along the way, even if it was by challenging my ability to do it in the first place. This also includes the friends I've made from the project; those who have supported me in the continuing journey to become the person I want to be.

My Mum and Dad, who have always supported my decisions – even when they clearly haven't understood the actions or intentions. I'm sorry if anything I said in the book caused you pain, that's never been my intention.

Thank you Glenn Manton, Kathy ver Eecke, and Beth A Grant who helped mentor and encourage me to move forward with this story in different ways over the last year and a bit. I doubt I would have created this book without the words of wisdom from these wonderful people – whether they realise that or not. A huge thank you also to Kate Torgovnik May, for supporting me through the TED Blog; I appreciate you including my story on the site I hold so dear.

My lovely editor, Merridy Pugh, who had the undesirable task of trying to proofread this book; and not losing her grammatical mind with how I write. Since this was the blog turned into a book, there was not a lot of editing in the process, but what did occur was essential to giving you something readable. There was another team that helped get this book out into the world in a very public way; thank you to the wonderful women of Sans Pareil for the promotional support for the book. Frederica, Caroline and Anne, your guidance and professionalism made a world of difference to the difficult process of being a fairly newbie self-publisher.

A massive thanks and enduring gratitude goes to TED and the TED speakers involved in this project. I've made mention a number of times in this book, on the blog, and in my own TED Talk, about the important role I think TED has played; not just in my life. As a resource that is freely available to the world, I think it's a fantastic way of bringing ideas and understanding to people who would not otherwise have had access to these brilliant speakers. I mentioned a couple of times that this project was designed to honour the *ideas worth spreading* ethos of TED. Taking these ideas and using them to improve my life was only one aspect of the project; sharing the experience and helping other people realise they aren't alone in their brokenness was the more important element.

Thank you Chris Anderson, for realising that the incredible resource you possessed in TED Talks was worth so much more when set free to the world – it's truly an inspirational resource.

Of course I need to thank the TED speakers themselves; this includes everyone who is brave enough to stand on the red dot and share their idea with the world, not just the speakers whose talks formed part of my project.

It was part of My Year of TED to contact every speaker to let them know I used their talk. There were two I could not find any contact details for, but for everyone else there was an email, contact form message, or social media message at the least. Probably about half of the speakers contacted me back at some stage, usually providing words of encouragement or well wishes – which was wholly unexpected when I started contacting them. Those responses from people whose talks meant so much to me, and were about to mean even more to my life, definitely helped get me through some of the low points of the project.

Some speakers truly engaged with the project, and have continued to support and encourage me. A few even agreed to an interview with me in the middle of last year; we discussed their TED experience, their talks, how I used them in the project, and whether they felt they were living their purpose – heads up, I might ask other speakers to participate in this as well.

I've been turning some of those insights into *Huffington Post* articles; there are more to come; other parts of the discussion will be in the next book. I'd like to take the opportunity here to thank that small group; your ongoing support has meant a lot to me – thank you Richard St John, Barry Schwartz, Carl Honoré, Dave Logan, J D Schramm, Derek Sivers and A J Jacobs.

My heartfelt thanks go out to all of the speakers whose talks I used in My Year of TED, whether we have had personal contact, or you didn't even know the project existed. Your ideas have become an important part of my life, and have allowed me to start reclaiming my life for myself. Thank you for your ideas: A J Jacobs, Adam Savage, Alain de Botton, Alan Siegel, Barry Schwartz, Bill Strickland, Brené Brown, Carl Honoré, Caroline Casey, Chade-Meng Tan, Chimamanda Ngozi Adichie, Dan Dennett, Dan Phillips, Daniel Goleman, Daniel Kahneman, David Logan, Dean Ornish, Derek Sivers, Elizabeth Gilbert, Eve Ensler, Graham Hill, J D Schramm, Jessi Arrington, Joachim de Posada, John Maeda, Joshua Foer, Julian Treasure, Karen Armstrong, Kathryn Schulz, Lakshmi Pratury, Laura Trice, Mark Bezos, Matt Cutts, Matthew Childs, Neil Pasricha, Nic Marks, Nigel Marsh, Philip Zimbardo, Ric Elias, Richard St John, Rory Sutherland, Sandra Fisher-Martins, Seth Godin, Shawn Achor, Sheena Iyengar, Simon Sinek, Sunni Brown, Susan Cain, Tony Robbins, and Ze Frank – and now Amanda Palmer.

Last, but certainly not least, the readers of the blog – and now this book. I continue to be surprised that people turn up and read the content I produce; and I am completely humbled by that experience. Whether you were here early on in the process, and have stuck around to watch the trainwreck; or you joined my tribe later in the piece – thank you all for listening. I truly hope you got something meaningful out of it.

About the Author

Kylie refers to herself as a recovering judgemental, perfectionist control freak – although she readily admits to relapsing.

Born in Wollongong, NSW, the middle child of a working class family, Kylie never knew what she wanted to be when she grew up. The result was living a life based on other people's expectations – resulting in two failed marriages and a number of largely unfulfilling careers. That all changed after making the tree change to Tasmania with her wonderful partner Derek.

After the rollercoaster of her life changing My Year of TED project, Kylie now lives so far outside her comfort zone it is often a speck on the horizon – at times she doesn't recognise herself in the new life she has created. Now a TEDx speaker, trainer, consultant and published author, Kylie focuses on trying to help other people rediscover their authenticity, understand their own courage, and become better decision makers.

She does this with the loving support of her partner Derek and their beloved crazy dog Lily; in the comfort of the house they built together in Tasmania's Huon Valley.